Community Police Administration

Jack L. Kuykendall
*Associate Professor, Criminal Justice Administration,
San Jose State University*

Peter C. Unsinger
*Assistant Professor, Criminal Justice Administration,
San Jose State University*

 Nelson-Hall Law Enforcement Series
George W. O'Connor, *Consulting Editor
Superintendent of Public Safety, Troy, New York*

Nelson-Hall / *Chicago*

Library of Congress Cataloging in Publication Data

Kuykendall, Jack L
  Community police administration.

  (Nelson-Hall law enforcement series)
  Bibliography: p.
  Includes index.
  1. Police administration. I. Unsinger, Peter C.,
joint author. II. Title.
  HV7935.K9   350'.74   75-2119
  ISBN 0-88229-158-0

Manufactured in the United States of America

Contents

Preface

All books are written with the assistance of individuals who deserve credit beyond any that might accrue to the authors. In the case of this book, these individuals include past teachers and criminal justice practitioners with whom we have had contact. While many of their names are, quite frankly, forgotten, their ideas are frequently expressed in the pages herein. In this sense we only synthesize, a task that takes considerable time and some creativity, but that is hardly original.

We would also like to express our thanks to special people who sustain us.

For Peter Unsinger, Charlene, the kids, and his parents, who bore the brunt of prolonged absences. To Klopfenstein, Vogel, Hosack, Duncombe, Borning, and Caldwell; to Jerome, Hudson, Russell, Clift, Pierson, Shipley, Tafoya, Guardino, Lavoie, and

Miller; and to the hundreds of middle managers and executives who educated him in many ways.

For Jack Kuykendall, those special people include wife, Mary, and parents. My parents encouraged me to go to college and to stay in. If this book can be considered an accomplishment of which I can be proud, they deserve the credit for giving me the opportunity and motivation to write it.

Last, and perhaps most immediately important in actual preparation of the manuscript, is Mrs. Pat Patrick. She endured, pleasantly, one grumpy author and two with poor handwriting. She did an excellent job and deserves many kudos for patience and fast and accurate work. She is appreciated and thanked.

CHAPTER 1

Management of Community Police Agencies

The purpose of this book is to present and analyze selected contemporary management concepts and methods as they relate to the administration of community police agencies. Although most of the material is applicable to all law enforcement organizations, the emphasis is on community police—that is, county and municipal, or local, law enforcement agencies—because of the diversity of problems with which community police are faced and the diversity of methods they use in attempting solutions to those problems.

The text covers both theoretical foundations and specific methods for use by the police manager. Theoretical foundations are included because application of contemporary managerial

---

Material in the section "Styles of Community Policing" is adapted from a chapter written by the authors for an introductory textbook to be published by John Wiley. Permission to reprint has been granted.

methods is more effective if the manager understands how such methods were developed. It is not uncommon for managers in any kind of organization to attempt a new managerial practice and then discard it because it does not seem to "work." The problem, however, is often in the manager's lack of understanding of the ideas or theory on which the new practice is based. With only minor adjustments the new practice might well suit the organization in question, but such adjustments are not possible unless the manager understands the theory behind the practice. Theories, or *management concepts*, as they will be called, are only generalizations about the real world in which the manager works and as such are a practical beginning for determining what a manager should do and how he should do it.

The word *management* is often used to apply to private business and industrial organizations, while *administration* is used to apply to public ones such as police agencies. Despite the distinctions between public and private organizations, the terms *administration* and *management* will be used synonymously in this book, because the concepts and methods of both are generally interchangeable. The differences between public and private organizations are substantial, however, and merit a brief discussion. These differences include accountability and responsiveness and the nature of the goals of each kind of organization.

Even though private organizations are increasingly concerned with social responsibility, the very essence of a public organization is public accountability in behavior, activities, and expenditures. The democratic process requires that public organizations be subject to public scrutiny in order to insure responsiveness to the needs of citizens. Community police agencies, as public organizations, have a dual accountability. Not only are the police accountable to the rule of law in a democratic society, but they are also accountable to the "public interest" in their own communities. For community police, organizational activity and the individual behavior of policemen must satisfy both the law and the expectations of the community. This dual accountability creates some rather complex and difficult problems for police administrators.

In terms of goals, private organizations tend to be profit-oriented, while public organizations are intended to be service-oriented. In pursuing profits, similar private organizations are often in competition with one another, and each has a clientele that has chosen its products or services from among those of several organizations. In addition, private organizations often have only a special or limited interest and may serve only selected individuals or groups in a community. Public organizations are not, or should not be, in competition. All citizens are their "clientele," and the citizens have no choice of organizations from which to select services. Public organizations must be concerned with the interests of *all* citizens, not just special interest groups. Furthermore, community police organizations have a clientele—the citizens—who may not *want* some of their services (a traffic ticket or an arrest, for example) and may even find them unpleasant and undesirable. This latter factor is unique to law enforcement organizations and certainly makes management more difficult.

The management of police organizations is a very responsible task, perhaps the most responsible of any management position in any organization. The continued success of democratic government will depend, in large measure, on the competent and conscientious behavior of police organization managers. The rapid pace of social and technological change in society has made managerial competence difficult to maintain. Hopefully, this book will help not only to maintain but to increase the quality of police managers.

Management and Administration

Management and administration may be explained in many ways. One practical approach is to analyze management in terms of goals, resources, and activities. Management involves attempts to achieve the *goals* of an organization through the use of available *resources*. Resources, generally speaking, can be classified as either physical (machines, raw materials, funds) or human (people). In other words, management involves those efforts or *activities* directed toward accomplishing goals through the use of people, equipment, machines, buildings, and so on. Management activities are actually a process with several discernible stages, or functions. The managerial process includes the general functions of planning, organizing, motivating and leading, and controlling. This process approach to management is the basic framework for this book.

Two other important characteristics of management are problem-solving and decision-making. Throughout the management process, police managers must continuously attempt to solve organizational problems and must constantly make decisions. Often they must solve problems and make decisions in stress situations—that is, under pressure. A good "test" of a police manager is his ability to do so effectively.

Figure 1 shows the functions and the characteristics of the functions of the managerial process as defined in this section. The overlapping circles show the interrelated nature of the functions. Three of them—planning, organizing, and controlling—are ongoing activities and often occur together. The fourth, motivating and leading, concerns the behavior of the police manager and is part of all the other functions, as are problem-solving and decision-making. The broken lines in the figure depict information flow. Everything the manager does is based on the information available to him. The more accurate, complete, and reliable the information, the more effective is the practice of management.

For example, a police manager functioning as a shift or watch commander goes through the entire managerial process each watch he works. The manager must *plan* some of the activities of his personnel, and he must *organize* those personnel in terms of units, areas, and perhaps teams. As activities begin on the shift, he *controls* them by comparing what is happening with established organizational plans and by trying to take corrective action if deviations occur. As the shift progresses, he will undoubtedly be faced with problems, possibly including crimes in progress, high-speed chases, and unusual calls for service. He must analyze these problems and devise solutions. Some of the solutions will be based on existing plans and organizational structure, while others may require innovative approaches.

The planning, organizing, controlling, and problem-solving activities of the manager all require him to make decisions and often require him to take a leadership role in directing and motivating his personnel. All these activities are based on the information available to the police manager. This process is continuous and ongoing, and its component parts are difficult to separate. In Figure 1, the overlapping circles and unbroken lines illustrate the integrated nature of the managerial process.

Figure 1
Management Functions

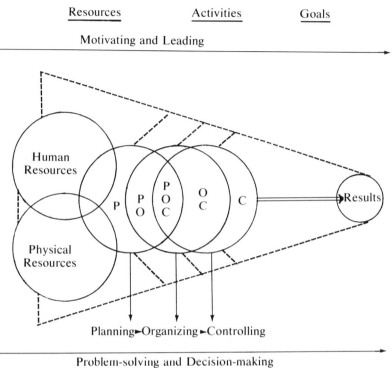

Resources   Activities   Goals

Motivating and Leading

Human Resources

Physical Resources

Results

Planning→Organizing→Controlling

Problem-solving and Decision-making
(Stress and Nonstress)

Historical Development of Management Thought

To understand contemporary concepts and methods of management, the reader should be aware of the historical continuity of their development. This section presents a brief and general overview of that development.

Present management knowledge has historical antecedents in church and military organizations. Development of a formal body of knowledge began with the rapid industrial expansion of the late nineteenth and early twentieth centuries. Frederick W. Taylor was a primary contributor to this development with a scientific study of the processes of work. Taylor's purpose was to obtain greater industrial efficiency through the systematic observation and measurement of work. He believed in standardizing work methods and conditions. Taylor and other advocates of *scientific management*, as it is called, were concerned with time-and-motion studies, physical plant layout, planning and controlling the production processes, and motivating employees by relating financial incentives to output.

Taylor and his disciples have made significant contributions to management theory. Systematic and logical analysis of work and organizational activities has continued and has become increasingly sophisticated. Presently, the term *management science* applies to logical and rational, or scientific, analysis of organizations and management practices. While management science is much broader in scope than was scientific management, they both emphasize systematic analysis of organizations. Management science emphasizes the importance of quantitative, or mathematical, analysis of organizational problems and decisions. A major part of the management science area of knowledge is *operations research* (OR). Techniques of operations research that have been applied to police organizations include probability theory and queuing theory. Probability theory has been applied in the allocation of police patrol resources by using historical crime data to predict the probability of the occurrence of crimes at certain times and in certain areas. Queuing, or waiting line, theory has been applied in trying to determine the number of radio channels a police agency should have based on the volume of radio traffic. These theories will be discussed later.

Taylor and proponents of scientific management have been criticized for not properly considering people, or the human organization. This may be somewhat unfair, because Taylor's approach to people at work was to provide them with a clean and safe environment and to reward them financially for their output. Both of these provisions were consistent with the needs of workers during the period in which scientific management developed. Man, however, is far more complex than Taylor realized, and rational organizations are often improved or short-circuited by the social, emotional, and, at times, nonrational nature of man.

Management awareness of the complex nature of men at work was initially stimulated by the Hawthorne Studies, which began in the late 1920s and were described by Elton Mayo. The findings indicated that man was influenced by factors other than the physical environment and, presumably, financial incentives.

These additional factors included his work group or peer group and others' expectations of his performance. This was the beginning of the *human relations* school of management. This school continues today, expanded by the growing body of knowledge resulting from studies conducted by researchers in the behavioral sciences—sociology, psychology, and social psychology. Presently, the emphasis on this dimension of management is called the *behavioral science* approach.

Behavioral science studies have resulted in the identification of many important factors that managers must consider. These include the impact of the informal organization; the importance of communication, motivation, and leadership; and the value of increased participation by employees in organizational activities. Increasingly, management theorists and practitioners are realizing that work is accomplished through people, and that people, or human resources, often have an untapped potential for improving organizational performance. The behavioral science study of management is attempting to tap this reservoir of human energy.

Modern management encompasses both a systematic and logical approach (management science) and an awareness of the complex nature of man as he influences organizations and is influenced by them (behavioral science). Managers must be knowledgeable and skilled in both areas if they are to be their most effective.

As the two major bodies of knowledge in management began to evolve, theorists needed a framework to integrate and relate the knowledge. Henri Fayol, a French industrialist in the late nineteenth and early twentieth centuries, was a major contributor to the *functional*, or process, approach to management. For Fayol, administration included the functions of planning, organization, command, coordination, and control.

The process approach to management, modified in various ways, has been the basis for numerous books. Luther Gulick and Lyndall F. Urwick described the popular and widely used administrative process, PODSCORB, for public organizations. The acronym PODSCORB stands for the administrative processes of *P*lanning, *O*rganizing, *D*irecting, *S*taffing, *C*oordinating, *R*eporting, and *B*udgeting. The process approach of this book is more general than PODSCORB, but it incorporates all those and other activities of management under one of the four functions. Numerous contributions to management thought are not discussed in this section, of course. Perhaps the most obvious omissions are theories of the ways organizations should be structured, but the development and contemporary concepts of organization are covered in a later chapter. Some of the more recent management concepts are also covered in later chapters; these include management by objectives, systems analysis, and relevant concepts and methods for each of the managerial functions, as well as specialized areas of police concern. Just as general management has important historical precedents, so do many administrative practices in community police agencies. The next section is a general analysis of that historical development.

Development of Community Police Administration

Man is a social animal and needs to associate with other human beings. As man evolved and formed societies, he also evolved customs that were designed to assure peace among the members of society. Even in so-called primitive societies, anthropologists have found rules of conduct and definite enforcement of norms of conduct.[1] As societies grew in complexity and became involved with one another, definite specialized law enforcement functions developed. From simple systems of order maintenance, modern forms of law enforcement evolved.

In ancient societies, two distinct law enforcement patterns emerged: centralized and decentralized. In China, Egypt, and Rome, law enforcement was centralized, often under the military. This central direction can be found in many parts of the world today; although it is not part of the heritage of American law enforcement, instances can be found increasingly in North America. The tradition of law enforcement in the United States has been one of decentralization and fragmentation.

Despite the diverse ethnic composition of the United States, the development of American police administration can be traced back to English law enforcement. The community policing found in America grew out of Anglo-Saxon and Norman traditions. This heritage, in combination with geographical isolation and the philosophy that governed early American governmental growth, resulted in the consideration of policing as a local matter that reflects, to a large degree, local preferences. While some impetus toward standardization exists in the form of standards and training commissions in various states, community policing is still primarily under local control. It is so localized, in fact, that estimates place the number of policing entities at approximately forty thousand. The exact number cannot be established, since not all agencies cooperate in making themselves known—a reflection of the inherent American dislike and distrust of "big government."

The heritage of small units of government and fear of centralized government started in England, which, shortly after the withdrawal of the Roman legions, suffered a series of incursions by various peoples. Invasions by Picts, Scots, and Vikings fragmented the population and led to dependency on local governmental arrangements; local answers were found for local problems. In order to provide domestic security, local peoples had no alternative but to maintain the peace by being responsible for other citizens. Given the relative isolation and sparse population of communities, the system of "peace of the folk" proved to be fairly successful. The customs were known to all, and everyone knew what was expected of him. Mutual expectations and reciprocity required everyone to assist in curtailing criminal activity. These various practices and customs were formalized when central authority was imposed again during the reign of King Alfred the Great (871–899 A.D.) and tithing was introduced.

For defense from foreign invasions, for tax collection, and for internal security, families were grouped into manageable units of ten families, each group known as a tithing. An individual was chosen to be the group's representative and direct its activities. Larger units, such as shires, were formed on a geographical basis, and leaders for them were selected as well. The term *sheriff* comes from this period; the *shire reeve* was a leader who directed the activities within the shire. Many of the functions now associated with the criminal justice system were performed by this official.

The Norman influence was mixed with the Anglo-Saxon when William the Conqueror gained control of England in the eleventh century. Capitalizing on the tithing system already in existence, William further strengthened this system and introduced the constable in areas of dispersed population in an attempt to maintain the peace and to collect taxes. Thus, the shire reeve and constable became firmly established in England and would eventually be copied when English governmental forms were adopted by the colonists in America.

Another feature of English law enforcement was the development of community watches. As towns began to develop, new forms of security were needed for the inhabitants. Among such forms were security patrols for both daylight and night hours. In London during the reign of Edward I, watchman-citizens were supervised by an alderman in a "watch and ward" system. Watchmen made arrests and brought violators before the alderman, who acted in a judicial capacity. Each of the twenty-four wards in London had to supply six watchmen every evening. Marching patrols were assigned to particularly troublesome locations. During this period, variations of the English system existed on the European continent, and when the American seaboard was settled, most settlements formed watch systems. The same was true of Spanish and French colonial areas.

The American preference for decentralized law enforcement was transplanted from England after England's experience with Oliver Cromwell. During the Cromwellian Protectorate, centralized law enforcement appeared in the form of mounted military police, who were disliked intensely by the people. Among the colonists, the same distaste for military and centralized control of police was coupled with their own preference for local government. Later, of course, the struggle for local control by the colonists helped cause the War of Independence. The memory of that struggle between local and centralized control and the experiences with centralized police reinforced the American desire to keep their law enforcement agencies restricted and responsive to local controls.

The American colonies therefore had law enforcement systems similar to those abroad, particularly those of England. Jamestown, Virginia, and the Massachusetts colonists each had parish constables. The duties of these officials and their places in local government closely paralleled those of officials across the

Atlantic. The southern colonies relied more on the sheriff than on the constable, but the forms of law enforcement were similiar. The institution of tithing, the use of watchmen, and, in particular, the philosophy of local control proved adequate to meet the colonists' needs while villages were small and populations homogeneous.

The American people have a heritage of electing the keepers of the peace, and they still elect sheriffs and constables. Efficiency experts have argued for years that this practice is archaic, but Americans have always wanted to exert influence over their officials, and the local election is an instrument for exercising this influence. One of the costs of this privilege has been politics in and over police departments. Most histories of early American police document political influences at work. A few political problems were election of watchmen, rotation of entire departments when administrations left office, and promotions based on "friends downtown." On occasion, two police departments have existed simultaneously in the same jurisdiction![2] The question of just who will control what in American local government has played an important part in the history of community police administration.

Few if any researchers in the nineteenth century published systematic studies of the administration of community police forces. Most materials published were memoirs of police careers or journalistic accounts of sensational criminal cases. The investigative commissions that existed devoted their attention to making political capital for a party or an interest group. They focused on corruption and proposed solutions ranging from outlawing "demon rum" or prostitution to demanding that law enforcement be directed by city hall one minute and by the state capital the next. Few police administrators or theorists gave serious consideration to the questions of administration. Even if some enterprising sheriff or police chief had taken the time to analyze or conceptualize his activities, the results probably would have fallen on deaf ears.

Historically, Americans have not been interested in policemen's doing an effective job, but in their avoiding unnecessary intervention in private matters. The public was simply unwilling to pay the costs, monetary and other, for adequate and well-managed law enforcement. The changes that did occur were not from rational and thoughtful planning, but from upheavals, scandals, and politics.[3] It was the beginning of the twentieth century before the field of police administration was touched by ideas not strongly influenced by politics.

The first third of the twentieth century witnessed a new interest in police management. Instead of concentrating solely on politics and corruption, writers such as Felix L. Fuld, Raymond B. Fosdick, and Elmer Graper emphasized functional specialization, training, selection, and service distribution. August Vollmer's experimentation in Berkeley, California, produced many new ideas as the technology of the industrial era was applied to the operational needs of police. The dawning of the twentieth century forecast a new era in American law enforcement.

The new era was slow in developing, however. Public attention focused on the First World War (1914–1918) and the glamor of the twenties. The depression, however, returned the public's attention to matters of government as law officers began to argue that they should be a separate body with a distinct purpose within local government.[4] Federal law enforcement gained acceptance, and the publicity-conscious Federal Bureau of Investigation began convincing the public of the policeman's uniqueness; the International Association of Chiefs of Police was instrumental in developing the Uniform Crime Reports that focused public attention on one aspect of the quality of living; and professionalism for policemen was encouraged by new university programs at San Jose and Berkeley, California. In the late 1920s and early 1930s, the problems and hopes of local police received wide publicity through various state crime commissions and the Wickersham Commission (National Commission on Law Observance and Enforcement) inquiries in 1931. Negative ideas were gradually being replaced by an optimistic desire to upgrade the quality of police services.

This impetus slowed again during the Second World War. Theorist Bruce Smith's work received some attention in the 1940s, but people were preoccupied with the war and then with the postwar desire to return to normal lives. Meanwhile, however, city management was becoming more professionalized, and the International City Management Association recognized policing as a distinct function. The Association's "green bible" of municipal police administration (now in its sixth edition) was published in 1943 and reflected the thinking of many public administrators concerning the law enforcement field. V. A. Leonard and O. W. Wilson began to create a distinct body of knowledge for police administration.

The most significant changes in American law enforcement administration occurred in the 1960s and continue today. Cities have experimented with agency consolidation and contract law enforcement as the centuries-old concept of local control and fragmentation has been tested. (In contract law enforcement, one community contracts with another for police services. Most often, a larger city or county provides designated services to a smaller one for a given cost.) Writings on police administration have multiplied. John P. Kenney and Harry W. More, among others, write of new and exciting management concepts; sociologists, political scientists, and even physicists, attracted by police problems, criticisms, and federal monies, diagnose police roles, equipment, and methods, and many policemen seek innovations when and wherever they will assist in the police mission.

Despite the proliferation of writings, equipment, and programs, American law enforcement remains essentially as it was when it was transplanted from England—fragmented and local in nature. (It remains to be seen whether this is desirable or undesirable.) Presently, police administrative concerns appear to be leaning toward a positive goal of doing the job better rather than the former negative one of keeping criticism away from the department. This change has been rather slow, but it is, nevertheless, a distinct change. The major bodies of management knowledge that provide impetus for that change are derived from general business management and public administration, plus numerous special studies of police. This knowledge is the basis of the content of this book.

The Environment of Community Police Administration

Every law enforcement agency is affected to some degree by the environment in which it operates. Each and every action, intended or not, that police undertake influences or alters in some way the world surrounding the agency. In some instances this interaction is highly visible, while in others the impact is very subtle and often goes unnoticed. It is present nevertheless, and must be recognized by the police manager if he and his agency are to be successful in achieving the goals of the organization. For example, police decisions to enforce or not to enforce certain laws affect the activities of citizens. The allocation of police manpower, especially uniformed officers, determines which areas of a city will receive the most service and, perhaps, the greatest protection. This in turn may influence insurance rates for homeowners and businessmen, determine the desirability of living in various neighborhoods, and generally affect the character of the community.

For our purposes, the environment of the manager is the community and the areas immediately adjacent. In actuality, of course, his environment is far larger than the city, town, village, suburb, or county, for events taking place at the state, federal, and even international levels all have an impact even in local areas. The intensity of their effect depends on the closeness of the relationship. As noted, however, the environmental context used here is the local community and the local persons and events that immediately affect the police manager and his agency.

The police manager normally considers the community to be his jurisdiction, so the jurisdiction will be the focus of the environmental analysis. A useful framework for environmental analysis has been provided by Roland L. Warren.[5] Through a series of systematic questions, Warren's methodology can be used by the police manager to help him visualize many of the elements and forces that are at work molding and modifying the agency and the community. The subjects emphasized by Warren's questions are discussed in the following paragraphs. With imagination and thoughtful analysis, the police manager can see the impact his organization has on the community and the impact the community has on the organization, and he can plan those "grand strategies" necessary to achieve agency goals.

One of the first prerequisites to an understanding of the agency's environment is a knowledge of its geography—the streets, housing patterns, traffic generators, meeting places, and centers of human activities. Geographical data are basic to police planning because they define the configuration and activity of the community.[6]

The police manager must also have a knowledge of the people, or citizens, in the community. In recent years "the people" has had a variety of definitions. In the context used here, "the people" refers to everyone residing in, visiting, and passing through the jurisdiction. Most managers know very well the individuals they see every day, but police managers need to have a thorough knowledge and understanding of *all* the people and their history, traditions, and values. In order to fully understand the environment, the manager must come to know the culture of those in the jurisdiction, even of those groups who pass through on vacations or for employment. Such information is important, because communities differ and have differing expectations about policing.

These differences in communities and their expectations concerning policing can be seen in the work of Albert J. Shafter. He examined two small communities in the same subcultural area of rural Illinois.[7] The communities had similar populations, yet their police departments differed in number of personnel and the way the personnel were deployed. Shafter found that the organizational differences were related to such factors as the isolation of the community, the presence of minority groups, attitudes toward vice, and whether the area was "dry" or "wet" in liquor sales. John A. Gardiner, although he did not fully identify his findings, found drastic differences in traffic enforcement policies among certain suburbs and towns in Massachusetts.[8] Each community and its people are unique, and the manager must know the jurisdiction and the people to respond appropriately.

The manager must also understand the community's economic life. Such conditions as chronic or seasonal unemployment directly affect the vitality of the community. Extractive industries such as mining and lumbering often suffer from the vagaries of the marketplace, and, partly because of the dangerous nature of the work, can attract workers who are prone to behavioral excesses. Strikes or other labor problems in industry and business can often create special needs within the law enforcement agency. In addition, each business has its unique problems, ranging from shoplifting to bad checks. Familiarity with market trends will often allow the manager to anticipate problems; when meat was in short supply, for example, it was possible to predict increases in the number of cattle thefts. Suburban police problems with bicycle thefts can be attributed to changes in consumers' tastes. Even missing lawn mowers and thefts of certain foreign car engines could have been forecast by the craze for go-carts and dune buggies. Economics plays an important role in today's crime problems.

Another important part of the police agency's environment is other governmental units. Each unit interacts with other units, and the manager must be thoroughly familiar with these interrelationships. A new housing project sponsored by one agency affects not only police services, but water supply, streets, and recreational facilities as well. The manager must know the effect of each governmental service on the quality of life and the delivery of other services.

Still another important environmental factor is the politics of the community. Harold D. Lasswell has referred to politics as the "who gets what, when and how."[9] The political directors of communities—the city councils, mayors, boards of commissioners or supervisors, and so on—are those who ultimately approve or disapprove the direction and management of police agencies. Familiarity with the forces at work in the political sector is important if the police manager is to be responsive to the public. One of his most serious problems is his role in the political environment. It is not the purpose of this text to suggest guidelines for the manager, since one could not devise universal rules other than the most obvious. But the manager must recognize that allocation of scarce community resources is politically determined. The people make a variety of demands, some consistent and some fickle, on their governmental representatives. Police services are only one of the many important services provided, and governmental resources must be shared and applied in ways determined by the people's representatives. The manager must provide information for the politicians' deliberations and abide by their decisions.

The community's law enforcement system is also a part of the larger criminal justice system. The manager needs to know fully the impact of his agency's actions on the other segments—the courts and corrections—as well as the impact of their actions on the police agency. All too often law enforcement personnel state their opinions about the other segments of the justice system without being fully aware of the problems and perspectives of the other agencies in the system. A thorough knowledge of, and trust in, the capabilities of the courts and corrections can relieve some of the joint problems facing the entire justice system and help in meeting the mutual objectives of serving the people.[10]

Another important consideration related to the environment is community planning. Knowledge of the needs, the kinds of planning activities, the planning processes, the participants, the interrelationships of agencies and jurisdictions, zoning, land use, capital improvement plans, and public attitudes toward the jurisdiction's planning function all permit the police manager to be aware of the future hopes and aspirations of the people in the jurisdiction. The manager should be part of the community's planning efforts in order to make the experience, knowledge, and desires of the criminal justice system available to others in the community. If the police manager does not share his knowledge, then he will have to manage the police services for a future design developed by others.

For example, many city planners are seriously studying types of housing in relation to the quality of life in communities. Certainly the relationship between certain types of crime and building design is a part of this quality of life. Buildings with dark corners and corridors and inadequate security hardware invite criminals and juveniles engaging in illegal behavior. Police officers should contribute to the design phase of projects if their experience is to be used in avoiding the failures and mistakes of the past.

For some communities, another important environmental concern is recreational activities. Is the town a "watering spot," where taverns and their problems demand constant attention? Is it a focal point for the area youth to "tool around" in their cars? Is it a tourist center whose small population swells to tens or even hundreds of thousands on a weekend? In many areas such features cause problems for the police manager, even though recreation has often been considered an alternative to crime. It is not some inherent conservatism in policemen that makes them worry about large throngs of people and large accumulations of unattended vehicles. Each form of recreation, while beneficial to the many who take advantage, creates certain conditions that are suitable for the criminal activities of a few. Law enforcement officers are aware of both the benefits and the problems of recreation. Familiarization with related problems allows for the development of effective countermeasures.

Other aspects of every jurisdiction are also included in the police environment—the health of the people, the provisions for special groups (the handicapped, migrants, the elderly), and the friendliness of diverse groups toward one another. The police manager should understand as many of these factors in the environment as possible so he can know how the police agency is affected by each one. Such an understanding permits the manager to determine the needs and expectations of the community and to define the role of the police agency.

The Role of Community Police

A *role* can be defined as the part an individual or organization is expected to play. Community police have a role in both society and government. In terms of society, police have traditionally been regarded as an organization of *social control.* Every society has rules, or norms and laws, to regulate the interrelationships of the members of that society. When these rules are violated, action often must be taken. Law enforcement agencies are rule-enforcing bodies and, as such, have been called *social control organizations.*

This analysis of the police role in a democratic society is somewhat misleading, however. The success of democratic government depends, in large measure, on the voluntary compliance of citizens with society's laws and norms of conduct. The desire to comply voluntarily is imparted during the individual's formative years through the family, school, church, and peer groups. These institutions are actually the means of developing social control. Police agencies are more concerned with social *accountability* than with social control. The police agencies' basic job is to prevent rule-breaking if possible, and, if they cannot, to hold accountable those who are responsible for violation of the law.

The role of the police in government is primarily a legal one in terms of crime, but police agencies traditionally have performed a wide variety of community services in addition to enforcing the law. A common method of defining the multifaceted role of police is to identify the goals of a police agency. Some outstanding authorities on police have used the goal-identification method to define the police role. Table 1 summarizes the role definitions of several of these authorities.

The table shows a general agreement on many of the traditional goals of community police agencies. In the 1960s, however, a rising crime rate and civil disorders stimulated a rethinking of the police role. The new emphasis has been on making the police function more compatible with a democratic society. Police in a democracy are in somewhat of a dilemma, for in a free society there is a delicate balance between enforcing laws and maintaining order effectively on the one hand and being repressive on the other. Following is an example of a democratic role definition for community police.

Democratic Role Definition for Community Police

1. Acts as a democratic role model for citizens in society by being impartial, fair, and objective, showing restraint, compassion, and tolerance.
2. Practices consistent enforcement of the laws.
3. Investigates crimes and apprehends suspected criminals.
4. Educates the public to protect themselves and their property.
5. Attempts management of interpersonal and intergroup conflict with minimal reliance on force.
6. Works with other community and criminal justice agencies to alter the causes of crime and to cope effectively with its occurrence.

The basic difference between the goal-oriented role definitions of Table 1 and the democratic role definition just described is that the latter defines how police should behave in a democratic society—they should be fair and consistent in the exercise of their law enforcement discretion, and they should rely on the use of force only when absolutely necessary. The increasing concern for

Table 1

Goal-Identification Role Definitions of Community Police

Goal	Authority
1. Control, prevention, or repression of crime	John Kenney, J. Edgar Hoover, V. A. Leonard and Harry W. More, O. W. Wilson, International City Management Association (ICMA)
2. Control of conduct, maintenance of peace and public order	Kenney, Leonard and More
3. Protection of life and property	Leonard and More, Hoover
4. Traffic control	Leonard and More
5. Arrest, apprehension of violators, recovery of property	Hoover, Wilson, ICMA
6. Enforcement of laws and ordinances	Hoover
7. Regulation of non-criminal activities	ICMA, Wilson, Leonard and More
8. Provision of miscellaneous services	ICMA, Kenney
9. Safeguarding rights of individuals	Hoover

SOURCES:

John Kenney, *Police Management Planning* (Los Angeles: Jack Kenney, 1956).

Y. A. Leonard and Harry W. More, *Police Organization and Management*, 3rd ed. (Brooklyn: Foundation Press, 1971).

O. W. Wilson, *Police Administration*, 2nd ed. (New York: McGraw-Hill, 1963).

J. Edgar Hoover, *Should You Go into Law Enforcement?* (New York: New York Life Insurance Company, 1961).

George D. Eastman and Esther M. Eastman, eds., *Municipal Police Administration*, 6th ed. (Washington, D.C.: International City Management Association, 1969).

a democratic emphasis in the police role is reflected in the following policies of a community police agency of moderate size in the western United States. These policies essentially define the role of the police agency:

1. The department will serve the entire populace of the com-

munity, will provide continuous protection and the highest possible level of service.

2. All laws and ordinances relating to the control of crime and regulations of conduct shall be enforced in a responsible and prudent manner with emphasis on violations which present a substantial threat to life and community peace.

3. All persons shall be treated equally and with fairness, dignity, and respect regardless of age, sex, social status, ethnic group, race, or creed. Constitutional provisions defined by judicial decisions relative to individual civil liberties and civil rights shall be observed.

4. The department will seek support and cooperation from the community while developing an awareness of, and assistance from, the community as to the nature, role, purpose, and scope of law enforcement.

5. The department shall act in a manner that assures citizens that orderly and legal community activities may proceed without disruption from criminal elements, and that freedom will not be curtailed by illegal police action.

6. The department recognizes in its efforts to achieve excellence that the right to peaceful dissent is an indispensable ingredient of a free and healthy society. The community interest and responsibility are essential to effective law enforcement.

7. The department will actively cooperate with citizens, organizations, and units of government in addressing criminal and other problems of community interest.

8. The department will be flexible and innovative in attempts to find superior methods of serving the populace and alleviating the problems of the community. When the need and value become apparent, this department will not hesitate to experiment with new roles, programs, and procedures for fear of failure, nor will it feel compelled to adhere strictly to historical definitions of police work.

Another approach to defining the role of police is to determine what is actually done. The part an organization plays can be related to the tasks or activities in which it engages. Project STAR (Systems and Training Analysis of Requirements for Criminal Justice Participants) conducted a task analysis of police in California, Texas, Michigan, and New Jersey. The following police tasks were identified in interim reports of the project:

1. *Advising* by providing information in the form of constructive guidance or recommendations.

2. *Booking and receiving prisoners* by transferring or accepting custody of suspects or offenders and completing jail or prison intake procedures.

3. *Collecting and preserving evidence* by acquiring and protecting all evidence.

4. *Communicating* by transmitting and receiving information in the form of written reports, oral messages, or telecommunications.

5. *Controlling crowds* by handling small or large groups of people involved in potential or actual disturbance situations.

6. *Defending self and others* by engaging in the necessary verbal and physical actions to protect himself and others in the presence of physical threat.

7. *Deterring crime* by attempting to foresee and prevent the occurrence of crime-related activities or rule infractions.

8. *Interacting with other agencies* by maintaining communication with criminal justice or private agencies to exchange information.

9. *Interviewing* through verbal interaction with individuals, witnesses, victims, suspects, or offenders.

10. *Investigating* by inquiring into possible law violations, obtaining and verifying factual information from involved persons, analyzing obtained verbal and physical evidence.

11. *Making arrests* by determining existence of probable cause, identifying and taking suspects and offenders into physical custody.

12. *Managing interpersonal conflict* by seeking to resolve disputes between two or more persons.

13. *Moving prisoners* by maintaining security and safety of individuals in custody and being moved.

14. *Participating in community relations/educational programs* through meeting with citizen groups.

15. *Participating in pretrial conferences* through meeting with various criminal justice personnel to discuss specific criminal cases.

16. *Patrolling/observing* to determine the existence of actual or potential troublesome or crime-related situations during routine vehicle or foot surveillance.

17. *Preparing reports* in accordance with agency procedures and maintaining personal records to assist the conduct of the agency's functions.

18. *Providing public service* by initiating public service activities and responding to requests from persons for information and assistance.

19. *Regulating traffic* through monitoring and directing vehicle and pedestrian traffic, and by enforcing traffic regulations.

20. *Searching* persons, vehicles, premises, or areas to determine the presence of individuals or illegal activities or articles.

21. *Testifying as a witness* by presenting factual information in court on field observations and investigations of criminal cases.

22. *Training* by observing and instructing less experienced individuals in the classroom or while on the job.

23. *Using equipment* by utilizing a variety of types, devices, and apparatus in day-to-day activities.

A role definition of the police in every community is an important consideration. Only when the agency's part is known and understood by all concerned can the manager be effective and consistent. All police managers should formulate a role definition either by identifying goals, tasks, and policies or in some other manner. The process by which that role is formulated, however, must include participation by the community. Each community has a different environment and will probably have different expectations of its police agency. These expectations will generally differ as to how laws will be enforced, whether certain laws will be enforced at all, and what services are to be provided. The different expectations of communities, along with other factors, have created distinctive styles of policing in the United States.

Styles of Community Policing

Community police agencies often have distinctive philosophies and characteristics of policing. The style of an agency is the result of different expectations concerning role performance—expectations derived from the police agency, the law, and the community (that is, political, socioeconomic, and racial-ethnic interest groups and the administrative suprastructure).

The role conflict generated from different expectations concerning performance requires that the police officer and organization make some kind of adjustment. For the police officer, the adjustment is related to discretionary behavior. For the police organization, the adjustment can be related to managerial decisions concerning the policing methods that will be used.

Several authors have analyzed the adjustment the police officer makes to role conflict.[11] James Q. Wilson, in his analysis of eight community police agencies, used police officer responses to police-citizen encounters to formulate three organization styles: *watchman, service,* and *legalistic.*[12] The police-citizen encounters were characterized as *order-maintenance* and *law-enforcement* kinds of situations.

Order-maintenance situations are related to disturbances of the peace or minor conflicts between two or more people. Examples of the former might be a noisy drunk, a panhandler, or a loud radio; examples of the latter might be a tavern fight, a family disturbance, or a landlord-tenant dispute. In such situations, a policeman must do more than simply apply the law; rather, he must interpret the law and attempt to determine who is wrong and how to respond. He may make an arrest, but frequently he does not.

Law-enforcement situations usually are more serious and/or are those for which a regular pattern of police response already exists. In a robbery, burglary, or serious assault there is little doubt that the officer will make an arrest if possible; very seldom must he interpret the law. Similarly, a serious traffic violation, such as speeding in a school zone, will almost unquestionably result in a ticket. In other words, while traffic violations are not as serious as robbery and burglary, some violations are so serious that the response of the police officer is predetermined.

In studying order-maintenance and law-enforcement situations, Wilson found differing emphases primarily in the order-maintenance situations. In the *watchman* style of organization, the police tended to view order maintenance as their primary function. In this style there is a tendency to overlook, tolerate, or ignore many minor violations of the law or to handle them short of arrest. The patrolman is encouraged by the organization to follow the path of least resistance. While many minor crimes are ignored, however, the police tend to take a "get-tough" approach when they think certain activities are getting out of hand —for example, when juvenile rowdiness threatens to develop into gang fights.

In the *legalistic* style, the police organization encourages the patrolman to take a law-enforcement view of as many situations as possible. In other words, the patrolman is encouraged to see every situation only in terms of legal alternatives. The legalistic department acts as if there were a single standard of conduct— the law—for the whole community and generally only one appropriate solution—a legal one—for each situation.

The *service* style takes seriously all situations encountered. Patrolmen in a service style department, however, do not formally apply the law as frequently as do those in a legalistic style department. In order-maintenance situations, alternatives other than arrest are often used—referral to a social service agency or the development of a special police program in traffic education or drug education, for example, to cope with order-maintenance problems.

A useful example to contrast these three policing styles is their respective responses to order-maintenance situations involving juveniles drinking beer. The tendency of a policeman in the watchman style organization would be to ignore the situation or perhaps to confiscate the beer, pour it out, and tell the juveniles to go home. A member of a legalistic style organization would probably arrest the juveniles and confiscate the beer for evidence. A policeman in a service style department would probably confiscate the beer for evidence and take the juveniles home to their parents, and might suggest attendance at some kind of program that would educate the youths in the problems related to drinking alcohol. On the other hand, in a law-enforcement situation involving a "robbery in progress" call, all three organizations would undoubtedly attempt to arrest the suspect, as there would be little difference in community expectations of the police in such a situation.

Wilson's style model is based on individual officer responses to police situations. While the response of the police officer is undoubtedly strongly influenced by the police organization, response patterns can vary considerably within each organization. Instead of viewing organization styles in terms of the responses of individual officers, it is useful to consider policing styles in terms of policing methods. Methods involve decisions of the police manager as to how most effectively to allocate resources to accomplish organizational goals. In the next section, community policing styles will be analyzed in terms of policing methods.

Policing Styles Model

A *model* is an example for explanation or, perhaps, imitation. For purposes of this book, a model is a verbal representation of the subject or topic under discussion. It identifies some of the important factors, and their relationships, for consideration in studying that particular topic. When a police manager develops an organizational chart on paper, for example, he is drawing a model representing the relationship of his personnel and activities to the organizational objectives. Models are useful ways of thinking about or *conceptualizing* the real world; they are usually not complete but can be an important basis for discussing police management topics.

An assumption of the policing styles model discussed here is that the most important goal of police is to reduce crime and maintain order in a way that establishes a trusting relationship with the great majority of citizens, and furthermore that the development of this trusting relationship will insure community support in the effort to reduce crime. The legal expectation of the police role is reflected in the concern for crime; the need for community support reflects a concern for community expectations of the police.

As the police go about trying to reduce crime and maintain community order, they can employ a variety of methods. Generally speaking, these methods are directed at two factors related to deviant behavior: (1) the *opportunity* to engage in deviant behavior and (2) the *desire* to engage in deviant behavior and the reasons for that desire. The word *motive* will be used here to apply to both the desire and the reasons for the desire to engage in criminal or disorderly behavior. The methods police select to deal with crime and disorder can be directed at opportunity or motive or both. From the standpoint of the general community, methods generally can be classified as either positive or negative in nature. Positive methods are those that the general community sees as helping them solve their problems and encouraging, supporting, and assisting in community efforts to deal with criminal and disorder problems. Negative methods are those that the general community sees as "punishing" them or providing negative sanctions—arresting citizens or giving tickets. An example of a positive method would be for police to respond to a rash of juvenile traffic violations with a driver training course; a negative method would be to issue more traffic tickets to juveniles. The former method places the police in a positive relationship with the community in that it is helping, in a nonpunitive manner, to deal with a problem. The latter method places the police in an essentially negative relationship with the community in that it emphasizes punishment.

Some typical methods employed by community police organizations are described below:

1. *Education.* Police organizations can educate members of the community to protect themselves and their property and keep the community informed in such matters as drug problems. The contemporary concept of crime prevention often involves educational programs encouraging the citizen to engage in "target hardening" (that is, increasing protection for home or business). Educational programs designed to harden targets primarily concern reducing the opportunity for crime; programs designed to educate about drugs concern preventing the development of motives. Education is essentially a positive method because it places the police in a supporting, helping relationship with the citizens in the community.

2. *Apprehension.* Apprehension includes making arrests and giving tickets, applying negative sanctions for behavior. Apprehension is the "catching" role of the police and involves normal investigations (in which the intent is to arrest), undercover work, stake-outs, raids, and so on. Generally, apprehension is negative

for the general community because of its punitive nature and because it includes the issuance of traffic tickets, which usually constitutes the most frequent police contact with citizens.

3. *Deterrence.* Deterrence is essentially prevention. One common method is patrolling—having visible police in uniforms and/or marked mobile units to limit both the opportunity and motive to engage in inappropriate behavior. The uniformed walking beat officer, the marked police car, and the helicopter are the primary means of deterrence. This is both a positive and a negative method, because while police presence reassures some citizens, it frightens or creates anxiety for others.

4. *Saturation.* Saturation, an extreme form of deterrence, means flooding an area with police officers. It is usually directed at areas that are troublesome from a police viewpoint, and it is directed at both opportunity and motive. The saturation method usually involves very aggressive patrolling and interrogation by police. The usual aggressiveness of this tactic and its frequent emphasis on arrests make it primarily a negative method.

5. *Mediation.* Mediation is also called conflict management, crisis intervention, or violence prevention. Essentially, it involves police officers' acting as mediators in interpersonal and intergroup conflicts. An example is a family disturbance in which the officer acts as mediator by reducing tensions and attempting to discover the reasons for the conflict in order to reduce the likelihood of its recurring. Since the police are placed in a helping relationship with the citizen, mediation is primarily a positive method.

6. *Referral and Diversion.* Referral is turning over individual problems to community agencies outside the criminal justice system. A referral to a family counseling center might be an alternative for a family disturbance after mediation has taken place. Diversion is providing an alternative to entry into the criminal justice system; it is most common in juvenile and drug cases. Both methods are designed to deal with the motive for inappropriate behavior rather than the opportunity. They are positive because of their helping orientation.

This list of police methods certainly is not all-inclusive, but these methods are the ones most used by community police agencies. Figure 2 summarizes these methods in terms of their relationship to opportunity or motive and in terms of their general positive or negative impact on community perceptions of police.

The distinction between opportunity and motive in policing methods is also important in the realization of organizational goals because it relates to the personalization of police activity and behavior. Police methods that are designed to impact on motive are, generally speaking, personalized in nature. Education, mediation, and referral and diversion methods generally involve face-to-face contact, and therefore tend to personalize police-citizen encounters in a positive way. Such individualized responsiveness by the police may generate stronger support for the police and may even have greater predicting power in crime control because of such support. Conversely, negative sanctions aimed at motives, because of their personalized nature, may tend to generate strong antipolice attitudes.

Figure 2
Categories of Police Methods

Deviant Factor at Which Method is Directed		General Community Reaction	
		Positive	**Negative**
	Opportunity	Education Deterrence	Deterrence Saturation
	Motive	Education Mediation Referral and Diversion	Apprehension Deterrence Saturation

Police methods, both positive and negative, that are designed to reduce opportunity tend to be impersonal. While often used, these methods seldom result in intense reactions to the police because they are not personalized.

Generally speaking, the police can place themselves in a positive or negative relationship to the community depending on the methods they use to deal with law-enforcement and order-maintenance problems. The different emphasis given to these methods reflects and determines the style of the police organization. The personal-impersonal nature of the method influences the strength and intensity of the community response. For purposes of developing a model of policing styles, the word *coun-selor* will be applied to the role of police using positive methods, and the word *enforcer* will be used to apply to the role of police using negative methods. The police, generally speaking, can be perceived as taking counselor or enforcer roles in the community. In Figure 3, these two basic police roles are used to identify styles of community police organizations. Each role is viewed in terms of its response emphasis—proactive or reactive. Proactive responses are those that are initiated by police in anticipation of, or to prevent, problems. Reactive responses are those made after a problem has occurred or after notification by a citizen in the community.

Depending on the type of response in the enforcer and counselor roles of police, several styles of community policing can be identified:

Role Combinations	Policing Style
Reactive Counselor and Enforcer	Passive
Reactive Counselor, Proactive Enforcer	Punitive
Proactive Counselor, Reactive Enforcer	Social
Proactive Counselor and Enforcer	Integrated

Passive policing is similar to the watchman style described by Wilson. Generally, passive police have a tendency to ignore many violations and avoid initiating any active programs to deal with crime problems. The reason is often excessive political influence in the police department and the pressure placed on police when they become too aggressive. The opposite extreme occurs when pressure is put on the police to do something about crime. The normal reaction of the passive police organization is to become rather *punitive.* From an overall organizational perspective, punitive policing usually does not last long, Historically, the more aggressive and negative the police become, the more the community resists and forces the police to become passive. The passive-punitive cycle is not uncommon in some cities in which there is considerable political influence in the police department.

Social policing is often dominant in small communities where police officers and citizens know one another very well. In small communities, people are regarded as individuals; in large com-

Figure 3
Counselor-Enforcer Model of Policing Styles

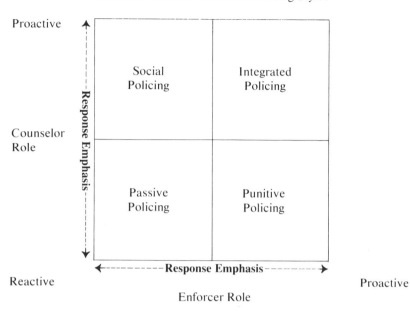

munities, people are known by their position (that is, a person is "a police officer," not John Doe) or by their visible status (that is, a person is a member of a minority group or a social or business organization, not an individual). This familiarity with citizens by police results in decisions based on the person *and* the problem rather than on just the problem itself. For example, in social policing, juveniles are likely to be taken home to their parents and not arrested.

The problem in social policing is that decisions made by police may often reflect a helping role (and therefore be related to a counseling role) that may not be at all objective. It is one thing for a police officer to refer a person to a family counseling center to help solve a personal problem; it is quite another matter to do nothing because he and the individual are friends. Another problem in social policing is that "favorite" groups may develop. In communities with diverse racial populations, middle-class whites may be known and treated favorably, while the racial minority might suffer from strict, punitive enforcement. In cases like these, social policing represents a helping relationship only with select-ed groups in the community.

Integrated policing represents a balance between the enforcer and the counselor roles. This balance, and the tendency and willingness to act out both roles proactively, can produce a "professional" approach. *Professionalism*, as used here, is based on a systematic and objective analysis of problems in an effort to determine the most efficient and effective method or methods to accomplish organizational goals. All methods identified here are included in the manager's "tool bag," and they will be used singly or in whatever combination is necessary to attempt to control crime while maintaining community trust and support.

The police manager should make a concerted effort to deter-mine what style of policing the community expects. It is sug-gested here that the integrated, or balanced, use of methods is the most effective and will insure continued community responsive-ness to the police. The analysis of styles in this section may prove useful for the manager in determining what organizational style presently exists and which one is a desirable goal. This analysis is certainly not definitive, however. Styles can be characterized in various ways; what is important is not necessarily what the styles are called, but rather that distinctive styles do exist and are important considerations for police managers.

Structure of the Book

As previously mentioned, the framework for this book is the management process. In addition, separate consideration is given to selected topics involved in police management and recent management concepts. The motivating and leading function of the management process is discussed next because of the impor-tance of the "human organization" to managerial success. After that is a chapter on management by objectives and results (MBO/R) because of the importance of establishing goals, or objectives, to provide an organizational purpose. The next four chapters concern the planning function, and following that are one chapter on organizing, one on managerial problems in per-sonnel selection and training, and one on evaluation and control. The final chapter on evaluation and control discusses the importance of determining and measuring effectiveness and productivity and the importance of police professionalism.

Each chapter of the book will follow the same general outline. The purpose of the chapter will be explained; theoretical foundations or concepts will be discussed; where appropriate, methods applicable to police agencies will be described; and a brief summary section will provide a recap. At the end of each chapter is a suggested reading list to help the reader explore the vast body of knowledge in the field of management, which can only be touched on in one book.

Suggested Reading

Barnard, Chester I. *The Functions of the Executive.* Cambridge: Harvard University Press, 1938.

Eastman, George D., and Eastman, Esther M., eds. *Municipal Police Administration.* 6th ed. Washington, D.C.: International City Management Association, 1969.

Fayol, Henri. *General and Industrial Management.* New York: Pitman, 1949.

Fosdick, Raymond B. *American Police Systems.* Montclair, N.J.: Patterson Smith, 1969. (Reprint; original published in 1920.)

Fuld, L. Felix. *Police Administration.* New York: G. P. Putnam's Sons, 1909.

Graper, Elmer. *American Police Administration.* Montclair, N.J.: Patterson Smith, 1969. (Reprint; original published in 1921.)

Gulick, Luther, and Urwick, Lyndall F. *Papers on the Science of Administration.* New York: Institute of Public Administration, 1937.

Kenney, John P. *Police Administration.* Springfield, Ill.: Charles C. Thomas, 1972.

Lane, Roger. *Policing the City: Boston, 1822–1885.* Cambridge: Harvard University Press, 1967.

Leonard, V. A., and More, Harry W. *Police Organization and Management.* 3rd ed. Brooklyn: Foundation Press, 1971.

Mayo, Elton. *The Human Problems of an Industrial Civilization.* Cambridge: Harvard University Press, 1933.

National Advisory Commission on Criminal Justice Standards and Goals. Reports: *A National Strategy to Reduce Crime; Police; Community Crime Prevention.* Washington, D.C.: U.S. Government Printing Office, 1973.

President's Commission on Law Enforcement and Administration of Justice. *Task Force Report: The Police.* Washington, D.C.: U.S. Government Printing Office, 1967. (See also *The Challenge of Crime in a Free Society.*)

Reiss, Albert J. *The Police and the Public.* New Haven, Conn.: Yale University Press, 1971.

Smith, Bruce. *Police Systems in the United States.* 2nd rev. ed. New York: Harper & Row, 1960.

Taylor, Frederick W. *Scientific Management.* New York: Harper & Row, 1947.

U.S. National Commission on Law Observance and Enforcement (Wickersham Commission). *Report on the Police.* Washington, D.C.: U.S. Government Printing Office, 1931. (See also the report on *Lawlessness in Law Enforcement.*)

Vollmer, August. *The Police in Modern Society.* Berkeley: University of California Press, 1936.

Wilson, O. W., and MacLaren, Roy. *Police Administration.* 3rd ed. New York: McGraw-Hill, 1972.

CHAPTER 2

The Human Organization

People are the most valuable resource in community police agencies, for all organizational activities are accomplished through or by people. The body of management knowledge that has developed about the complex relationships of men in organizations has come primarily from behavioral science studies of management. The major areas of emphasis in such studies include communication, motivation, leadership, the informal organization, and concepts of role and status. Three of the principal areas of study have been communication, motivation, and leadership. This chapter will discuss these three areas in terms of effective management. The other areas mentioned above will be discussed in the chapter on organization.

The purpose of this chapter is to present concepts and methods of communication, motivation, and leadership that will be useful to the police manager. While each area will be presented separately, the three are almost always interrelated in practice.

Communication

The discussion in this section will emphasize interpersonal communication; organizational communication is analyzed in a later chapter.

Communication is the exchange of information intended to transfer meaning. Generally, communication takes place through the use of symbols—spoken or written; however, gestures, facial expressions, and body position can also transfer meaning. Communication takes place when an impression results from what is seen or heard.

The basic communication process is depicted in Figure 4. In the first phase, one individual has an idea that he intends to communicate. In the second phase, he encodes the idea by determining the symbols or words to use. In the third phase, he transmits the message by some method to the individual or individuals who are the intended receivers. In the fourth phase the receiver receives the message, and in the fifth, he decodes it, or decides what it means. In the sixth and final phase, some action takes place as a result of the communication. The communication also normally includes a feedback cycle—that is, the receiver of the communication indicates that the message is received and/or requests clarification of its content or purpose. Each phase of the communication process presents problems that merit discussion; managers should be aware of these potential pitfalls in order to facilitate effective communication.

Idea

A sender or communicator of a message, be it verbal or written, should have a purpose in mind when sending a message. The idea determines the content of the message, and it is important that the idea be well formed by the communicator. If an idea is clear, it will be easier to put into words, and the receiver will understand it better. The first step to effective communication is to think through carefully what you intend to say and logically

Figure 4
The Communication Process

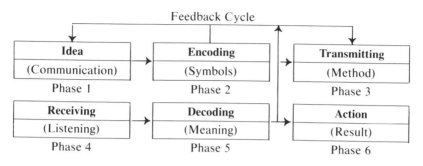

arrange the ideas so they make sense. If the communication concerns other people, seek their advice as to the content and logical development of the facts.

Encoding

Once the purpose, content, and structure of the message are thought out, the message must be encoded into symbols, or words. There are approximately 600,000 words in the English language, approximately 2,000 of which are used in daily conversation by an educated person. For the 500 most frequently used words, however, there are approximately 14,000 dictionary definitions! For example, the word *round* has 79 different dictionary meanings.[1] The word *police* has approximately 15 different dictionary definitions.

Semantics, or the scientific study of communication symbols, provides a useful framework from which to view words selected for use to encode messages. Two broad categories of words are abstract and concrete words. Abstract words concern *concepts*, such as *justice, power, equity, professional,* and so on. Concrete words stand for *objects*, such as *car, pistol, handcuffs.* and so on.

Abstract words can be further divided into connotative and denotative words. Connotative abstract words are given meaning by an individual based on his own experience. The words *fear* and *justice* are essentially connotative words, and they may mean different things to different individuals. Denotative abstract words have somewhat more specific meanings because they have generally the same meanings to many individuals. Examples of such words are *management, arrest, deterrence,* and *prevention.*

In an encoded message, the kinds of words that result in the fewest communication problems are, in order of accuracy: (1) concrete words, (2) abstract, denotative words, and (3) abstract, connotative words. As the sender moves from concrete to abstract, the probability of the receiver's misunderstanding the message increases. The context of the message in which words are used, of course, can help compensate for the possible misunderstanding. For example, if a police manager asks a subordinate to insure that a citizen is treated "fairly," the manager should make sure that the subordinate's meaning of fairness is compatible with the manager's, or the manager needs to be much more specific in the message. In one case with which the authors are familiar, a chief of police delegated to a lieutenant the responsibility for disciplining a patrol officer for driving outside his assigned area to visit his girlfriend. The chief told the lieutenant not to be too harsh in the disciplinary action and to treat the officer "fairly." The lieutenant's concept of fairness in reference to harshness of punishment was considerably different from the chief's. To the lieutenant, "harsh" punishment would be dismissal, while "not too harsh" would be a thirty-day suspension without pay. To the chief, "harsh" punishment would be suspension without pay for a few days while "not too harsh" would be a written reprimand or perhaps one day off without pay. Obviously, the chief of police and the lieutenant had different concepts of fairness in this situation. Initially, the patrolman who was the victim of this misunderstanding was suspended for thirty days; however, when the chief was told of the decision by the lieutenant, he changed the punishment to only five days.

Two other points that merit discussion are the selection of words whose meanings are commonly known and understood and the avoidance of slang. The communicator should not assume that if the receiver of a message does not know the meaning of a word he will look it up in a dictionary (even if he did, the dictionary would probably provide several meanings). The communicator should use words that he believes are commonly understood within the work situation. If he has doubts, he should provide definitions or get enough feedback from the receiver to insure that meanings are understood. He can also "reduce" words to their simplest form. Examples of reducing words to avoid misunderstanding are to use *forbid* instead of *proscribe; bulge* or *swelling* for *protuberance; noisy* or *troublesome* for *obstreperous,* and so on.

Likewise, the use of occupational slang, or "in" words, should be avoided. Occupational words develop in nearly every organization. For example, the word *perpetrator* is often used by police to mean an individual committing a crime. This meaning is understood by those within the police organization, but may not be understood by people outside. It is particularly important not to use such words in communications with nonpolice individuals or groups.

General slang should also be avoided. Slang words usually have only temporary popularity. For example, *rip off* became a popular word for "steal" in the 1970s; in the 1960s *lift* was a word for "steal." Because their meanings can change, such words can easily be misunderstood.

Here is an example that illustrates the problem of language unique to the police organization. A new and untrained policeman was assigned to a patrol car by himself one night during a manpower shortage. Shortly after leaving the station, he was assigned to a disturbance call, and on the way he had a flat tire. Wondering what to do, he looked at his Ten Code Sheet and saw that Code 30 meant "Emergency—Officer Needs Help." This new officer picked up the radio, said, "Code 30," and gave his location. He then got out of the car to direct traffic around his vehicle. Shortly after that, he heard sirens and wondered what was happening. He soon found out. Within minutes, several police cars came screeching up to his location. This new officer learned a valuable lesson in communication when he was informed by his supervisor that a flat tire was not a Code 30! Fortunately, the lesson was not without positive consequences for the police department. The importance of communication, training, and the meanings of words in a work context was made most explicit by this incident.

Transmitting

Once a message is encoded, how will it be transmitted? Generally speaking, messages are verbal, written, or both. Transmission of either kind of message can also have technological assistance —a telephone, television, films, and so on. As a general rule, if a manager wants his communication to be fully understood, he should transmit it verbally, elicit a discussion of the message (feedback) from the receiver to clarify the meaning, and provide a written document to support the verbal communication and to help the receiver remember it.

Receiving

The receiving phase of the communication process concerns whether or not the intended receiver hears or sees the message. Several problems can arise, some of which are related to organizational problems (geographical distance, the number of organizational levels, or the number of channels). Again, such organizational problems will be discussed later.

In terms of interpersonal communication, it can be assumed that the sender will have contact with those intended to receive the communication. This really leaves only one major receiving problem: *Is the receiver listening?* The communicator can facilitate good listening by being a good listener himself, by selecting a place and time as free of distractions as possible, and by carefully observing the attentiveness of the receiver. Since attentiveness can be deceiving, however, the sender should look for questions or comments by the receiver that indicate a grasp of the material communicated; if they are not forthcoming, he should ask questions or request comments from the receiver. These need not be abrupt, but can be such questions as "What do you think about this?" or "Is that your interpretation?" or "Would you give that back to me as you understand it?" A good listener hears the words, attempts to understand them, and evaluates the message to insure that the transfer of meaning is complete. The manager should remember that communications may not be fully understood, so he should do everything he possibly can to make sure the message is received and decoded properly.

Decoding

This is perhaps the most crucial stage in the communication process because the receiver, not the sender, interprets the message. No matter how carefully ideas are thought out, encoded, and transmitted, the receiver, for a variety of reasons, is often likely to interpret the message somewhat differently from the way it was intended to be interpreted. Some of these factors will be discussed later, but first let us analyze the importance of feedback.

Feedback from messages is absolutely crucial if the intent of a communication is to be understood as fully as possible. A simple exercise will illustrate the importance of feedback. Figure 5 shows two sets of five connected boxes. To illustrate the importance of feedback, verbally describe to one or more individuals how these boxes should be drawn, and request them to draw the boxes as you describe them. For the first set of boxes, do not permit any questions or discussion of your instructions. After you have finished, draw the boxes of Set 1 for the participants to see. You will find that most, if not all, of them will have drawn the boxes differently. Then repeat the experiment with Set 2, but permit questions about your instructions. The results will be quite different. All, or most, of the participants will produce a drawing exactly like the one you described.

Other experiments to illustrate the importance of feedback, and even supporting written material, are easy to devise. The reader need only develop a series of fairly complex instructions typical to a work situation and ask an individual or group to carry them out, using a variety of communication methods: (1) verbal with no feedback, (2) verbal with feedback, (3) verbal with feedback and a supporting document, (4) written document only. It might prove interesting for a manager to determine which of the four methods of communication, given the complexity of the message, produces the best results.

As noted earlier, other important problems arise in decoding. The first concerns the perception of the receiver concerning the sender. The receiver perceives the sender's status—that is, his organizational position. He also perceives his personal qualities —for example, he may respect the sender's knowledge in an area

Figure 5
Communication Experiment

Set 1   Set 2

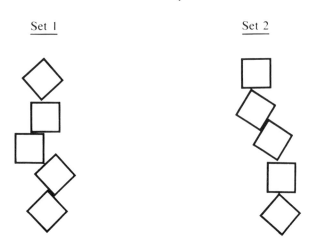

or subject, share his values and/or interests, or simply have personal rapport with him. Negative perceptions in any of these areas can tend to discredit the communicator, and therefore his message, while positive perceptions may result in poor evaluation of the message while listening. A manager should be aware of the listener's perceptions of him when communicating and overcome negative perceptions through sound, well-researched communication. In addition, a manager should insist on evaluative feedback, particularly from those who have only positive perceptions of the manager.

Another factor, somewhat related, is the "psychological distance" between the receiver and the sender in terms of attitudes or values. The closer the sender and receiver are in shared attitudes or values about the message, the less the psychological distance. Two conservative policemen discussing Warren Supreme Court decisions of the 1960s are likely to have little psychological distance; their values are the same. A conservative policeman and an attorney from the American Civil Liberties Union probably are separated by considerable psychological distance, and each may misunderstand or disregard what the other is saying or simply "tune out" the message. Psychological distance can be a real problem in police organizations because of the rapid changes that have taken place in the last decade. As opinions concerning the police role, methods, and behavior become more diverse within police organizations, psychological distance becomes a serious communications problem. Managers should be aware of those who are thought to be so psychologically distant that meaningful communication presents a problem. Greater efforts are needed to transfer meaning and intent. One reaction can be simply to dictate, or require, that those who disagree must comply; this, however, is only a temporary solution and often creates serious organizational consequences (see the section on leadership). Those who act out of personal belief are usually more productive employees than those who are coerced or required to act in a certain manner.

The other extreme of the psychological distance problem is for a communicator to be too quick to stereotype a receiver or place him in a category based on his perception of the receiver's attitudes and values. Here is an example of what can happen. A young police officer was called in by his watch commander (that is, his shift commander or station commander), told to get a haircut, and then dismissed. The officer, quite competent and dedicated, promptly resigned. The officer explained later that he had developed the reputation of being too rebellious and that he believed a moderation of some of his ideas was necessary. He had been prepared to get a haircut and had intended to tell the watch commander that when he was called in for the meeting; however, without any discussion at all, he had been ordered to get the haircut, and, thinking this unfair, he became angry and quit.

The problem was that the manager, recalling the past performance of the policeman, expected to have no basis for communication and decided to resolve the problem by a direct order (always the easiest and sometimes necessary, but seldom the best way out of a difficult problem). The patrolman, wanting to change but at the same time expecting to be treated as a mature person, believed he was given no opportunity to change voluntarily. He lost his temper (a human failing, but unwise under the circumstances). The result was that the manager had done his job poorly, the resigned officer may have been lost to police work forever, and the organization lost a valuable human resource. Certainly the patrolman must share a large part of the responsibility, but he presented a communication problem that, if properly handled, could have been resolved without the worst results. In any communication situation where the manager perceives the likelihood of a problem of psychological distance, he should make sure the problem exists before reacting as if it were a reality.

A final problem in decoding messages concerns the receiver and his acceptance of the message. A receiver is more likely to accept the message and carry it out with full support and in keeping with both its substance and its intent if the receiver believes he has influenced that message. When the receiver makes the communication his own by having some influence on its content, full commitment is more likely.

Action

In the final phase of the communication process, the activity and/or behavior that the message is intended to accomplish occurs. The intended result is more likely to occur if the barriers to effective communication that have just been described are considered. Feedback is especially important to the effective transfer of meaning. However, feedback continues even after the decoding phase, for the manager needs information concerning the activity and behavior itself. Obtaining this information or feedback is related to the controlling function of management and will be discussed in a separate chapter.

When the manager desires to communicate with another person or group, he should be aware of the problems that interfere with effective communication. In addition, he should consider the following guidelines for effective communication.[2]

1. Determine the purpose of the communication before encoding the message; think through the ideas intended for communication.

2. Make sure that the purpose, or goal, is not too broad. The more complex or the broader the message, the greater the possibility of a communication failure.

3. Confer with others who have information about the communication. Be sure the facts are correct.

4. Consider the timing and setting for the communication.

Deliver it at a time and under circumstances that are likely to favor understanding and retention.

5. Be aware of the overtones of the message. A serious message should not be delivered with a mocking tone of voice or a cynical expression. The listener's receptiveness to a message can be strongly influenced by such overtones.

6. Give constant attention to establishing a trusting relationship with those with whom you are to communicate. Make a concerted effort to understand those individuals and develop a relationship that will facilitate open and candid communication.

7. Follow up your communication by asking questions and soliciting comments.

8. Communications of any magnitude should be considered in terms of long-range organizational objectives and past practices. Messages that do not conform to goals, or are departures from established policy and procedures, can create serious problems.

9. As a manager and leader, make sure your actions support your words. Be a role model, or an example, of those messages concerning individual performance or behavior. If the manager believes something and acts it out, others will usually consider more seriously what he says.

10. When appropriate, be a good listener by[3]

    a. Not talking when the other person is
    b. Putting the talker at ease
    c. Looking and acting interested
    d. Not engaging in distractions
    e. Trying to see the talker's point of view (even if you disagree)
    f. Being patient
    g. Not losing your temper
    h. Asking questions

Motivation

Communication and motivation are closely related. To perform to maximum capacity, employees must not only understand what is expected, but they must also have a strong desire and commitment to perform. Understanding comes through sound communication; desire and commitment come from motivation.

In practice they are often inseparable, but for purposes of study they can be discussed separately.

Motivation in Organizations

Motivation can be defined as energy in the form of behavior and/or activity that is directed at some goal. The energy is provided by the physical, emotional, and intellectual capacity of a person as that person attempts to fulfill a need or a desire. The goal selected by the person represents, when realized, the fulfillment of the need or desire. An individual is motivated to the greatest extent, in terms of performance defined by an organization, when the manager in the organization creates conditions of work in which all the needs of the employee are satisfied. Motivation is certainly no easy task for the manager.

Depending on the degree to which needs are fulfilled, employee motivation can be described as (1) unacceptable in terms of work output and performance, (2) acceptable, or (3) high. Most employees fall into the second category, being motivated enough to put in an acceptable day's work however it is defined by the organization. The real challenge for the manager is to increase the number of employees who are highly motivated and minimize the number whose level of motivation is unacceptable. A typical, and unfortunate, approach to motivation is to discipline and eventually discharge those at the first level of motivation and to be satisfied with motivation at the second level. An effective manager who desires to realize the most effective organizational performance possible, however, will make a concerted effort to move as many employees as possible to the third level. Although it may not be possible to move all employees to the third level, many can and will improve their output and performance if proper motivational methods are used.

A closely related issue that will be discussed later is the appropriateness of motivated activity and behavior. (Defining appropriateness is a function of the planning phase of the managerial process.) Without guidelines for highly motivated activity and behavior, the results could harm organizational performance. For example, for a policeman to increase the number of arrests of suspected felons is desirable unless those arrests involve insufficient or manufactured evidence or violation of the suspects' rights. Motivated behavior requires direction by the organization and manager.

Motivational Theories

To fully understand how employees are motivated, one must understand something about people's needs. Several theorists have made important contributions to the understanding of people's needs and how they relate to motivation considerations for managers.

A. H. Maslow has described what he calls man's need hierarchy.[4] According to Maslow, man's needs are fivefold: basic, safety, belongingness, ego-status, and self-actualization. Figure 6 depicts the relationships of these needs and the goal-related behavior that is associated with each need level. Any need, to act as a motivator, will usually operate to drive a person only when his lower order needs are fulfilled. For example, an individual will not strive for meaningful work relationships (belongingness) if he is not reasonably secure in his job (safety). In the United States and many other countries, basic needs and safety needs are fulfilled in most organizations, including police departments. There are exceptions, however—both in some police agencies most of the time and in all police agencies in some situations. For example, some police organizations have such inadequate salaries, fringe benefits, and working conditions that employees may have to take a second job ("moonlight"), be tempted into corruption, or leave the police field. Such poor conditions can generate considerable "turnover" in an organization. In organizations with adequate salary, fringe benefits, and working conditions, basic and safety needs are usually reconsidered on a regular basis. So while basic and safety needs are generally met, they do act as motivators periodically and in some situations.

Generally speaking, however, it is the three higher-level needs —belongingness, ego-status, and self-actualization—that are the most important factors for managers to consider in employee motivation. In this regard, David C. McClelland and J. W. Atkinson have found that employees respond to three work-related motives:[5]

Figure 6
Maslow's Need Hierarchy and
Related Motivational Goals

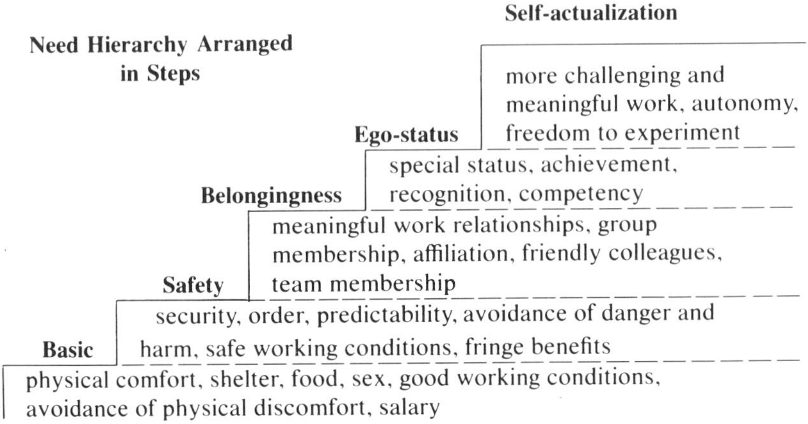

Self-actualization

**Need Hierarchy Arranged
in Steps**

more challenging and
meaningful work, autonomy,

Ego-status | freedom to experiment

special status, achievement,

Belongingness | recognition, competency

meaningful work relationships, group
membership, affiliation, friendly colleagues,

Safety | team membership

security, order, predictability, avoidance of danger and

Basic | harm, safe working conditions, fringe benefits

physical comfort, shelter, food, sex, good working conditions,
avoidance of physical discomfort, salary

Related Motivational Goals

1. *Affiliation.* This is similar to the belongingness identified by Maslow and is a dependence of the employee on a friendly work group for satisfaction.

2. *Achievement.* This is related to ego-status and self-actualization and is a desire to get ahead and achieve recognition.

3. *Power.* This is related to ego-status and self-actualization and is a desire to control and influence or take charge.

Different employees have different needs in a work situation. A manager must be aware of the needs of employees and be able to respond, if possible, in an appropriate manner. Individuals can be motivated as follows by one or a combination of the three needs identified by Atkinson and McClelland:

1. The employee who needs *affiliation* wants others to like him, needs friendly interaction with other employees, and wants interpersonal competency, the ability to relate well to others.

2. The employee who needs *achievement* wants tasks that are challenging and require some risk, wants personal responsibility in solving problems, and needs feedback, or recognition, for performance.

3. The employee who wants *power* has a desire to influence others or to control the means by which people are influenced. This person is often forceful and outspoken.

Atkinson describes a model to explain how these three needs can act as motivators for employees. This model includes the strength of the basic motive or need, the expectancy of obtaining the goal that would fulfill the need, and the perceived incentive value of that goal. This model adds an important dimension to the problem of employee motivation—the *expectations* of the employee. A person may have a strong need for power, but if promotion is the perceived and valuable goal that would increase power, and if promotion is not believed to be possible, then motivation in the direction of promotion will not result. However, the seeker of power *will* take on another goal, perhaps leadership in a police association or union. Some such leaders may have believed that the realization of power was not an achievable goal in the police organization (certainly there are other reasons for association leadership, too).

The expectations of the employee concerning the organization rewards (money, status, power) and the possibility of getting those rewards act as motivators. The rewards become the goals that, when realized, fulfill the need. If the goals are not perceived to be possible, however, they will not act as motivators. In a recent study of a police department, a graduate student of the authors' found that the greatest cause of dissatisfaction and low motivation of employees was lack of promotional opportunities. The police department in question had only thirty men and consequently a limited number of promotional opportunities. Several policemen who had worked in the department for several years could not have their need for achievement recognized through promotion; they did not perceive that promotion was possible. This fact not only decreased their motivation but made them dissatisfied with their jobs and the organization. Most of these policemen were seeking other jobs, and all of them were performing at unacceptable or barely acceptable levels.

Also important to motivation is the value of the goal for which the worker is striving. For example, in the case of wages and fringe benefits, increasing conflict has arisen in many police agencies over appropriate wages for police officers. How do these differences in value expectation develop? Normally, wages and fringe benefits are related to those received by other police organizations or other occupational groups in the community. The salaries and fringe benefits suggested by city or community administrators and those expected by the employees may be far apart. As most police managers are aware, this often creates conflict and can result in demotivated employees. There is no easy solution to the expectation problem, and until police salaries are more standardized, this particular conflict will continue.

Management Methods to Improve Motivation

To maximize motivation, managers must address the problem of need expectations and value of rewards or goals. A first step in considering specific methods for police managers is the work of Frederick Herzberg.[6] His research indicated that man's needs in terms of job satisfaction can be grouped into *maintenance factors* and *motivating factors.* In essence, Herzberg said that an employee will perform an acceptable day's work if his basic, safety, and belongingness needs are met by the organization in relation to the employee's expectations. Among the factors that will maintain performance Herzberg placed employee satisfaction with organizational policy, administration, supervision, salary, interpersonal relations with workers, and working conditions. Given these factors, the employee maintains satisfaction and does an acceptable day's work. High levels of motivation and performance are related to other factors, however; these are associated with ego-status and self-actualization needs. Factors here include achievement, recognition, responsibility, chance for advancement, and the rewards inherent in the work itself.

Police managers must be concerned with both maintenance and motivating factors. The fact that maintenance factors appear to be acceptable to most workers does not mean that their expectations and values will not change. Herzberg said that maintenance factors are like eating; once you eat, you're satisfied for a while, but you get hungry again. This is true of employees; they may be satisfied with maintenance factors at any given time, but because their expectations and values associated with rewards (such as salaries) change, so will their satisfaction with the factors that exist.

Police managers must also give attention to motivators, the factors that get employees to move beyond an acceptable day's work to high levels of performance.

A useful way for a manager to think of methods to motivate employees is in terms of their intrinsic and extrinsic qualities. *Extrinsic* methods of motivation, generally speaking, are not self-motivators. They are associated with work but are not the *work itself.* Extrinsic motivators include money, fringe benefits, recognition, status, promotion, good equipment, and safe conditions. They generally lead to an acceptable day's work and sometimes beyond. *Intrinsic* methods, which should always be used with extrinsic methods, are related to the work itself. The word *intrinsic* means "inherent," and, applied to work, means that rewards are derived from the *work*, not from external factors. A job that is intrinsically satisfying fulfills a worker's need for self-actualization and has, perhaps, the greatest potential for self-motivation of workers. Intrinsic rewards for employees are challenge, latitude in decision-making, opportunity to do work that one really wants to do, and general personal satisfaction with work.

Motivational Problems for Police Managers

Perhaps the most serious problem for police managers is that they do not always control to a significant degree many factors, or rewards, important to worker satisfaction and motivation. Police organizations are part of a larger organization, the community government, that frequently depends on approval of elected officials for resources, wages, fringe benefits, and even organizational practices and policy. The greater the extent of the control outside the organization, the less the ability of the police manager to motivate employees. The authors recognize an analogous situation at the university at which they teach. While the authors' manager, the department chairman, is responsible for determining tasks and evaluating performance, he has *no* influence on salaries, fringe benefits, or working conditions. All of these are *extrinsic* factors. He does, however, control the subjects taught and various other work-related activities. These *intrinsic* rewards are very strong motivators for the authors.

The police manager is likely to have the greatest control over the factors that provide intrinsic rewards for his officers—what work is done and how. If the manager listens to his employees to determine their expectations from their work and helps create challenging job situations, he may be able to overcome some of the difficulties of not being able to influence all the extrinsic rewards of the job. The police field has attracted many highly committed individuals who, for intrinsic rewards associated with work, have given up some expectations concerning extrinsic rewards. Hopefully, the time will come when this is not necessary, but in the interim, the police manager may have to concentrate on intrinsic rewards in police work. Here are some specific examples of ways to increase intrinsic rewards:

1. If a person has limited responsibility, the manager can enlarge the job by giving him more to do and decreasing his specialization. Highly specialized tasks (fingerprint analysis, dispatching, directing traffic) can become boring. Of course, some workers may "fit" such positions and find them fulfilling. But the manager should remember that there is a difference between being highly motivated in a position and just getting by.

2. If an employee is ready, the manager can enrich his job by giving him more freedom and responsibility. He might also assign more complicated tasks and requirements. The employer should be sure, however, that the employee is ready to handle the job and has the skills and training required.

3. The manager can rotate certain jobs unless it means simply replacing one boring job with another. A clerk-typist who is bored with typing is likely to be just as bored with typing one type of crime report as another. If he or she enjoys typing, however, he or she may welcome the change. The typist who is bored probably needs a periodic change to a different type of job or an enlarged or enriched job.

4. For the worker who gets great rewards from working with others, a job may be made more meaningful by putting him on a team or instituting a group effort.

5. In general, increasing the employee's participation in decisions concerning the nature of the work will make it more meaningful. However, not all employees are mature enough in an organizational sense to be allowed participation. These employees need to be developed so they will become capable of such participation. (This development is discussed in greater detail in the next section.)

6. Managers always should do what they can to provide recognition for effective performance through whatever means are available—personal attention, commendation, promotion, or desired assignments. While not an intrinsic reward, such recognition almost always motivates workers.

For further ideas about motivating employees, refer to the suggested readings at the end of the chapter.

The final motivational problem to be discussed concerns the civil service or merit system in many police organizations. Originally designed to employ only the most qualified applicants and to provide job security, civil service systems now provide a haven for nonmotivated employees. Some individuals, if not most, in such secure positions have exhausted any challenge the work has to offer. Many simply do the minimal work necessary to "get by." To change such a system is usually beyond the influence of police managers, but they should certainly try. This does not mean that employees should be arbitrarily discharged; rather, continued employment should be contingent on satisfactory performance that is evaluated throughout each employee's career.

If the civil service and merit systems cannot be revised to provide for ongoing and meaningful evaluation of performance during the organizational career of an employee, the manager must not avoid problems created by nonmotivated employees; he should confront them. To some degree, careful selection and career development will preclude such problems, but people can change markedly over a long career and may develop a "hold on" attitude about the job and organization. It is the manager's job to confront the problem through candid discussion, encouragement, reassignment, retraining, or whatever else is necessary. If desirable performance does not result, then the manager is faced with accepting the employee or attempting to make a case for termination. Making such a decision is certainly not an easy task and should be done on an individual basis.

Leadership

Communication and motivation are essential to effective management. The process by which they are implemented in practice is leadership.

Leadership can be defined in many ways, and a useful approach to defining it is to consider the activities of a leader. These activities include communicating, motivating, inspiring, coordinating, directing, commanding, influencing others, setting goals, and making decisions. Each manager develops a management style. He has his own personal leadership characteristics and behaves in his own way as he carries out managerial activities. In this section, the term *internal leadership* will mean the manager's style or behavior with the police agency. *External leadership* will mean the police manager's leadership role in the community. These two leadership roles are largely interrelated and overlapping, but each requires separate discussion.

Before examining internal and external leadership roles, however, let us look at power and authority as related to leadership and summarize the development of leadership theories.

Power and Authority

The concepts of leadership, power, and authority are closely related. Leadership has been and will continue to be analyzed here; authority is the *right* to lead, compel, or motivate another person to do certain things. In the police organization, the *right* to lead is normally granted to the manager by the police agency, which gives him rank and official status. The designation of sergeant, lieutenant, captain, chief, or sheriff indicates that the holder is a manager of people and resources and therefore is in an official leadership position.

This official, or formal, method of giving authority explicitly assumes that the organization has the right to designate leaders, which it does; further, it implicitly assumes that the members of the organization will accept the formal authority and follow the dictates of those in authority. This latter assumption is not always correct, because authority in an organization is determined not only from the top of the organization, but also from the bottom up, or by the consent of those in the organization. In other words, the leaders in any organization have only as much authority as the people in the organization are willing to give them. After all, if the employees will not do as they are expected, the leaders for all practical purposes have no authority. Of course, such a leader could say that if the employees do not respond, just get rid of them, but this assumes that there is no union or association or civil service to preclude such action and that there are capable replacements.

Most employees accept authority at times and reject it at other times. Most of the rejecting takes place when they are not being "watched." Usually there is much time not officially supervised in police organizations when employees can hide actions that reflect a rejection of the official authority of the agency as represented by the desires of the official leaders. The authors have both had experience as police officers and have observed, and in some cases practiced, behavior that reflects a lack of motivation and a disregard for authority. Some common practices *observed* include visiting friends, frequently of the opposite sex, and sleeping in an isolated location, perhaps after jacking up the back wheels of the car to keep them turning in order to build up mileage on the car.

The importance of employee acceptance of authority raises the issue of power. While authority is the right to command, power is the ability to command, or more accurately, to influence others. Power is given by those employees who are influenced by a leader or manager. Power can be granted to an individual on the basis of his knowledge of the job, his interpersonal style, or personality, his friendship and associations, the length of his service in the organization, or a combination of these factors. Any characteristic that puts an individual in the position of being able to influence others gives power. Those managers who have both the authority of the organization and power, accepted by the employees, usually are the most effective leaders. The "ideal leader" has both power and authority.

No discussion of leadership and authority would be complete without a brief consideration of delegation of authority and responsibility and the concept of accountability. Delegation of authority is the basis for building organizations. When a one-man police department hires a second man, certain authority, or right to act, is delegated to him. Delegation continues as the organization grows. Delegation of authority is usually paralleled by a delegation of responsibility, and ideally, the authority must be commensurate with the delegated responsibilities. For example, when a police manager delegates to an employee the responsibility for determining the type of vehicles to purchase and for purchasing those vehicles, he must also grant him the authority to disburse funds. Delegation should not be confused with displacement, however. If the employee fails to purchase good cars, the manager must take some of the blame, since *he* delegated the responsibility. The essence of management is to seek, accept, and effectively meet the responsibility of the position. All activities taking place in the manager's organization or unit are his responsibility; he can delegate, but ultimately, he is responsible. Managers can, however, hold accountable those employees to whom responsibility and authority were given. As the manager is responsible for all those under his command, he holds those under him accountable for their delegated responsibilities.

Leadership Theories

Theories of leadership include the "great man" approach, the trait approach, the situational approach, and the systems approach.

The *"great man"* approach to leadership holds that leadership qualities can be determined by studying great men to determine the reasons for their success, and then using the characteristics identified to select, or develop, leaders. The "great man" approach has generally proved unhelpful, however, and is not popular today.

The *trait* approach is to observe or study effective leaders to determine the traits of those in leadership positions. Two subschools exist, differing in their approach to determining the traits. The *intuitive trait* approach is based on general observation and judgment. The problem with this approach is that identified traits can be general and hard to define—industriousness, sincerity, character, dependability. The *research trait* subschool is more systematic in that careful consideration is given to both definitions and meaning of traits. Some of the traits of effective leaders that have been identified by using this approach are the following:

1. Intelligence (above the average of his followers)
2. Skill in verbal and written communication
3. Confidence in self (healthy self-concept)
4. Competence in task or activities performed
5. Perception of and insight into problems
6. Sensitivity to individual and group feelings
7. Moderate boldness in social situations (somewhat extroverted)
8. Emotional maturity
9. High tolerance for frustration
10. Breadth in interests and activities
11. Strong motivation for achievement
12. High concern for the feelings and needs of people in the organization

Of course, an individual who does not possess all these traits might still be an effective leader, but these traits should be considered in identifying leaders in an organization.

As study of leadership continued, researchers realized that they had to look beyond the man himself in order to learn what makes a leader. This realization led to a look at the situation in which the leader was involved. The *situational* approach to leadership holds that the style and behavior of the leader should change when the situation changes.

In the late 1940s and early 1950s, Ohio State University conducted leadership studies that identified a fourfold classification of possible situations confronting a manager:[7]

1. Situations primarily concerning an individual
2. Situations concerning relationships between or among individuals
3. Situations concerning the task or job

4. Situations concerning the relationships between or among tasks or jobs

In other words, each situation or problem with which the manager is faced can be classified in those terms. In the first situation, the managerial or leadership style should be *individual-centered* and personal attention given. *Individual-centered* leadership is appropriate in a situation involving the personal problems of an employee. If a patrolman is having problems with his wife, for example, the manager should make every reasonable effort to respond to his needs, including temporarily lessening work requirements if necessary. In a situation involving relationships between people, such as a patrolman and his working partner, the manager's style should be *group-centered.* If conflict and resulting poor performance exist in such a situation, the manager should emphasize the relationship between the two individuals in attempting to deal with the problem. Although the needs of one or both individuals may be part of the problem in such a situation, the relationship itself should be emphasized.

In situations involving a task or job, such as a patrolman having difficulty investigating a traffic accident, the manager should take a *task-orientation* and help the patrolman develop the expertise needed to solve a particular problem. In a situation involving relationships among tasks—for example, if several officers are dealing with a minor civil disturbance or a crime in progress—the manager would take a *task-relationship orientation* by assigning and coordinating the various tasks necessary to deal effectively with the problem.

Another major contributor to the situational approach is Fred E. Fiedler.[8] The basis for Fiedler's ideas is a twofold leadership style—one that emphasizes task (production, organization goals) and one that emphasizes human relations (individual goals, relationships among people). Using these two styles, Fiedler characterized the situations facing managers by (1) the strength of the leader-employee relationship, (2) the degree to which the work or task is structured or spelled out, and (3) the degree to which the leader has the authority and power formally attributed to the leader's position. When the leader-employee relationship is strong, when the work is structured, and when the leader has authority, the leader should use the task-directed style. He is accepted and liked, and the employees need and want direction. The leader also should use the task-directed style when situational conditions are unfavorable, because the employees do not want to work and *require* firm direction. When tasks or activities are not highly structured and/or the leader's relationship with employees is not well established and accepted, the leader should use a human relations approach, showing more concern for relationships, for the people involved, and for cooperation in determining what the tasks and activities will be.

A *systems* approach to leadership suggests an optimum, or absolute, style for managerial effectiveness. One such approach, to be discussed in the next subsection, is the *grid system* of management. Another is that of Rensis Likert.[9] Using seven factors to evaluate the management systems of organizations, Likert suggested four systems of management:

1. Exploitive autocratic (authoritarian)
2. Benevolent autocratic (paternal)
3. Consultative
4. Participative (democratic)

Likert's system, however, is more than just an effort to appraise managerial style; it is an attempt to analyze and develop a management system for an organization. Likert's research is too extensive to present here, but it is most interesting, and the reader is encouraged to consult Likert's book.

Internal Police Leadership: A Suggested Model

Optimum motivation for employees can be achieved if individual goals and organizational goals can be integrated. These two goals can be used to develop an internal leadership system for police and are closely related to the variables in the Ohio State University and Fiedler studies. Robert Blake and Jane Mouton have used these two variables to develop a grid system of managerial styles (or internal organizational leadership).[10] Using the variables or factors (1) *concern for people* (or individual goals) and (2) *concern for production* (or organizational goals), Blake and Mouton designate a high concern as 9, a moderate concern as 5, and a low concern as 1. They identify five leadership or managerial styles:

1. The 9/9 style (high concern for production and people) reflects managerial values and actions that lead to an integration of task and human requirements in realizing goals.

2. The 5/5 style (moderate concern for production and people) reflects managerial values and actions that lead to an emphasis on production but also an awareness that morale should not be ignored. This leads to pushing just enough to get the work done but not so much that morale is adversely affected.

3. The 9/1 style (high concern for production, low concern for people) reflects managerial values and actions that lead to a strong emphasis on production. Managers tend to concentrate on planning, directing, and controlling the work.

4. The 1/9 style (low concern for production, high concern for people) reflects managerial values and actions that lead to conflict avoidance and efforts to promote good fellowship. People are considered all-important, and organizational requirements are minimized.

5. The 1/1 style (low concern for production and people) reflects managerial values and attitudes that lead to a general indifference toward people and production in favor of "the book" and organizational procedures and ritual.

According to Blake and Mouton, the most desirable style is the 9/9, in which the leader shows a high concern for both people and production. The 9/9 style is similar to Likert's participative or democratic system of management mentioned earlier.

The grid system also has been used by Jay Hall, Jerry B. Harvey, and Martha Williams to develop an evaluation instrument to measure the styles of leaders or managers.[11] Their instrument evaluates styles in the four major areas of a managerial process:

1. *Philosophy of management* concerns the basic set of attitudes and assumptions the manager holds about people.

2. *Planning and goal-setting* concern making decisions, determining work plans, and establishing evaluation criteria.

3. *Implementation* involves the actual translation of plans into actions to accomplish tasks.

4. *Evaluation* concerns the review of work accomplished to correct problem areas.

Table 2 is a breakdown of Blake and Mouton's five managerial styles by each of the four areas listed above. This table provides a useful way for the reader to compare management styles in each phase of the managerial process. More detailed information can be obtained from sources in the suggested readings listed at the end of this chapter.

Table 3 is a breakdown of the primary and back-up styles of seventy-six police managers who were evaluated by Hall, Harvey, and Williams. The primary style is the one most frequently used, while the back-up style is the one a police manager may resort to under stress. Table 4 is a breakdown of styles by managerial activity. The primary styles are somewhat misleading, because the style of the most effective managers tends to change as the activity changes. The change is most significant when moving from the thinking phase (that is, philosophy and planning and goal-setting) to the acting phase (that is, implementation and evaluation). Police managers need to give careful attention to this material in determining the style they will employ. Comparing Tables 2 and 4 will provide a characterization of the police management styles that have been analyzed by the authors. Table 2 provides brief descriptions of each style, and Table 4 provides the managerial style results of the police managers studied. When the reader compares these two tables, he can see the kinds of styles police managers employ and how they change as the manager performs various activities.

While the grid system is a useful starting point, it does not incorporate much flexibility for police managers. If possible, the manager should be concerned for both individual and organizational goals, but he must consider other factors in dealing with different types of situations. He should take into account the employee's organizational maturity and the stressful and nonstressful nature of any given situation.

Paul Hersey and Kenneth H. Blanchard suggest that the organizational maturity of an employee is an important factor in deter-

Table 2
Style Characterizations by Managerial Component

Style	MANAGERIAL		COMPONENTS	
	Philosophy of Management	Planning and Goal-Setting	Implementation	Evaluation
9/9	Mature individuals desire meaningful work; integration of individual and organizational needs (people and production) results in optimal performance; use of teams important in integrating needs.	Manager works with all individuals who have relevant data to set goals, make decisions, and so on; goal commitment is realized through participation.	Manager acts as a member of implementation group contributing his resources; he is familiar with progress and assists with problems, lends support, and so on.	An ongoing process with implementation; manager views candid and open critique as a learning experience; gives basic team recognition and also recognizes outstanding individual performance.
5/5	Organization and individual needs are in conflict; moderation and compromise are the most effective strategies; people are practical as they realize some effort is needed.	Manager decides on plans and goals but listens to opinions of others; tries to obtain agreement through a "tell and sell" method.	"Open door" policy is typical here; manager is on call if problems occur; he keeps up with work, gives positive suggestions if difficulties arise.	Manager emphasizes mistakes and successes; tends to underplay evaluation; reviews successes in group setting and mistakes on a one-time basis; holds discussions for reasonable suggestions for improvement.
9/1	Organization and individual needs are in conflict; people do not like work and are incompetent; they should minimize attitudes and feelings, as they get in way of work.	Manager keeps planning decisions to self; believes uniformity of action via own guidelines is the key to success.	Manager gives close and constant step-by-step supervision; appears to be ever-present; authorizes changes as needed.	Manager emphasizes mistakes in one-to-one meetings; is concerned with fixing the blame and handing out penalties.

Table 2
(Cont'd.)

Style	MANAGERIAL		COMPONENTS	
	Philosophy of Management	Planning and Goal-Setting	Implementation	Evaluation
1/9	(Same as in 9/1 style except emphasis is on people so as not to hurt morale; manager wants acceptance of group. wants to "help.")	Manager abdicates to group. even subjugating his own desires; makes broad plans and assignments and leaves it to subordinates to do the job.	Manager supports morale and technology needs of people; leads rather than pushes; gets what employees need and relates in terms of gentle persuasion.	Manager avoids discussion of mistakes to preserve morale; tends to deemphasize critiques, to have fun, and not say anything unless it is "nice."
1/1	(Same as in 9/1 style except manager tries to avoid conflict; emphasis is on formal rules and regulations; manager believes in and goes by "the book," does not like or want to cope with uncertainty.)	Manager avoids personal involvement; does no more than supervisor or job description requires.	Manager gives directions and does not get involved unless major problem arises; believes in little action unless required; people are free to solve own problems.	Manager does not evaluate unless required by policy; when required, he emphasizes "objective" checklist of performance indicators; tries to avoid blame for mistakes.

SOURCE: This table was developed from Jay Hall. Jerry B. Harvey, and Martha Williams, *Styles of Management Inventory and Interpretive Score Sheet* (Conroe, Texas: Teleometrics International, n.d.); and Robert Blake and Jane Mouton. *The Managerial Grid* (Houston: Gulf. 1964).

Table 3
Police Management
Primary and Back-up Styles
(N = 76)

Style	Primary		Back-up	
	Number	%	Number	%
9/9	53	69.7	12	15.8
5/5	7	9.2	24	31.6
9/1	13	17.1	15	18.4
1/9	2	2.7	24	32.9
1/1	1	1.3	1	1.3

Table 4
Police Management Primary Styles
by Activity
(N = 76)

Style	Managerial Activity							
	Philosophy		Planning and Goal-Setting		Implementation		Evaluation	
	Number	%	Number	%	Number	%	Number	%
9/9	57	75	54	71	25	33	17	22
5/5	10	13	5	7	15	20	7	9
9/1	5	7	12	15	28	36	21	28
1/9	4	5	5	7	3	4	29	38
1/1	0	0	0	0	5	7	2	3

mining a manager's style.[12] Organizational maturity is defined as the "willingness and ability to take responsibility." When an employee has low organizational maturity, the manager should structure tasks and control them closely. He should spell out work and direct it. At the same time, the manager should maintain concern for the individual and his needs; organizational needs are best served by structuring tasks for the employee. As the employee matures in developing skills and taking responsibility, the manager should continue to encourage his development by permitting him more and more participation in deciding what and how activities are to be performed. Eventually the employee will not need direction and encouragement, because he will have become organizationally mature. This means that the manager will have treated the employee in such a way that the employee will no longer require external control but will have self-control and self-motivation.

The organizational maturity of employees and proper response to their development are extremely important. Commonly, a manager never stops controlling an employee or laying out what is to be done and how. While such direction is desirable at first, an employee who is maturing will become unmotivated if the manager's style does not change as the employee does. In addition, a manager must positively support and encourage the employee's development by recognition and assistance. A manager who fails to do so will probably contribute to the creation of a dependent employee who cannot do anything on his own.

Stress is of special importance in community police organizations. Stress is normally present in dangerous situations involving possible or actual personal harm or property damage (crimes, riots, high-speed chases). Stress situations require a task-oriented manager. In the grid system, this is the 9/1 style. Fiedler has found that the task-oriented style is more effective in stress situations,[13] for strong and decisive action is necessary to provide direction and solve the problems at hand. Employees expect such behavior, and the situation requires such a managerial style. A task-oriented style during the course of a stress situation, however, should not be confused with the style used in planning what should be done. For example, in considering plans for riots, civil disorders, crowd control, and so on, mature employees should be consulted and allowed participation in plan development; when the policemen are handling the emergency, however, the manager should consider exactly what needs to be done in that particular situation and order it done.

As described, the internal leadership style suggested for police managers includes the grid system, the organizational maturity of the employee in terms of how that employee's work is structured by the manager, and the conditions of stress. Following are some general guidelines for the manager.[14]

Suggested Characteristics of an Effective Police Manager

1. Shows confidence and trust in employees as they mature
2. Acts in a supportive role to achieve goals

3. Attempts to understand individual and organizational problems and *never* avoids dealing with them

4. Provides the necessary training for employee development

5. Shares all important information about the organization

6. Is friendly and easily approached

7. Is generous in credit and recognition of successful performance

8. Employs constructive action instead of criticism

9. Respects others' ideas and criticisms without necessarily accepting them completely

10. Will not "walk over" others to achieve personal goals, yet still strives to "get ahead"

11. "Plays square" and does not "work angles" even for his own advantage

12. Bases managerial efforts on a coherent plan

13. Is objective and values facts and adequacy of information

14. Has positive, as opposed to negative, assumptions about people

The last characteristic merits a brief comment. The assumptions a manager makes about people often determine how he will manage. Douglas M. McGregor developed the concepts of Theory X and Theory Y to illustrate managerial assumptions.[15] Theory X managers tend to see people in a negative way—lazy, indifferent, disliking work, avoiding responsibility—while Theory Y managers have positive views of people—just the opposite of the negative characteristics. A manager's style and the way he plans, organizes, and controls work are influenced by such assumptions. A Theory X, or people-negative, manager is likely to emphasize close supervision and control, use strong discipline based on punishment, and generally attempt to obtain performance out of fear. A Theory Y manager generally has a freer style, respects people more, allows more participation by employees, and attempts to establish positive, open relationships. Theory X managers can be effective for short periods of time, but almost inevitably the results are unmotivated employees, high turnover, high absenteeism, and continued performance problems. As a rule, police managers should *attempt* to operate from Theory Y assumptions in terms of their managerial behavior toward people.

External Police Leadership

This subsection concerns the leadership role of the police manager in the community rather than in the department. In this respect a police manager, especially at the executive level, is a public official or administrator who is keeper of the public trust. How should a police manager carry out this most responsible role?

One basic distinction, already explained in Chapter 1, is that between reactive and proactive leadership in the community. Reactive leadership is almost a contradiction in terms. Can a manager be an effective leader when he only reacts to problems, offers opinions only when asked, or takes initiative or action only when requested or directed to do so? The authors think not. This is not effective leadership in terms of police-related problems in the community. More appropriate is proactive leadership, the opposite of reactive leadership. A proactive manager would be forceful and decisive in taking a leadership role in the community to develop support and resources, and offer alternative solutions to crime-related problems.

Here is an example of the difference between reactive and proactive leadership. Faced with a rising incidence of burglaries and larceny thefts by teen-agers, a reactive police manager would probably only report the increase and ask for more officers for patrol and investigation. A proactive leader might suggest increased recreational alternatives, seek changes in any school policies that could be giving school-age children the opportunity to engage in deviant behavior, recommend a curfew, develop educational programs (for all teen-agers) regarding the crimes, and/or develop prevention programs for citizens to help them avoid becoming victims.

Proactive leadership inevitably involves a police manager in the political processes of a community. For purposes of discussion, being involved in the political processes means having power or using power to get resources and support for a position. All police managers are faced with political situations. Being political does not *have to* mean that one loses objectivity or integrity or stops being fair and impartial; it simply means that one is aware that most solutions to community problems are more the result of political processes than of rational and systematic decision-making processes. If a police manager is to be effective in obtaining resources and support in a community, then that manager must have power—that is, the ability to influence.

Proactive leadership and its inevitable involvement in the political processes of a community have associated risks. When a manager seeks to influence or to obtain power, he often finds himself in conflict with others—elected officials, a public manager, a city manager, or a chief executive officer. Such conflict may even result in the police manager's being discharged. This is a risk that a proactive leader must take, and if organizations are to be as effective as possible, proactive leadership is necessary.

If a police manager assumes a proactive leadership role and obtains some measure of power in the community, what direction should that influence take? Surely a manager's role should reflect the democratic nature of the police function and a concept of the public interest.

The concept of the public interest is rooted in the idea that all citizens in a society have something in common; the public interest constitutes both guidelines and goals that govern societies and citizens. In a democracy the values of a police manager are most important in public-interest decision-making. Emette S. Redford has stated several tenets of democratic morality:[16]

1. Persons are the units of value in society; man is the ultimate measure of human value.

2. All men have worth and are deserving of social recognition.

3. Personal worth is most fully protected through active participation by individuals and groups in the decision-making processes of government.

In other words, the basic underlying principles of democracy are a belief in the value of all men and participation by persons in their own government. For the proactive police leader, an acceptance of these tenets would result in decisions generally consistent with the principles of democracy. In combination with a commitment to the rule of law, these principles form the framework for proactive leadership. The characteristics of a proactive leader are as follows:

1. He identifies and speaks out on all police-related community problems.

2. He offers alternatives to these problems consistent with democratic principles.

3. He advocates the rule of law.

4. He advocates active citizen participation in police policy formulation in areas that are not covered by legal rules.

5. He advocates fair and impartial policing for all segments of the community.

6. He seeks support for progress and solutions to problems consistent with democratic principles.

Summary

The human organization is the people who work for any company or institution. Major considerations in discussing the human organization in terms of management are communication, motivation, and leadership, all of which are closely interrelated when managers are carrying out their responsibilities. Effective managerial activity is, in large measure, the result of the manager's ability to communicate, to obtain top performance through motivation, and to provide leadership for the organization and its employees. This chapter covers only a small part of the material that is available to the manager who desires to be more effective; additional readings are suggested following this chapter.

Suggested
Reading

Atkinson, J. W. *An Introduction to Motivation*. Princeton: D. Van Nostrand, 1958.

Blake, Robert, and Mouton, Jane. *The Managerial Grid*. Houston: Gulf, 1964.

Davis, Keith. *Human Behavior at Work*. 4th ed. New York: McGraw-Hill, 1972.

Fiedler, Fred E. *A Theory of Leadership Effectiveness*. New York: McGraw-Hill, 1967.

Hersey, Paul, and Blanchard, Kenneth H. *Management of Organizational Behavior*. 2nd ed. Englewood Cliffs, N.J.: Prentice-Hall, 1972.

Herzberg, Frederick. *Work and the Nature of Man*. Cleveland: World, 1966.

Likert, Rensis. *The Human Organization*. New York: McGraw-Hill, 1967.

Litnin, George H., and Stringer, Robert A., Jr. *Motivation and Organization Climate*. Boston: Graduate School of Business Administration, Harvard University, 1968.

Luthans, Fred. *Organizational Behavior*. New York: McGraw-Hill, 1973.

McClelland, David C. *Assessing Human Motivation*. Morristown, N.J.: General Learning Press, 1971.

McGregor, Douglas. *The Human Side of Enterprise.* New York: McGraw-Hill, 1960.

Marting, Elizabeth; Finley, Robert E.; and Word, Anna. *Effective Communication on the Job.* 5th ptg., rev. ed. New York: American Management Association, 1963.

Maslow, A. H. *Motivation and Personality.* New York: Harper & Row, 1954.

Reddin, William J. *Managerial Effectiveness.* New York: McGraw-Hill, 1970.

Redford, Emette S. *Democracy in the Administrative State.* New York: Oxford Press, 1969.

CHAPTER 3

Management By Objectives/Results

Next to dealing with people, or the human resources in an organization, the most important undertaking of the police manager is to establish objectives that identify expected results. Objectives provide direction, stand as the basis for measuring effectiveness, and permit evaluation of performance when compared with results. The *management by objectives and results (MBO/R) system* has emerged as a separate area of study in the field of management and has become a method of managing entire organizations. As discussed in this book, however, MBO/R is not considered a separate system but is integrated with other activities in the managerial process.

Each managerial activity (planning, organizing, motivating and leading, and controlling) requires that the manager determine objectives to identify the results he expects. Generally, the formal process of setting objectives is related to long-range planning, but informal objectives are developed daily by most individuals. The purpose of this chapter is to analyze MBO/R concepts and suggest a system that can be used by police agencies.

MBO/R: Meaning and Purpose

Management by objectives is a management system that focuses on results through the joint establishment by manager and worker of the expectations of the worker's performance and those of the organization and its functional units. The expectation of performance, or results, is stated as an objective. Other words used for objectives include *goals*, *aims*, and *targets*.

The purpose of MBO/R is to develop cohesive organizational action—that is, to assure that everyone is working toward the same goals—to determine what the organization expects of employees and what the employees expect of the organization, to increase motivation, and to establish a basis for evaluation and control. When the objectives or goals are established, the organization's effectiveness can be determined in relation to the degree to which the goals or objectives are realized.

The motivational dimension of MBO/R is important. Figure 7 diagrams the potential motivational dimensions of an MBO/R system. As the organizational maturity of an employee increases, he should be permitted increased participation in setting individual and unit objectives. As manager and employee set objectives together, they learn what each expects. This active participation by the employee should increase his motivation and commitment and result in improved performance as a consequence of having specific objectives for which to work. The manager should appraise his performance, and, if it meets expectations, he should reward it to insure ongoing development and effectiveness. Effective action or performance, however, is also influenced by other factors. An employee without ability and training could work very hard toward an objective and the result could be totally inadequate. To be considered effective, performance requires more than just a "hard charger"; it requires competent "hard chargers" who know where they are going.

Ability and training are subjects for discussion in another chapter, but they are important factors in establishing objectives.

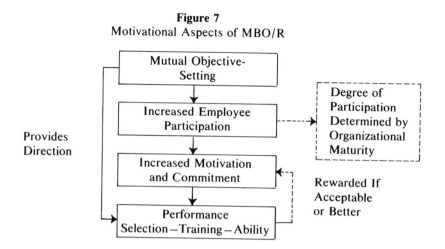

Figure 7
Motivational Aspects of MBO/R

MBO/R: Process

The development of an MBO/R system proceeds in several steps: (1) organizational effectiveness, (2) role and mission analysis, (3) establishing goals, and (4) establishing objectives.

Step 1: Organizational Effectiveness

As previously noted, organizational effectiveness is defined as the degree to which the organization's goals are realized. In considering the use of the MBO/R system, the police manager has two alternatives in this step. First, he can assume that the present methods of the organization are the most effective and develop the MBO/R system within the existing organizational system. Or second, he can systematically analyze existing methods to determine their relative effectiveness before attempting utilization of the MBO/R system.

The latter alternative is strongly suggested, for all organizations require periodic, systematic analysis to insure that they remain effective. If the manager has been involved in such an analysis, it would probably not be fruitful for him to do so before using MBO/R; if he has not analyzed his organization systematically, he might be in danger of establishing an objective for an organization unit, or employee, that has little impact on organizational goals. As community and legal expectations for a police agency change, police managers should respond in the most effective way possible. Ongoing evaluation of organizational practices is necessary to insure this responsiveness. If, for example, research studies indicated that police patrol deterred only certain types of crimes (burglaries) and not others (rape), it would not be appropriate for the manager to consider a police objective calling for increased patrol to deter rape. Without ongoing organizational evaluation, such an objective could easily be established.

Step 2: Role and Mission Analysis

As used here, *role* and *mission* apply to the same general question: what part the police organization is to play in the community. To a large degree, this role is determined by the traditional responsibility of police to enforce criminal laws and community ordinances. However, many departments have related activities that vary from department to department. The range of police activities in the United States includes animal control, fire fighting (public safety), health services, employment services, and day care centers. The list is almost inexhaustible. Because the role or mission of each police agency can differ with community needs and expectations, the police manager must systematically think through and analyze the role of his own agency.

The development of the role/mission perspective is essentially a thinking and discussion process with other community officials, citizens, and fellow police officers. It is a process by which the framework, or system, of the police organization is mentally outlined. This process focuses on such questions as the following:

1. What activities should the police agency be involved in?
2. What should the organizational (or departmental) style be?
3. What is the police organization's relationship to other community agencies and organizations?

4. As the community changes in population, industry, and so on, what process needs to be established to modify the role/mission of the organization?

By discussing these issues, the police manager, in cooperation with citizens and city government officials, can move toward the next step in the development of an MBO/R system—establish goals.

Step 3: Establishing Goals

It is not uncommon for the words *goal* and *objective* to be used interchangeably by managers. As used in this MBO/R system, however, they will have different meanings. As used here, a *goal* is a broad qualitative statement of organizational purpose that defines the role or mission of the police agency. (Refer to Chapter 1 for traditional and contemporary statements of police goals.)

An *objective*, on the other hand, is more specific and immediate. Objectives are steps toward goals. As an analogy, consider a professional football team. Its ongoing goal is to win the Super Bowl, to be champions. Yearly objectives are to win the division or league; shorter-term objectives are the winning of individual games; even shorter-term objectives are making first downs and touchdowns. Supporting objectives are completing certain practices by game time, securing certain personnel, and so on. This distinction between goals and objectives is useful for the MBO/R process described in this chapter, although not all advocates of MBO/R would agree with it.

The establishment of goals gives the police organization its direction. Goals are the basis for evaluating the organization's effectiveness. And, even more important, an MBO/R system has little use without goals, because unless the role/mission of the police organization is identified through a statement of goals, the objectives, which are directional statements of expected performance, have no real meaning. In other words, organization and employee performance must be given direction; goals provide a broad general framework, while objectives are more specific steps within the framework.

Step 4: Establishing Objectives

An objective is a general or specific statement that identifies expected performance. Objectives should be time-bounded—that is, a certain time period should be set for their completion—and may be either *quantitative* or *qualitative.*

Objectives are set in relationship to, and are compatible with, the goals of the organization. For example, one goal of a police agency commonly is "crime control." An objective might be "a 5 percent reduction of Part I (index) crimes over the next twelve months." This is a quantitative (5 percent), time-bounded (twelve months) objective that is related to the organization's goal of crime control. (Index crimes are those used by the Federal Bureau of Investigation to gauge the crime rate in the United States. The index, or Part I, crimes are murder, aggravated assault, forcible rape, robbery, burglary, auto theft, and larceny-theft.)

Qualitative objectives are difficult or impossible to quantify. For example, an objective for the individual officer might be "to improve courtesy in contacts with citizens over the next month." Courtesy is impossible to quantify; therefore, it is a qualitative objective. In this statement, however, it is time-bounded, for the improvement, the desired result, is expected within a given time period. Objectives should be quantified if possible, and both quantitative and qualitative objectives should be time-bounded. Quantifiable objectives are best because they provide a specific measure of results and a basis for control. The time frame for the objectives identifies periodic checkpoints for evaluation and development of new objectives.

The general categories of objectives to be developed by police agencies are (1) agency objectives, (2) unit objectives, (3) program objectives, and (4) individual objectives. The agency objectives are those directly related to the organizational goals. The number of unit objectives depends on the size of the organization. Units are the separate functional activities of the police organization—patrol, traffic, investigations, and so on. For example, a patrol division, or the patrolling function, would be a unit; or the day, evening, or midnight watch or shift could be a unit. In medium-sized and large departments, shifts or watches could even have smaller units, such as teams or groups covering certain geographical areas.

Program objectives are somewhat different. From time to time police agencies develop special programs on traffic safety, crime prevention, or another problem related to the department. If the activity is a continuous endeavor of the organization, it should be treated as a unit; if it has a definite life span, the objectives for that program should be established just for the life of the program. An ongoing effort to discourage high school students from alcohol abuse would be considered as a unit, but a state or federal grant for prevention of burglaries would be a program. The objective, of course, should be compatible with those of the organization. The program or project concept will be discussed later in the chapter on organization.

And, of course, individual objectives are for individual police employees. Individual objectives are of two kinds: one concerns the activity of the employee, and the second concerns the employee's development—his training, education, assignments to broaden his experience, and so on.

A Police MBO/R Example

Here is a brief example of an MBO/R system for police. The development of the system proceeds as follows: (1) identification of goals, (2) selection of one goal for objective development, (3) selection of one unit for objectives, and (4) selection of one employee for setting objectives.

Among the goals of the police agency (selected from Table 1, page 20) are control of crime, protection of life and property, provision of community services, and control of traffic and selected noncriminal activities. It would be possible, and even desirable, to be more specific in development of organizational goals; however, these goals are sufficient for purposes of the illustration. The one goal to be used for the development of objectives in this illustration is *control of crime.*

Agency-level objectives should (1) be related to specific crimes and crime-related activities and (2) be quantifiable if possible and cover a quarterly, semiannual, or annual time period.

Goal: Control of crime

Examples of Agency-Level Objectives:

1. Reduce burglaries by 10 percent over the next fiscal year. (The measurement is based on a comparison with the previous year's burglary rate. One must consider increased population, housing, industry, and so on. For example, if there were 10 burglaries per 1,000 population, or per 1,000 houses or businesses, then a 10 percent decrease would be 9 per 1,000. Even though the actual number may have increased, the *rate* of burglary would have declined.)

2. Establish an educational program for crime prevention for businesses in the next fiscal year. (Note that this is a qualitative, time-bounded objective.)

3. Increase the arrest rate for crimes of violence by 10 percent over the next fiscal year.

4. Increase the average visibility time of all patrol units to an average of 50 percent of the shift or watch time over the next fiscal year.

These are examples of agency-level objectives that could be set and that are supportive of the goal of crime control. The exact percentage, or other quantifiable objective, should be determined by the unique circumstances of each community. Of the four objectives, however, three are quantifiable, and all are time-bounded. (The time set is one year, but it could be less if the chief executive wanted a more frequent check.)

The next step is to take agency-level objectives and identify the unit objectives supportive of the agency objectives. The unit to be used as an example will be the patrol division. First, what can the patrol division specifically do to reduce burglaries? This raises an important issue that the manager should address—the difference between an objective that states what is to be done and an objective that states the methods to be employed. It is recommended that agency-level objectives be statements of *what* is to be done, such as objectives 1 and 3 above, while unit and individual objectives be statements of methods, such as objectives 2 and 4. Therefore, objective 1 will be used as an example here.

Objectives 2 and 4 should actually be objectives for units and individuals. Second, the manager must ask whether the method used to obtain the reduction is the most effective.

Agency Objective 1: Reduce burglaries by 10 percent over the next fiscal year

Examples of Patrol Unit Objectives for Agency Objective 1:

1. Establish an education program for *(number)* homes and *(number)* businesses by *(date)*. (As the program develops, more specific objectives should be established.)

2. Decrease average report-taking time per report by *(certain percent)* in the next *(time period)*. (Saving time here can permit investment of that time in some other activity.)

3. Establish an intelligence unit to identify and develop behavioral files on all known or suspected burglars by *(date)*. (All is 100 percent, so it is a quantifiable objective.)

4. Provide a special forty-hour training program for all patrol officers in special burglary investigation techniques within *(time period)*.

These are examples of *hows*, or *methods objectives* to accomplish *whats*, or *purpose objectives*. Accomplishment of these unit objectives would bring agency objectives closer to realization. These methods objectives are designed to give the patrol unit a greater influence on factors causing the burglaries. They focus on several different areas: (1) education, or crime prevention, which is emerging as a new police method, (2) saving time in one activity to invest it in a more productive activity, (3) taking a somewhat different approach to investigating burglaries by concentrating on individuals instead of separate cases, and (4) improving the skills of those investigating burglaries. These methods objectives represent both traditional and creative approaches to attempting to meet the agency objectives. The times and dates should be based on the resources and unique problems of the agency; generally, however, the time frame should be less than that of the agency objectives so more frequent checks can be made in case changes are necessary.

It is possible that additional unit objectives could be established, depending on the size of the police agency. As organizations increase in size, the objectives for lesser units can be the same as those for the larger unit but with shorter time frames, or they can be part of the larger unit objective. For example, one watch, or part of a watch, could develop educational material for the crime prevention program or methods for gathering intelligence files. On the other hand, objectives can be completely separate and unique to the problems of each unit or shift. For example, a midnight watch might be plagued by thefts from a new housing project, or an evening watch might have a nuisance problem. These special situations can be considered in setting unique objectives.

The final step in the MBO/R example is setting individual objectives for specific employees. Individual objectives are closely related to agency-level and unit objectives. Generally, the time frames are shorter, and individual objectives can be set for unique assignments or "beat" problems. In addition, objectives should be established for individual personal development. These can and should include participation in training and education programs to upgrade understanding and skills, individual study and reading, participation in professional organizations, and so on.

Figure 8 is a form that can be used for the development of individual objectives. It can be modified to fit any level of objective, but it is most appropriate on an individual level. It can also be the basis for a performance appraisal system. The form provides a space for objective identification, the standard of measurement, the time frame, and the type and frequency of progress check. Objectives and time frames have already been discussed, but standards of measurement need elaboration.

If an objective of a certain quantity is established, what should be the basis for comparison, or the standard of measurement? In the case of a 10 percent reduction in time per report, the basis would be the time per report for the last year, month, or week. In the case of the agency's objective to reduce burglaries, the basis is an absolute comparison (an actual numerical change) or a comparison based on ratio changes (the ratio of burglaries per 1,000 or 10,000 population) in one time period compared with

Figure 8
Manager-Employee Objective Development Form

Objectives for *(Name of Employee)* with *(Name of Supervisor)* Date:

Objective	Standard of Measurement	Time Frame	Type and Frequency of Progress Check

Progress Check for Objective _____

Analysis of Results:

Action: (Altered, New, or No Change) _____

another. Standards of measurement are important and require systematic consideration by the manager.

The time frame of individual objectives varies, but if the objective is part of a large one—a unit or agency object—the time frame should decrease as the objectives are set at lower levels in the organization. Shorter time periods permit a more frequent check and an analysis of problems as they develop. Such analysis in turn will facilitate accomplishment of the higher-level objectives. The frequency of checks can be the same as the time frame of the objective, but it does not have to be. It is a good idea to have periodic checks on all objectives prior to their time frame date in order to deal with unanticipated problems. The type of check can range from a highly detailed statistical report to a brief oral conversation. The type of check should be based on the level and frequency of the check. At some point, a written evaluation should be prepared, but the checks on progress can take the form of brief conversations or meetings. This is a matter for the individual agency and manager to decide.

The bottom of the form in Figure 8 indicates that for each check some notation should be made. This is a sound idea, for the analysis of results provides a place for a notation concerning problems, the reasons for them, the action taken, and the degree to which objectives are realized. It may be necessary to revise objectives or set new ones. In addition, the analysis and notation of problem areas provide a valuable learning experience and can result in the identification of important problems requiring separate study. Periodically—two or three times per year, or even more often—new forms should be developed for each employee. The regular process permits performance checks to provide an ongoing evaluation and analysis of efforts toward objectives.

Manager-Employee Objective-Setting Process

The employee, or worker, is the basic and most valuable resource in a police organization. The MBO/R process, if it is to be effective, must be successful at the manager-employee level of development. When mature employees have a direct voice in deciding what is expected of them, they tend to develop a feeling of participation in the organization's goals and objectives. The following examples describe the objective-setting process with three employees, each with a different degree of organizational maturity. It is assumed in each case that the manager and employee are familiar with the MBO/R system and have appropriate forms. In each case, Pete is the manager.

Situation 1: New Employee (Joe)

Pete: Joe, we're here to discuss your objectives for the next three months. You haven't been with us too long, so until you know more about the job, I'll be giving you more guidance than some of the other guys. Now here's what I have in mind for your objectives. [Presents objectives.] Any questions or suggestions?

Joe: No, not now, but I may have some later.

Pete: OK, just ask me, and remember that these objectives aren't fixed in concrete. We want you to do your best, but we don't expect the impossible. Let's get together every so often to see how you're doing.

Situation 2: Employee Who Is Moderately Mature as an Organization Member (Alec)

Pete: Alec, you know why we're here. I've got some possible objectives for you for the next six months. Look them over while I read the ones you've prepared. [Alec was requested to do this prior to the meeting.]

     I think your objectives are good and compatible with the ones I've developed; however, objective 4 seems to be too much to accomplish in that time period. [A discussion follows in which the men agree on specific objectives, times, and so on.]

Alec: The objectives look good; I'm still uncertain over the last two, though.

Pete: OK, let's keep a closer watch on the progress there, and if it looks as if you can't realize them, we can modify them later. OK?

Alec: OK.

Situation 3: Organizationally Mature Employee (Bill)

Pete: Bill, what do you have in mind for your objectives for this next year?

Bill: Here they are; I'd like to try some new things this time.

Pete: [Reads the objectives.] OK. You know the problems we've had with the first two before, so let's work together on these to try and see if we can't get them done. Let me know if you have problems on the others, and keep me advised on your progress.

Bill: OK.

In each of these situations the manager demonstrates a high concern for the individual and the organization and considers the organizational maturity of the employee in determining the degree of employee participation in the objective-setting process. Each situation shows the importance of the supportive dimension of the manager's role in encouraging and helping the employee mature into a highly effective and motivated police officer.

Criteria for Sound Objectives

Several important criteria should be considered in setting objectives in police agencies.

1. Is the objective quantifiable? If possible, objectives should be expressed in terms of numbers, ratios, percentages, and so on. Qualitative objectives are unavoidable in police agencies, however, so some objectives will inevitably be subjective and therefore more difficult to develop and evaluate.

2. Does the objective lead to improved performance? Objectives should lead to performance greater than an "acceptable day's work." They should be challenging but not so challenging that they become impossible to realize and therefore frustrating.

3. Are the objectives compatible and integrated? If objectives are compatible, they will not be in conflict. For example, a patrol objective to become more aggressive in enforcing some laws may be incompatible with a community relations objective to improve citizen relations with the police. Objectives should be compatible, or at least balanced. Lower-level objectives, if accomplished, should lead to the accomplishment of higher-level objectives and not hinder them.

4. Do objectives recognize constraints? Managers should not establish objectives that cannot be realized because of resources, social or political limitations, the law, community expectations, or other factors. Such objectives are frustrating and demoralizing for employees and often create excessive conflict. To some degree, conflict cannot be avoided in police work, but the greater the conflict, the greater the risk for the manager and the organization.

MBO/R as Used in a Police Agency

The foregoing approach for the development of an MBO/R system is, of course, not the only way to proceed. It is, however, a logical, step-by-step method that is useful for the manager to consider in objective development. Another approach, described next, was developed by a moderate-sized police department.[1] This police department established the goals of the organization, the objective or objectives for each goal, and the means and measures for each objective. Some of the objectives have more than one means. In the system described earlier, the means, or methods objectives, were at the unit level. In the system described next, the means would be assigned to various units in the organization. The means are not stated as objectives in the example, however, and they should be. Nevertheless, a valuable feature of the following approach is the specific identification of the measure, or standard of measurement of the objective.

MBO/R System for Police (An Example)

Goal I:	Provide for crime prevention programs utilizing all available manpower and other resources.
Objective 1:	Reduce residential burglaries by *(a certain percent)* during *(a certain fiscal year)*.
Means:	Implement an identification operation in *(number)* homes by *(a certain time)* through homeowners' groups, civic organizations, and so on.
Measures:	The rate of home burglaries in general, the rate of burglaries among homes participating in the program, and the recovery rate of property stolen from homes that participated in the identification operation. Comparison is with the same amounts in the previous time period.
Means:	Participate with city planners to review residential building codes regarding minimum standards for locks, windows, and other security devices.
Measure:	Burglary rates in reporting areas that meet security standards compared with those in other areas that do not.
Means:	Coordinate the identification and control of potential truants.
Measure:	The rate of daytime home burglaries.

Objective 2: Reduce commercial burglaries by *(a certain percent)* during *(a certain fiscal year)*.

Means: Develop a program for merchants identifying related factors causing commercial burglaries and techniques available to combat those factors. Prepare and gather brochures and visual aids for presentation to business groups. Provide manpower to tour business establishments and suggest burglary prevention techniques applicable to the location inspected. Provide follow-up checks with business representatives to determine what preventive actions have been taken.

Measures: Percentage decrease in burglaries of businesses adopting recommended crime preventive measures compared with those of merchants who did not follow recommendations; percentage of businesses receiving a prevention inspection that implement recommended measures.

Objective 3: Reduce *repeat* disturbance of the peace calls by *(a certain percent)* during *(a certain fiscal year)*.

Means: Implement a *(number)*-hour crisis intervention program for all operational personnel between *(time)* and *(time)*. Develop a referral system of agencies that provide various public services for use in crisis intervention programs. Implement crisis intervention by *(date)*. Develop a follow-up procedure on referred cases.

Measure: The rate of repeat disturbance of the peace calls between *(time)* and *(time)*, as compared to previous time periods.

Goal II: Provide aggressive, offensive measures against established criminal activities.

Objective 1: Increase burglary arrests by *(a certain percent)* over *(a certain time period)*.

Means: Organize special enforcement units to "stake out" high-burglary-rate areas. Coordinate all burglary reports with other forms of police intelligence (interview cards, suspicious circumstances reports, and so on) to develop a comprehensive burglary information system. Provide for exten-

	sive interviews of all burglar arrestees to develop data on *modus operandi,* location of stolen property, identification of additional suspects, and so on.
Measure:	Percentage increase of burglars arrested over *(a certain time period).*
Objective 2:	Increase the amount of stolen property recovered by *(a certain percent)* over *(a certain time period).*
Means:	Provide surveillance on known fences, pawn shops, and flea markets. Compile comprehensive lists of stolen property, emphasizing those items readily identifiable (by serial or ID number, complete description, uniqueness, and so on). Provide extensive interviews of all suspected thieves arrested. Follow up on all thefts, emphasizing accurate property description.
Measure:	Percentage increase of recovered stolen property over *(a certain time period)* as compared to previous time periods.
Goal III:	Provide thorough and lawful police-related investigations.
Objective 1:	Significantly increase the development of investigative leads.
Means:	Develop and implement a total information system capable of effectively gathering, collating, storing, and disseminating criminal intelligence by *(a certain date).* Establish an intelligence unit to develop a prototype intelligence system. Establish a report technique to be utilized by field personnel in preparing intelligence reports. Implement critiquing meetings between shift personnel with an intelligence monitor to record pertinent data. Establish an intelligence file system that will make total intelligence packages (suspect histories, acquaintances, vehicles, *modus operandi,* cross-references) readily available. Contact neighboring communities and agencies to tap their criminal intelligence for inclusion in departmental files and reports.

Measure: Percentage increase in clearance rates resulting from utilization of criminal intelligence files during *(a certain fiscal year)* as compared to previous fiscal years.

Objective 2:   Improve investigative cost effectiveness by decreasing the ratio of investigative hours expended to cases cleared.

Means: Establish criteria for determining case expenditures that will provide for the greatest degree of successful case dispositions and manpower utilization by *(a certain date)*. Analyze case variables to determine the probability of a successful investigation. Develop minimum standards for case investigations such as level of investigatable elements available, working caseload, time in relation to investigatable elements, and so on.

Measures: Percentage decrease in man-hours expended on noninvestigatable cases; percentage increase in cases cleared in ratio to intelligence manpower expended.

Problem Areas in MBO/R

As is the case with most management systems, MBO/R is not without pitfalls. There are two principal areas for consideration in this regard: (1) objectives, or "quotas," and (2) output and outcome objectives.

When a police agency establishes an objective that is quantified and related to arrests or tickets, for example, some citizens consider it a quota. Officers themselves, if they know they are to be rewarded by realizing the objective, can be motivated to give tickets or make arrests when they would not normally do so. Officers and citizens should be carefully cautioned that objectives are to be fulfilled within legal and departmental guidelines. If policemen understand this and if the objectives are realistic and the manager is systematic and fair in his analysis of the reasons why objectives are not realized, the "quota" problem will be minimized.

It is questionable whether all citizens will ever accept the fact that objectives are not quotas, especially if these citizens are arrested or given tickets. If, however, the objectives are established within legal and policy guidelines, the police manager should be able to defend the use of the MBO/R system adequately.

The output and outcome problem is somewhat more complicated. As used here, police *outputs* are the things police do (investigate, patrol, and so on), and *outcomes* are the results of what police do (changes in crime or citizen attitudes and so on). Police agencies tend to set agency-level objectives in terms of outcomes and unit-level objectives in terms of outputs. The problem that arises is the relationship between what police do and crime, citizen attitudes, and so on. If the goal is crime control, the agency-level objective is a 10 percent reduction of crime. What happens if the police cannot influence the crime rate—no matter what is lawfully done—by 10 percent? Obviously, the goal the agency-level objective is a 10 percent reduction of crime, what happens if the police cannot influence the crime rate—no ing what police do and what happens as a result of what they do is just beginning to be explored systematically. The police manager should be aware of this problem and the ever-present temptation to manipulate data to appear to obtain the desired outcome. Changes in police department reporting policies can change apparent crime rates. If an MBO/R system is to have meaning, this should, of course, not be done. Rather, managers should attempt to develop an understanding of the relationship between police outputs and outcomes.

Here is a brief example of one police department's experience with MBO. As in all management systems, some problems developed.

The city in question employs 167 people, 48 of whom are policemen. The city manager instituted MBO throughout the entire city. Both he and the police chief were committed to trying it. At the beginning of the program, the city spent a considerable sum of money instructing the administrative staff in the background of MBO and the proper method for instituting it within each city department. The problem was that no such instruction was held for the remainder of the employees who were expected to participate in the program. On completion of the training for the administrative staff, the patrol commander issued objectives to each individual. Unfortunately, he held no discussion regarding the objectives for which each officer was to be held accountable. Nor did he and his employees agree on what the objectives would be. The officers resented this and considered MBO just another way to check up on them.

A few city employees agreed with the principles of MBO. The remainder, because MBO was new and would result in their having to change their behavior, were resentful. Also, many division and department heads did not understand the concept or how it should be implemented. In plain language, most of the people were afraid of the concept just because it was something new.

Many supervisors believed that an employee should not have a voice in deciding how to do his job. Supervisors were also afraid of the idea of actually having to sit down and discuss jobs with their employees. Morale was low, as the officers believed that they were not really part of the organization because they were not allowed to participate in any of the decisions that were made regarding their job functions.

Because of these problems, a training session was begun on a weekly basis over a four-month period. All officers and supervisors were required to attend. Additional training was given to the supervisors to insure that they were familiar with the proper method of reaching individual objectives with the officers. Each watch was also required to decide on watch objectives that were to cover a six-month period.

The consequences of full participation in MBO appeared to improve the situation. Each officer began to participate fully and agree on the individual objectives that he was expected to accomplish, and he knew exactly what the watch objectives were. Supervisors began communicating on a regular basis with their men on matters relating to the job.

MBO is not without problems, but it can be effective. The manager considering use of MBO, however, should consider all the potential problems suggested in this chapter and the examples just cited.

Summary

This chapter has described an MBO/R system that can be utilized by police. Important considerations are the process of MBO/R development, the motivational dimensions of the system, the quota relationship, the differences between output and outcome objectives, and the issue of organizational effectiveness.

MBO/R has tremendous potential for police organizations and managers. The variations on the method described in this chapter are numerous. Each organization can develop an individualized system. The purpose of MBO/R is to get the organization and the individual to identify a purpose (goal or objective), analyze how best to realize that purpose, make it specific enough to be measured, and continuously evaluate the progress toward the realization of the purpose in order to establish new goals and increase effectiveness. This evaluation process will be discussed in more detail in the chapter on controlling.

Suggested
Reading

Hughes, Charles L. *Goal Setting.* New York: American Management Association, 1965.

Mali, Paul. *Managing by Objectives.* New York: John Wiley, Interscience, 1972

Reddin, W. J. *Effective Management by Objectives.* New York: McGraw-Hill, 1970.

Valentine, Raymond F. *Performance Objectives for Managers.* New York: American Management Association, 1966.

CHAPTER 4

Planning
Concepts
and Methods

While the planning phase of the management process includes goal and objective development, planning itself is much broader in scope. Planning includes the development of a broad outline of how the agency intends to achieve its goals and objectives. Once the broad plans have been agreed on, the finer details are worked out so that each person involved will know exactly what is expected of him. In addition, planners must identify and allocate material and human resources as plans are developed. Planning in a police agency, at its simplest, is deciding *who* will be doing *what*, *where*, *when*, and often, *how*. Throughout this chapter, the words *planner* and *manager* will be used interchangeably. Often separate planning units exist in large agencies, but this is not true in smaller ones; managers are the planners there, and, to a lesser degree, even in the larger agencies.

97

Planning as an Intellectual Process

Planning is, in essence, an intellectual activity. Planners literally think through each step of possible routes by which the agency can achieve its goals and objectives. In order that the decision-makers have sufficient choice, planners often must think through a variety of ways to reach these goals and objectives. Sometimes the paths planners create intellectually are familiar in that others already have experimented with the procedures considered; at other times plans are innovative and untried. Generally, small police agencies have more difficulty being innovative because of their limited resources, so the techniques and processes used by other police agencies are often adjusted to local conditions and then implemented. In order for this process of imitation and occasional innovation to be successful, a thorough understanding of the agency's environment is necessary. Such an understanding is a prerequisite for effective law enforcement planning, for the manager simply must know whether the impact achieved elsewhere or forecast by theorists elsewhere will in fact be the same in his city or county. No two places or populations are exactly alike. The local manager should not continually copy the efforts and successes of others, because such imitation can destroy or stifle creativity in the organization. In addition, copying may not always result in the most effective plan. The planning process is improved significantly if the administrator is, and encourages others to be, as creative as possible instead of relying solely on the plans of others.

Some patterns of creativity are already well known to law officers since many of their operations, such as investigations, are scientifically based. The same patterns apply to the planning process of management. For instance, police officers use logic when they investigate a case. Deductive reasoning (moving from general to specific principles) and inductive reasoning (moving from specific to general principles) are often employed. The use of *modus operandi*, reasonable cause, and other familiar principles and investigative techniques are examples of a type of logical thinking employed by police. Another pattern of creativity is idea linking. In order to attain a certain objective, many different ideas are needed. Many of these, if viewed singly, would contribute little toward the goal, but when viewed together in a logical pattern and bearing on the desired achievements, the value of linked ideas is evident. An example is the application of general managerial concepts to police agencies. The ability to obtain and link often diverse ideas calls for a variety of perspectives and experiences. One of the most effective mechanisms for obtaining diverse ideas is the free association process often employed in the preliminary phases of the planning process. A modified form of free association can be found in some departmental staff meetings where the manager encourages a free flow of ideas when discussing departmental goals or problems. Some departments even sponsor a fishing trip or a retreat to get key personnel away to an isolated location for an intensive session in which ideas are exchanged freely and plans developed. The inclusion of some nonstaff personnel (patrolmen) often proves highly rewarding, since persons at that level often have valuable perspectives and ideas. Regardless of how the ideas are obtained, planning is an intellectual process that is aided by a freedom to suggest and explore diverse ideas.

Police organizations have had a pattern of duplication, or copying, and some innovation. As federal monies have become increasingly available, innovation has increased. Still, it has had only limited impact on community police agencies. All community police agencies should constantly seek innovative methods for solutions to community police problems. This does not mean that being aware of, and even using, the methods of other police agencies is inappropriate, only that effective management is, in large measure, the result of constant innovation to meet new problems effectively.

Purposes and Values of Planning

Ideally, what should the purpose of planning be, and what value will accrue to the police agency that plans its activities? By planning activities, the organization usually increases both its efficiency and its effectiveness. Planning also provides direction (goals and objectives) and means for goal-realization. The planning process and the plans developed from it help the organization move along predetermined pathways approved by those responsible for the agency and its activities. Once managers have thought through the steps to be encountered and executed, problem areas can be anticipated and preparations made to overcome hazards. Surprises, and often crises, can be avoided.

Planning also helps employees at the various levels of the agency know how to think and act, since familiarity with overall goals and plans provides a useful frame of reference for them. Involvement in planning helps employees link all the parts to the whole and stimulates cooperation, integration of functions, and enthusiasm, particularly if personnel at many levels within the agency have participated in the setting of goals and the related planning activities. Last, planning allows the agency to make a plan of action designed to achieve its goals and relate activities to useful results. With detailed steps outlined, the manager and personnel can see progress when and where it occurs and also discover deviations. (As will be discussed in the chapter on controlling, planning also provides the base line for corrective action by the manager.)

The ideals and purposes of planning can become reality for the manager when he encourages cooperation in planning and implementing. Every agency, and every community as well, contains a wealth of perspectives and experience. These resources should be used in planning whenever feasible. And, to reemphasize, those employees in nonstaff, service-delivery-level positions should not be overlooked. Participation, although somewhat time-consuming, almost always results in better plans and, equally important, motivated employees. Planning, to be of value and to achieve its purpose, must be participative.

The Planning Process

The planning process is a series of steps that resembles decision-making and policy formulation processes. All the difficulties and problems to be discussed in Chapter 5 occur when taking the steps described in the following paragraphs. These steps are the normative ones often prescribed in the management literature of law enforcement, public administration, and business.

Stage 1 is the determination of goals and objectives and/or the recognition and definition of problems and/or the determination of opportunities to be explored. In this stage, the planner decides just what it is that the agency wants to accomplish. This stage can also include the recognition of a problem, such as an alarming rise in a particular criminal activity. It may be that the agency's goals and objectives already cover this phase. If so, this stage involves definition and assessment of the planning problem that exists. Whether determining goals or objectives, the planner in this stage is trying to find out exactly what it is that is to be done.

Stage 2 is scanning and forecasting, gathering the data or information needed to help define the exact nature of the problem now and at some future time, and even the related environmental impact. The kind of information collected will depend on the objective of the planning process, the problem to be solved, or the opportunity to be seized. Planners should collect as much data or information as resources permit and as they can effectively analyze.

Stage 3 is analyzing the data. The interpretation of the facts, both qualitative and quantitative, is vitally important to planning. Often the manager must judge what facts are the most important and what weight should be given to the data or information in the determination and final selection of plans. Subjective hunches should not be overlooked in analyzing the data. The interpretation of data or information is very important, because those interpretations become the planning assumptions and influence the predictions and expectations about the future. Planning assumptions are the "truths" the planner accepts. For example, many planners accept the assumption that patrol deters crime. Other assumptions, perhaps concerning predicted crime five years in the future, could determine plans for resources.

Stage 4 is the determination and exploration of all the possible alternatives. This stage requires creativity. Every conceivable way of solving the problem, meeting the objective, or seizing the opportunity should be fully explored. Every cost and gain should be examined. If feasible, the alternatives should be tested. If not, the planners should test each alternative in their minds. The person in the department most opposed to each alternative can play "devil's advocate" with the suggestion he opposes. The manager should utilize all the participants' expertise and viewpoints and should not automatically preclude the most outlandish solutions. Each can contain some element useful to the planning process.

Stage 5 is the selection of the most appropriate alternative. This is the decision phase of the planning process. The decision will be based on a variety of considerations, including available resources, costs, organizational acceptance, community acceptance, predetermined impact on goals and objectives, type of changes needed, and so on.

Stage 6 is developing support for the plan. Generally, it is impossible to include the entire department in the planning process that occurs before the decision is made. But the success of the plan and the other stages in the process involve those who were excluded from those earlier steps. All persons who will be concerned with the subsequent phases can be involved in developing support for the plan. Developing support involves explaining its essentials. Every actor in the plan must be briefed about his role in achieving the plan's objectives. Many managers will "sell" the plan by allowing subunits to help flesh out the skeletal idea. Whatever method is employed, the executors of the plan will accept it more readily if they are convinced that what they will be doing is important and will contribute to their own and the organization's goals.

Stage 7 is the actual execution of the plan. The plan is put into motion and becomes operational. As the plan is implemented, the planners should scrutinize each phase to make adjustments as necessary.

Stage 8 is review and control, the constant monitoring of the plan in all parts of the organization. Part of the planning includes the development of indicators to measure the progress of the plan. As part of the control phase of management, the entire environment should be scanned and particular attention devoted to the indicators within the department. Unexpected benefits, or problems, can be discovered during the monitoring phase of the planning process.[1] It is important for managers to include monitoring as a normal part of the police agency's management program. Hopefully, the manager will have an openness in the organization that will result in all personnel feeling free to tell him when events are not occurring according to plan.

Stage 9 is changing the original plan as necessary. Once set in motion, plans should not be followed slavishly if modifications or cancellation proves to be necessary. Planning is a continuing process in that new circumstances and unforeseen problems are encountered, or other priorities arise. Plans should be continually reviewed and updated even while they are being implemented. Control feedback should be reviewed constantly, and if it is necessary to alter, modify, renew, or stop a plan, the manager should be prepared to take rapid, but deliberate, action. As mentioned in the introduction of the book, the environment of law enforcement agencies is not static, and plans therefore should never be cast in concrete.

Characteristics of a Good Plan and of Good Planning

One of the major characteristics of a good plan and good planning is that the objectives to be achieved are clearly defined and understood by everyone. If the plan includes the public, they should be generally aware of the reasons for, and details of, the plan. For instance, in traffic enforcement the public should be advised of the dangers of driving under the influence of alcohol and of the fact that the police will be specifically looking for intoxicated drivers. Persons inside the agency should also be aware of organizational plans and what they are intended to achieve. A good plan should include methods to insure this familiarization.

A plan should be comprehensive and outline the actions necessary to achieve objectives. For example, efforts to increase clearance of cases by investigators should include the delineation of the role of the uniformed patrol division. Patrolmen should know what investigators will be needing in preliminary reports, field interrogations, and so on if the new plans call for changes in standard operating procedures. Although aimed at the investigators, the plan would include the actions expected of others. Since most functional activities require the support of many other functional units, necessary interrelated supportive action should be spelled out and understood; the hierarchy of plans within the organization should be integrated. To insure that plans and planning have a maximum chance to achieve objectives, comprehensive integration is needed in all activities related to the problem with which the plan is concerned.

Probably the most crucial consideration by managers in planning is feasibility, especially in terms of available resources. When plans are developed, new resources usually must be obtained or taken from another activity. This means that a "new" plan affects an "old" plan. The manager must consider the trade-offs of one plan against the other.

Another important factor in planning is the assessment of the impact of present accepted plans on future courses of action. This requires not only a thorough knowledge of the present environment, but also the ability to forecast environmental and organizational changes. Present plans are decisions about the future.

Flexibility in planning is also important; it involves a consideration of alternative plans related to the original should conditions change or unforeseen developments occur. The plan might contain an appendix laying out alternatives for accelerating the plan to a rapid conclusion, shifting resources elsewhere to meet the unforeseen, suspending the plan and its activities, or perhaps winding down the plan. A good plan includes a mechanism for changing direction as a changing environment requires.

Time, Detail, and Responsibilities in Planning

Much terminology exists concerning the time frame of a plan. Generally, the detail of the plan is related to the time frame. A short-range plan is usually for less than a year; an intermediate-range plan is for from approximately one year to as long as five years; and anything longer than intermediate is classified as long-range. Some plans are held in anticipation of certain problems and their length or duration depends on the persistence of the problem. These, often called *contingency plans*, are activated when the problem for which they were designed appears and deactivated when the problem disappears.

Some plans are written in general terms while others are quite detailed. The extent of the detail depends on the level in the hierarchy at which the planning occurs and the time frame of the plan. Generally, the longer the plan's time frame and the higher the level in the organization, the more general the plan; the shorter the plan's time frame and the lower the level in the organization, the more specific and detailed the plan. Everyone in the organization is involved in the planning process, but what is expected of them varies. Here are three levels of management in an organization and the general planning responsibilities of each:

1. Top management is concerned with long-range considerations and general planning, and considerable time is invested in planning activities. In large police departments, top management is placing increasingly greater reliance on specialized planning and research units.

2. Middle managers participate in development of all ranges of plans in the agency, oversee the short- and intermediate-range plans, develop many of the details in long- and intermediate-range plans, and usually play a key role in making adjustments in the execution phases of plans.

3. Supervisors participate in the planning process by overseeing operational plans, and in many small police departments may perform the functions of middle management as well; they also assist in developing the specifics or details for translation of plans into action.

Operational personnel participate in the planning process if administrators encourage them; they may also develop detailed plans in small departments. They are directly involved in implementation of formulated and approved plans and often are the first to know when plans are succeeding or failing.

The planning responsibilities in an organization can be diagrammed as follows:

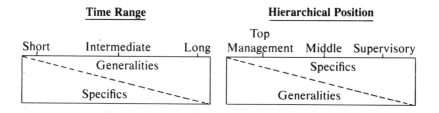

Categories of Plans

Plans can be classified in many ways and put into many categories. Here is one such classification:

1. *Standing Plans.* Standing plans are used each time a given situation is encountered and are those used as the framework for the agency.

    a. General Mission Plans. These include the philosophies as to function and role that give personnel a general sense of direction.

    b. Policies. These are general and broad guidelines or statements that assist each decision at all levels in the organization.

    c. Procedures. These are guides to action, the exact steps to be taken when action can be exactly prescribed; the standard operating procedure (SOP) to be followed in such matters as records, dispatching, handcuffing, and so on.

    d. Methods. These are explanations of how the exact steps of procedures are to be executed.

    e. Rules. These are the very definite "do's and don'ts" of various jobs or tasks.

2. *Time-Specific Plans.* Time-specific plans are those that are aimed at a specific objective and terminate at the achievement of the objective, when feedback is negative, when objectives are changed, or at a specified time.

    a. Programs. These are specific investments of resources to achieve specified goals. The program usually spells out what is to be accomplished, its costs, necessary training, and whatever else is needed. A time phase and evaluation mechanism are often specified.

    b. Projects. A project is a part of a program that is usually of shorter duration. The project often involves a broad spectrum of people who return to their normal functions at the completion of the project. At times the terms *project* and *program* are used interchangeably.

    c. Budget Plans. These are the financial plans of the department.

    d. Contingency Plans. These are outlines of action to be taken at a specific location, under certain circumstances, and with designated personnel.

3. *Functional Plans.* Functional plans are the general work plans of the line divisions (the patrol or uniformed and investiga-

tive divisions); they include the goals and objectives, resources, and general methods of action for achievement. Standing plans are normally employed in conjunction with general functional plans.

4. *Supporting Plans.* Supporting plans are related to any of the others and assist in their development, implementation, or achievement.

Extradepartmental Planning

From time to time law enforcement agencies must plan activities with other agencies. Extradepartmental planning can be comprehensive criminal justice planning for a region—for example, development of a regional training center; joint programs or projects among similar elements of the system—for example, a county-wide auto theft unit; projects among diverse agencies on a common problem—for example, a joint juvenile probation and police diversion program for juveniles; or joint tactical plans aimed at a particular law enforcement problem—for example, civil disturbances. In extradepartmental or joint planning, police managers should consider the following factors.

The planners or managers of the joint activity want to be sure exactly what each means by the words he uses to describe the goal of the activity. Often the same phrases are used by the participants, but each interprets them differently. Joint plans should spell out exactly the goals of the plan and the resources to be expended. One person should direct the project and have the authority to act. Personnel involved in the joint activity should know that the director is empowered to act and has the support of the executives or top managers. Those involved in the various organizations should communicate openly and cooperate. If resources have been allocated, each should do his part to assure delivery unless overpowering circumstances intervene. The planners should agree on definite time phases for review of the program's development, and if a modification is necessary, as much lead time as possible should be given the other agency or agencies involved so that they can make adjustments in their activities. All the mechanisms and experiences from the field of diplomacy in international relations should be applied to the planning and implementation of plans among agencies. Diplomats have a vast experience that can be tapped to guide the relationships between the parties involved.

Planning Methods and Personnel

Planning units are usually called planning and research units, and it is not without reason that the function of research is combined with the function of planning. Planning is based on knowledge of the agency's environment and the operations it conducts within that environment. In order to develop the methods whereby the organization achieves its goals and objectives, planners must know exactly what is occurring at the time and have some ideas about the potential for affecting the future. Planning and research go together. Planning methods are, therefore, part of research methodology.

Planning units in law enforcement agencies are a fairly recent innovation. For instance, in cities of over 1 million population, the average age of planning units is a scant fifteen years. The average size of the staff is about thirty. In cities with populations of 100,000 to 250,000, the average unit age is about four years and the average number of personnel is two.[2] The belief in the value of a planning unit is only now being emphasized. As noted previously, in small agencies the manager and planner may be one and the same.

The greatest impetus for planning has probably been federal monies that were made available and administered by the Law Enforcement Assistance Administration and various state planning agencies. Although programs carried out with these funds have been criticized severely because of their emphasis on short-term planning and equipment,[3] rapid success in gaining equipment and satisfying immediate needs made people realize that by rationally planning activities to meet certain goals and objectives, police agencies were able to achieve a great deal more than before. Many small agencies, while unable to develop a unit or assign a planner full time, are attempting to practice some degree of planning in their activities. The planning pump has been primed.

Whether planning is conducted by a full-size unit or by a single officer or manager on a part-time basis, the duties are approximately the same. The planner is responsible for developing and updating policies, procedures, rules, and directives as well as developing short-, intermediate-, and long-range plans. Specific plans could include an annual report for the community and government officials. Studies could also be developed—to identify changes in the environment or to evaluate operational practices and management. The variety of duties and activities would depend on the resources allocated to planning.

An important factor for the manager to keep in mind is the stimulation of planning throughout the entire organization. The patrol and investigative units may consider planning to be of only subsidiary importance. Like intelligence, planning is a valuable tool in helping these units accomplish their goals. Planners not only "sell" individual plans but must also foster planning and research concepts. Some planners have undertaken specialized projects to open the door for later acceptance of the concepts and practices of planning. Success with specialized studies requested by patrol and investigation can make this "selling" easier at some later date. If planning is to play a major role in the management of the police agency, it must be accepted.

Methods and Techniques of the Planning Process

In order to set or help set objectives, to detect and understand problems, and to recognize opportunities when and where they occur, the police manager must have a base of data or information. A manager's intuitive feelings about the environment are valuable but can be misleading because his information may be incomplete. The business of planners includes providing the decision-makers with adequate information on which to make their decisions.

Information comes from a variety of sources. Many kinds of data are generated within the department itself. The entire records system provides valuable input to the manager: complaints, field interrogations, calls for service, arrests, and so on. The same is true of the information and data available from other agencies, private and public, in the community—businesses, schools, and firms collect a myriad of data for their individual needs, and these data are potentially useful for the police and other criminal justice agencies in planning their services and activities. Some such information is available on a regular basis and is complete, while other data are collected sporadically and may be incomplete. The information and data of use to the community police planner will also vary with the passage of time and the shifting of societal priorities. What was unimportant yesterday may take on importance today. Each generation has a different set of questions to ask and demands to make. The planning units and their personnel should accumulate and store as much data as they can feasibly process and interpret while also knowing other sources of information outside the agency. Keeping future data needs in mind is also important.

Just what information and data should be collected is, of course, a matter that each police or sheriff's department must decide for itself. Some suggested types of information appear in Table 5, but the list should not be considered the maximum or the minimum. The trial-and-error method is the only sure way to determine what data are valuable.

Analyzing the Data

The data collected by the planning unit for the manager are used to assist in the identification of problems and their causes, the opportunities available, and the indicators of successful planning. All quantitative data should be subjected to statistical analysis or mathematical computation and should be explored by all the scientific means available. Qualitative data—subjective, historical, descriptive, or based solely on experience—should be recognized as such and used cautiously. New approaches, such as placing data into some schematic design so that the logical and patterned flow of all important variables in the environment can be observed, should also be employed for more effective management. Whatever the technique employed, all data and information by themselves are useless unless they are interpreted, understood, and used meaningfully.

Many specific methods of data analysis are used. The most common is employing the accumulated experience of personnel

Table 5
Types of Information Potentially Useful to Police Agencies

1. Criminal Activities
   a. Type *b.* Location *c.* Time of occurrence (time of day, day of week, month) *d.* Response time *e.* Time required for handling *f. Modus operandi g.* Personal data on suspect *h.* Personal data on victim
2. Noncriminal and Related Activities
   a. Same data as above
   b. Nature of calls for services the agency *could not* initiate or complete
3. Population trends
4. Population composition
5. Income levels
6. Housing and building characteristics
7. Industrial and commercial growth
8. Potential annexations
9. Geographical information
10. Climatic conditions as they influence operations
11. Neighborhood characteristics (problems, services)
12. Political climate
13. Power structure (including behind-the-scenes leaders, minority spokesmen)
14. Citizens groups (attitudes, power, needs)
15. Data from criminal justice agencies
16. Governmental and quasi-governmental organizations (operations, clientele, leadership)
17. Fiscal matters (sources of revenue, attitudes toward new sources of revenue, future growth or decline of revenue; current expenditures, trends, potential new or increased demand for services)
18. Problem areas (potential disorders, attitudes toward governmental action)
19. Community attitudes and opinions on all issues, particularly those affecting the agency
20. Current and potential legal decisions (state and federal trends in courts)
21. Internal health (turnover, illness, absenteeism; cynicism from role conflict and negative supervision)
22. Attitudes and opinions of personnel
23. Current trends and innovative practices in other law enforcement agencies
24. Intelligence data on activities of professional criminals

and knowledgeable persons in the community. Intuition about past situations and current or future problems can be valuable. Every perspective and viewpoint should be sought, and analyses of past operations, problems, and cases should be explored for their future value. Debriefing sessions should be conducted regularly to get "readings" by those closest to the action, and definitely conducted when new or strange situations occur that are beyond the experience of all personnel. (It is important to remember, however, that these sessions are for learning, and not to find a scapegoat.) Attitude and opinion surveys also can give the planner the views of others on important issues. General statistical techniques such as analyzing percentages, rates, ratios, means, medians, modes, and correlations can quantify the data and make trends readily visible.

Of particular importance in data analysis is understanding the police agency's operations. Controlling and experimentation are particularly useful to the manager and/or planner. If plans are to be realistic and effective, the planner must take more than a passing interest in the agency. Often he can develop models so the interrelationship of important variables can be better understood and sometimes predicted, and he must understand cause-and-effect relationships in order to reduce guesswork.

Operations research (OR) is a growing field that offers many techniques that are applicable to planning. Common operations research techniques are listed in Table 6.[4] Other activities useful to the agency (time-motion studies, analyses of physical layouts, flow diagrams, form control/design, management/fiscal audits, information system analysis, and equipment evaluations) are described in sources listed at the end of the chapter.

GANTT and PERT/CPM

Certain planning problems in law enforcement have two critical aspects—time and money. Various operational research techniques have value for the law enforcement planner in estimating the most effective uses of these short items. The techniques that have considerable interest are GANTT, PERT/TIME and PERT/COST. As a "spin-off" from the PERT system of planning, CPM as it pertains to time and cost also has considerable value. Each of these techniques is explained below.

GANTT

The forerunner of this whole methodology in managing and planning systems was the GANTT chart. Henry L. Gantt, an

Table 6
Techniques of Operations Research (OR)

1. *Probability Theory.* Based on past history of the agency, the probability of a certain event's occurring again can be determined. This planning method can be used to estimate future events; it is useful in reducing uncertainty about operations.
2. *Linear Programming.* Whenever the element of uncertainty is low and the relationship between all the variables is clear, a model of the problems can be constructed. From the model such things as the optimum allocation of resources to achieve a specific objective can be determined.
3. *Inventory Control.* Supplies and materials are stored by any organization and eventually used by personnel. While on the shelf, however, such supplies represent money spent and not used. Control techniques help determine the quantity to order and the time to order, allowing the space and money to be used elsewhere.
4. *Transportation Models.* These are used to minimize costs and reduce overloading at certain points; they are useful in planning booking and temporary detention facilities, locations, and workloads at other facilities.
5. *Nonlinear Programming.* Nonlinear programming is potentially useful if an agency has a variety of personnel, each with specialized functions; the proper mix is developed to meet demands for services.
6. *Gaming and Simulation.* These are the acting out of operations or techniques in order to understand fully the potential actions of others and the effect of a strategy, move, or decision. The methods can use a real game, a mental activity, or a mathematical model.
7. *Queuing Theory.* The waiting-line discipline has potential uses in determining patrol allocations. This method examines the manner in which services are called for to assure that a unit is available or to determine what must be available to meet a variety of demands.
8. *General Problem Solver.* Techniques are devised for a computer to be adaptive to reason according to means and ends and to solve problems through subproblems by adjusting to attainable objectives. The GPS instructions program the computer to go through the analysis and present the answer or answers.
9. *Best Route Theory.* This is a means of determining patrol routes and frequency.
10. *Venture Analysis.* This is a technique used in business; its potential application is to determine costs and results of providing new services against hiring another agency to deliver the service.
11. *Allocation of Sales Effort.* The agency can determine just how much time should be spent on which activity and set priorities between cases in terms of how much time to spend (for example, trying to concentrate on clearable cases).

associate of Frederick W. Taylor, worked during an era when managers were concerned with gaining the greatest return for the least amount of effort and waste. Gantt hoped to reduce delays and duplication of effort by observing the work of others and mapping out the steps involved in work processes to assure the smooth occurrence of all events. Rather than face a "hurry up and wait" situation, Gantt argued that by careful planning and scheduling, the workload could be evenly distributed and the efforts of all involved would be smooth and continuous.

Gantt wanted, in particular, to show the relationship of tasks within some visual framework of time. In the Gantt chart he attempted to meet that need. The chart (Figure 9) shows the work activity in relation to time. For instance, a Gantt chart could be drawn for a hypothetical sheriff's department undertaking the development of a new communications center for a county-wide network.

Figure 9
GANTT CHART

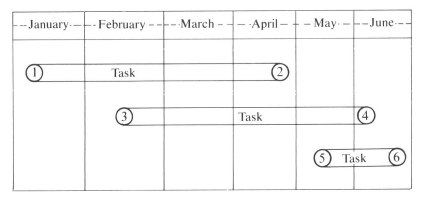

The building would have to be built (task 1–2; 4 months), equipment ordered and installed (task 3–4; 4 months), and the personnel trained and the equipment actually tested (task 5–6; 1¼ months) prior to the operational date. By knowing or estimating the time required for each task, the activities can be started in sufficient time and the sequence structured so that building, equipment, and personnel are neither lying idle nor being rushed. All will be available and operational on the same date. Each activity and event on a GANTT chart can be drawn so that the manager/planner can visualize all the components in relation to one another and schedule events to occur in a logical and economical fashion.

PERT

Program evaluation and review technique (PERT) is an extension of the GANTT chart concept. Developed in 1958 by the navy's Special Projects Office and the Lockheed Aircraft Corporation for missile projects, PERT allows the planner greater flexibility than did the GANTT chart. Essentially, PERT is an analytical device that shows all the work necessary to achieve a stated objective. At the same time, PERT allows the manager to predict time and costs under a variety of conditions while spotlighting those uncertainties or problems that might impede, delay, or frustrate the achievement of the goal or program.

The focus of PERT, like GANTT, is on events or activities. Each event is a specific achievement or accomplishment. The activity is the work that is necessary to achieve or accomplish each event. Unlike GANTT, the events and activities are laid out in a network instead of a bar/time graph. For the same hypothetical sheriff's department communications center (Figure 9), a PERT network would look like Figure 10. The information on this simple PERT network is the same as that in Figure 9 except that there is no time element or estimate. PERT must be carried further.

The very first step in PERT is developing the network. The planner estimates all the events and activities that are necessary to achieve a certain goal. In the hypothetical sheriff's department communications center, the steps could be:

1. Building—design and construct on county property.

2. Equipment—design; set specifications; accept bids; choose, order, receive, and install equipment in new building.

3. Personnel—train those presently employed on new equipment; train personnel transferred from other agencies in sheriff's department policies and on new equipment; recruit, select, and train the additional personnel to be hired.

The manager can make the PERT network as simple or as complex as he wishes. Often the general plan is kept simple and the appendixes to the plan contain the more complex steps. For purposes of this chapter, the network will be simple (Figure 10).

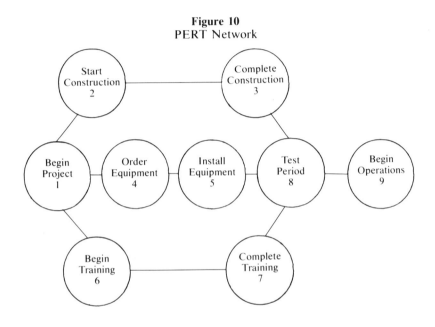

Figure 10
PERT Network

After the network's steps (events and activities) are laid out, the planner must calculate which steps can occur concurrently and which must await the completion of other steps. For instance, the hypothetical communications center cannot be tested until building, equipment, and personnel are ready. The acquisition of equipment can, however, occur concurrently with either the training of personnel or the construction of the building. It would be most desirable that the building's completion and the training of personnel be completed at the same time. That way the personnel and the building will not be sitting idle—a cost bearing little relation to the program.

Once the logical flow of events is laid out, the next phase is to collect information on timing. Those responsible (the contractor, equipment suppliers, trainers, and so on) are asked to estimate three time spans for completion of their part of the project. These are their *estimated optimistic time (to), most likely time (tm)*, and *pessimistic time (tp)*. These times are then written on the network in the *to-tm-tp* order. If the contractor for the communications center gives six weeks as his optimistic estimate, ten weeks as his most likely, and sixteen weeks as his pessimistic, these times would be placed on the network this way:

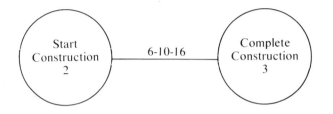

After times have been obtained from everyone responsible for an activity in the program, the network would look like Figure 11. The same unit of time (weeks) is used throughout. The reader has probably noticed that some activities have estimated times of "0-0-0" and "1-1-1." The "0-0-0" is simply a dummy activity inserted in the network to maintain the logical sequence of events. In activity 7–8, for example, no time is needed between completing training and the beginning of testing. The "1-1-1" of activity 8–9 simply means that the estimator is allowing one week for tests—no more and no less.

Figure 11
PERT Network

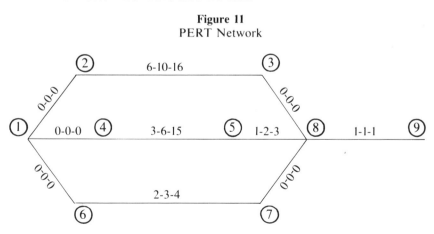

Because all of these times are estimates, the manager needs to know more precisely the amount of time each activity is expected to take. The *expected time (te)* is calculated from the *to-tm-tp* by using the following formula:

$$te = \frac{to + 4\ tm + tp}{6}$$

This formula is derived from empirical investigation and is the weighted average of all three times. The manager has an even chance that more or less time will be required, so the estimated time *(te)* for the times given by the contractor on the building would be determined as follows:

$$te = \frac{6 + 4(10) + 16}{6} = \frac{6 + 40 + 16}{6} = \frac{62}{6} = 10.3\ \text{weeks}$$

The manager will estimate the time from beginning of construction to completion as 10.3 weeks. If the formula is applied to the entire network, the network would look like Figure 12.

Figure 12
PERT Network

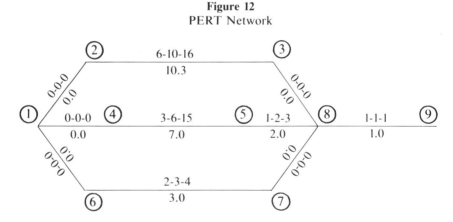

With the optimistic, most likely, and pessimistic times as well as the expected time available, the manager or planner can easily estimate how long the plan or project will take from start to finish. By simply adding up the times in the hypothetical case and using the largest figure, the planner will be in the ball park.

Notice that the times are added only for tasks that must be completed in sequence and cannot be done while other tasks are underway.

Path 1-2-3-8-9				Path 1-4-5-8-9				Path 1-6-7-8-9			
to	tm	tp	te	to	tm	tp	te	to	tm	tp	te
0	0	0	0	0	0	0	0	0	0	0	0
6	10	16	10.3	3	6	15	7	2	3	4	3
0	0	0	0	1	2	3	2	0	0	0	0
1	1	1	1	1	1	1	1	1	1	1	1
7	11	17	11.3	5	9	19	10	3	4	5	4

The expected time is 11.3 weeks, and if things do not go well, it may be as long as 19 weeks.

Several other calculations can be made by the manager using the PERT network. If he wants to know when an event can be expected to be completed, or the *earliest expected time of completion (Te)*, the manager simply adds up the expected times *(te)* that precede the event along the paths. So the earliest expected time *(Te)* for event 8 on path 1–4–5–8 is 9.0 weeks (0 + 7 + 2). For path 1–6–7–8 it is 3.0 weeks (0 + 3 + 0). The planner then knows he can begin the activities of path 1–6–7–8 *(Te = 3.0)* three weeks prior to the completion of path 1–4–5–8 *(Te = 9.0)*; to begin path 1–6–7–8 earlier would mean the people trained to communicate would "sit around" until the building was completed; this is a wasted resource. In addition, another PERT formula allows the manager/planner to know the time when each event should be begun in order to meet any "target" date for the project's completion.

CPM

The critical path method (CPM) is related to PERT. The critical path is the path with the longest times. It is determined by simply adding up all the expected times *(te)* of each path. The manager uses the expected time, since it is the weighted average. In the hypothetical case, the critical path would be 1–2–3–8–9, which has a total *te* of 11.3 weeks. If the pessimistic time were used, path 1–4–5–8–9 would be critical, but PERT planners have found the use of expected time more effective. Mathematical experts say the odds are that optimistic or pessimistic times rarely will occur in reality.

For the police manager who must accelerate a program to meet a newer and shorter deadline than originally anticipated, the critical path method indicates that he should concentrate resources on shortening the time involved in path 1–2–3–8–9. Placing resources elsewhere, while giving the illusion of speeding up the project, would not accomplish that purpose. The fact that activities are often speeded up on the wrong path has probably led to the fact that many workers must "hurry up and wait." By applying PERT to the activities, the critical path can be discovered and the pressure brought to bear on the right places when haste is required.

If PERT is employed to estimate times, the planner may want to use the visual network or tables to supply cost estimates as well. With this added information the decision-maker will be able to choose programs that fit the time and cost frames he has in mind. The planner can either display them on a table along with the times or write them directly on the visual network. The planner may even want to include "crash" estimates of the costs of each activity if no expense were spared in completing it. By estimating costs as well as times, the executive can make more realistic decisions regarding proposed projects.

Summary

This chapter has presented an overview of the planning process with a discussion of some specific methods. The content is, of necessity, somewhat general in nature, for the body of knowledge concerning prediction, research, data analysis, and so on is quite extensive. This chapter is designed to put planning into perspective for the manager. Like the managerial process, the planning process has several discernible stages. If the manager follows them, they will help him structure his thinking about the planning phase of the managerial process.

One of the most useful planning and controlling tools available to the manager is PERT/CPM. This approach to planning is very systematic and can be readily applied to planning and scheduling problems. Of course, it can become quite complex in its application, but PERT/CPM is a very useful way for the manager to oversee planning activities.

The next three chapters also deal with planning, but they are more specific. Each of those chapters addresses particular planning problems—policy formulation and decision-making, manpower determination and allocation, and budgets. Together, these four chapters provide a comprehensive, though general, coverage of police agency planning. For more specific material, consult the suggested readings.

Suggested Reading

Ackoff, R. L. *Design of Social Research.* Chicago: University of Chicago Press, 1953.

Ackoff, R. L., and Sasieni, M. W. *Fundamentals of Operations Research.* New York: John Wiley, 1968.

Backstrom, C. H., and Hursh, G. D. *Survey Research.* Evanston: Northwestern University Press, n.d.

Burroughs Corporation. *Simulation.* Detroit: Burroughs Corporation, 1967.

Churchman, C. W. *The Systems Approach.* New York: Dell, 1968.

Cleland, D. I., and King, W. R. *Systems Analysis and Project Management.* New York: McGraw-Hill, 1968.

Eris, R. L., and Baker, B. N. *Introduction to PERT-CPM.* Homewood, Ill.: Richard D. Irwin, 1964.

Ewing, D. W. *The Practice of Planning.* New York: Harper & Row, 1968.

Famularo, J. J. *Organization Planning Manual.* New York: American Management Association, 1971.

Jet Propulsion Laboratory. *Crime Prediction Modeling.* Pasadena: California Institute of Technology, 1971.

Kenney, J. P. *Police Management Planning.* Springfield, Ill.: Charles C. Thomas, 1959.

LeBreton, P. P., and Henning, D. A. *Planning Theory.* Englewood Cliffs, N.J.: Prentice-Hall, 1961.

Prince, T. R. *Information Systems for Management Planning and Controlling.* Homewood, Ill.: Richard D. Irwin, 1966.

Travelers Research Corporation. *Literature Review of Police Planning.* Hartford, Conn.: Travelers Research Corporation, 1968.

Vroom, V. H. *Methods of Organizational Research.* Pittsburgh, Pa.: University of Pittsburgh Press, 1967.

Warren, E. K. *Long Range Planning: The Executive Viewpoint.* Englewood Cliffs, N.J.: Prentice-Hall, 1966.

Wilson, Orlando W. *Police Planning.* Springfield, Ill.: Charles C. Thomas, 1958.

CHAPTER 5

Decision-Making
and
Policy Formulation

Many definitions of decision-making exist in police management literature. When these definitions are broken down into
their basic elements, however, certain similar features appear.
Decision-making is first of all a process that involves the selection of some course of action, usually from among several alternatives. Second, the alternative eventually selected is the most
practical and desirable and offers the greatest likelihood for
achieving the most desired consequences, or results, with the
least likelihood of undesired consequences or results. Decision-
makers try to select a course that will eliminate the original
problem without creating newer or greater problems. Decision-
making definitions, by and large, assume a great deal: that, faced
with a problem, the decision-maker will select the best course of
action to achieve his goal while avoiding those that will create

consequences detrimental to the organization. This certainly is not always the case, as will be discussed later.

This chapter is divided into two major sections. The first discusses several important aspects of the decision-making process in community police agencies. The second defines and analyzes policy and policy formulation and relates policy-making to the decision process.

The Rational/Normative Decision Model

The literature dealing with decision-making in the management field is quite extensive. Most of it is devoted to the rational and normative model in that the process advocated is one that is well reasoned and explains how managers should behave. Table 7 provides some examples of this rational and normative decision-making process. The steps are similar and are simple: define the problem, gather the pertinent facts, consider the alternatives, choose one alternative, and implement and monitor the decision. While useful in telling managers what should be done, the rational and normative model ignores many of the realities faced by those who must actually make decisions. The problems with the model will be explored later in the chapter.

Given an ideal situation, how should decisions be made? The process is the same as that employed in determining plans and choosing policies.

Step 1: Recognizing Organizational Goals or Objectives. In order that the decisions made by managers will be aligned with the goals and objectives of the organization, all decision-makers must be familiar with the agency's goals and objectives. Knowledge of just what the agency wants to achieve will determine to a large extent what alternatives are explored and which are accepted. Without this knowledge, the decisions will be random and without rationale.

Step 2: Constant Monitoring. The decision-maker must know when the time is near for making a decision, and he should know in general the nature of the decision that is to be made. Such decisions occur at the supervisory, middle management, and executive levels, and certain indicators will often show the level at

Table 7
Decision-Making Models (Rational/Normative Process)

1. George D. Eastman and Esther M. Eastman, eds., *Municipal Police Administration,* 6th ed. (Washington, D.C.: International City Management Association, 1969), p. 210.
   Discover the problem
   Isolate and clarify the problem
   Gather and analyze data; secure opinions
   Decide
   Execute
   Evaluate
2. N. F. Iannone, *Supervision of Police Personnel* (Englewood Cliffs, N.J.: Prentice-Hall, 1970), pp. 84–85.
   Be aware of the problem
   Gather the facts
   Evaluate and analyze
   Lay out all possible decisions
   Select suitable alternative
   Follow up
3. T. D. Cain, "Decision-Making," in Glen D. King, ed., *First-Line Supervisor's Manual* (Springfield, Ill.: Charles C. Thomas, 1961), pp. 59–65.
   Define the problem
   Secure the pertinent information
   Analyze the facts
   Find the answer
   Apply the decision

which action must be taken. For example, court decisions or new state legislation often indicates changing values in society. If the indicators are that society is changing priorities relative to police activity, then related decisions will be made at the executive level. If new kinds of services are being requested, then decisions will involve middle managers or, if major enough, the executive level. Changes in field practices may involve only the supervisors. Each indicator that results from monitoring will determine to an extent just who will be involved in the decision. The choice of indicators for monitoring is a matter for each department to decide and, of course, will depend on the resources available for collecting and evaluating data.

Step 3: Being Aware That Some Problem Exists. When it is clear that the agency is confronted with a problem, the problem must be identified. Police managers, from the executive to the supervisory level, have some idea of the standards for police activity. When monitoring indicates that a standard is not being met, managers must identify, locate, and describe the problems that confront the organization and determine the reasons for the deviation from the standard.

One approach to determining the causes of a problem is *force field analysis*, developed by Kurt Lewin. All persons associated with the problem should be involved in using this method. The first step is to attempt to identify the exact problem confronting the agency. Each individual writes a short descriptive statement of the problem, describing it and telling how he would like it to be resolved. One author suggests that the statement be no longer than a message in a telegram.[1] The next step is to list all the forces at work that are helping achieve the desired end and all those that frustrate the goal. From this point a plan is developed to offset the negative forces and accentuate the positive ones. This method is useful for analyzing problems and developing solutions for them.

Step 4: Laying out Possible Courses of Action. The decision-maker should think of each and every possible course of action, even those that do not appear to be feasible. No alternative should be overlooked or rejected. The alternatives range from doing nothing to dropping everything else and committing the whole agency to the alleviation of the problem. In between the "do nothing" and the "whole hog" approaches, of course, there are always numerous possibilities.

Step 5: Examining Each Alternative. With a knowledge of the agency's objectives, the decision-maker should set down the objectives to be achieved by the decision. If there are several objectives, they should be ranked in order of importance. Each alternative should be evaluated according to the degree to which it will achieve the objective of the decision, its possible future adverse consequences, the risks involved, internal and external factors being influenced by and influencing the decision, the resources to be committed, and any other factor important to the agency. Once this is done, the decision-maker can rank the alternatives.

Step 6: The Decision. After the objectives are determined and the alternatives ranked, the manager can make a final decision. If possible, that decision should be tested on a limited basis and all those concerned or affected by the decision should be advised of the impact the decision will have so that they can plan and coordinate their activities.

Step 7: Documenting the Decision Process. The reason for documenting or writing up the decision is simply that the span of memory is short, and the decision-maker will be able to justify the alternative he selects if he is questioned later. Other reasons for writing up the decision are to allow it to be criticized in order to improve the decision-making process, to provide a basis for minor changes, to provide the foundation for organizational memory, to help classify any jobs associated with the decision, and to provide material for training those already in, or planning to undertake, decision tasks. Documenting the decision should not be overlooked.

Step 8: Immediate and Long-Range Monitoring. Managers should expect problems after the decision is implemented and should monitor the results. Problems can arise because information is incomplete or misinterpreted, because personnel have implemented the decision incorrectly, or because the desired results are not achieved. The manager should monitor closely and take corrective action when required.

Management Styles and Decision-Making

The kinds of decisions made by managers depend on a variety of factors inside the organization. For instance, the leadership styles of the managers and the organizational milieu created by the hierarchy and co-workers will, in large measure, determine what kinds of decisions are made and how many. Patterns of leadership and supervisory styles have already been described in Chapter 2.[2] Here they will be examined in terms of their influence on the decision-making process in a police organization.[3]

The leadership style of the manager influences how decisions are made not only by him but throughout the organization. The *hard-boiled autocrat* makes all the decisions and rarely asks for advice. He demands complete and instant compliance of all subordinates and often makes decisions that should be made by supervisors or managers at lower levels in the organization. The *benevolent autocrat* behaves in almost the same way as the hard-boiled variety except that he attempts to convince subordinates and others of the wisdom of his decisions and the value of supporting them. Since this style is authority-oriented, subordinates may also pass the responsibility for decisions upward.

Another management style is the *consult and participate manager*, who, while still keeping the decisions in his office, will encourage open discussion and some initiative on the part of subordinates. The *democrat* encourages an even greater degree of employee participation, initiative, and decision-making. Occasionally a decision may be overridden, but this does not stifle initiative. Last, the *easygoing manager* can easily become dominated by subordinates and normally goes along with whatever his subordinates decide. A manager of this style will not have great problems if the personnel are well trained, thoroughly experienced, and usually make decisions that are morally, ethically, and legally sound. He will have problems, however, if he begins supporting unsound decisions of subordinates simply for the sake of backing them up.

Another approach to considering styles of police managers relative to decisions is the grid system described in Chapter 2. That system classifies organizations in terms of their concern for production and/or the morale and feelings of employees. The 1/1 style of management (low concern for production and people) is not conducive to decision-making. Key decisions will be relegated to others or perhaps left to the next watch in the organization. Any decision that cannot safely be avoided will be masked so that the decision-maker can remain anonymous. At worst, the manager will attempt to "cover his posterior" by having a ready supply of scapegoats available should the decision be interpreted as a poor one.

A manager of the 9/1 style (high concern for production, low concern for people) will consider only those alternatives that increase production; a manager of the 1/9 style (low concern for production, high concern for people) sacrifices production and concentrates primarily on decisions that will not hurt the feelings of subordinates; and a manager of the 5/5 style (moderate concern for production and people) will produce bland alternatives in an attempt to be all things to all people. The 1/1, 9/1, 1/9, and 5/5 styles of management encourage alternatives and decisions that prevent the agency from being a vital factor in the community. The 9/9 manager (high concern for production and people) is innovative and participative, considers numerous alternatives, and then makes the decision that will best accomplish the objectives in an atmosphere of trust and respect.

The Not-So-Rational/Normative World of Decision-Making

Police officers, from patrolmen or deputies to chiefs or sheriffs, almost all admit that the normative and rational decision-making model is excellent but say that very often they have to plan, make decisions, and formulate policies under less than ideal circumstances. Sometimes they do not have the time to explore fully all the possibilities. Sometimes outside pressures force consideration of policies that are not in the public's interest. Sometimes certain alternatives are unacceptable to the public even though they might be best in the long run. Information may be lacking and calculations must be based solely on hunches, or revenue forecasts do not permit effective programs to be developed or cause them to be terminated prematurely. Briefly, the real world of police organizations does not always, if ever, permit the use of the rational/normative model of decision-making.

Man has always tried to make his world a little better each day than it was before, to create the ideal model. The rational/normative model is one of these attempts. It is an ideal—something to try to achieve even though it is likely to be impossible in practice. The police manager needs a model or models that account for the real world he faces, whether he is planning, making decisions, or formulating policies. He must be aware of all limitations so he can know which ones have to be accepted and which can be modified, and which decisions can be made almost entirely through the rational/normative approach.

Two interesting theories concerning the modification of the rational/normative model are the "incremental" and "muddling through" theories explored by Charles Lindblom.[4] Decision-making has always been a problem for the manager. Lindblom argues that the decision-maker is always limited in terms of time—time he can devote to the analysis of the problem before him, time he can devote to weighing the various alternatives, time he has to implement the decision, and time he has to analyze the solution applied to the problem. The manager also usually has only partial information and limited resources, and many factors frustrate the decisions he must make. According to Lindblom, the decision-maker at best simply muddles through the problems he faces. Even though he may have time, resources, and full support, Lindblom contends, the manager will play it safe and opt for a bland decision that is only slightly different from those that have been made before. Changes are therefore incremental and come about very slowly. If he encounters difficulty after making the decision, the manager will return to the way things were before rather than push his decision through to conclusion. Lindblom's ideas have support; even such an avowed radical thinker as Chairman Mao is an incrementalist, since he advocates two steps forward and, when confronted by problems (foreseen or unforeseen), one step back. There is little doubt that managers, both public and political, have a tendency to play it safe when making decisions and formulating policies. Many police managers find Lindblom's theory to be a description of reality.

Another theory of decision-making that departs from the rational/normative model is presented by Robert E. Agger, Daniel Goldrich, and Bert E. Swanson.[5] Their research indicates that an interesting process occurs in decision-making, especially when policies are under consideration. These theorists argue that a problem really is not examined until someone believes it can be alleviated, solved, or prevented by some action—in other words, the problem is not confronted until someone has the solution. After the solution is proposed, its supporters assemble and examine facts supporting it, and a "ground swell" pressures the decision-maker to accept the solution. The manager never examines the full range of alternatives. Since most solutions mean that someone in the organization will lose something, such as status or resources, reaction sets in, and the opponents of the decision propose their own alternatives.[6] They begin mustering facts and support designed to negate or modify the proposed solution. The manager eventually makes a decision, but the matter is not really settled. The advocates who lost continue to provide feedback designed to reverse or modify the original decision, with varying degrees of success. Those who won must defend the decision and counter the opposition. Feedback becomes a game in which winners and losers bombard the decision-maker in attempts to modify his choice. Somehow, in this model, decisions are made through continued confrontation between factions; it is almost as if an adversary system were at work.

These theorists are not alone in supporting this approach. New texts in management, public administration, and law enforcement abound with modifications and suggestions that something other than the rational and normative model must actually be used. One must understand his agency's decision-making process before he can devise methods that are more nearly ideal. A good starting point is to understand the shortcomings of the rational/normative model.

Factors Affecting the Rational/Normative Model

The creator of a model or technique must make certain assumptions about the people and organizations in the model. Advocates of the rational/normative model of decision-making, for example, often assume that there is only one decision-maker. Any sheriff can tell you that he was elected to make decisions, but to get the resources to implement the decisions, he depends in turn on the decisions of a group of elected officials. Other assumptions are that a single set of values governs the decision,[7] that the full range of alternatives is known, that the "right" alternative can be recognized, that the alternative selected can be implemented, and that feedback can be interpreted accurately. In fact, the rational/normative model of decision-making, planning, or policy formulation is based on many assumptions; the problem is that the assumptions may not be accurate.

The first difficulty the manager faces in the implementation of a normative/rational model is defining the problem and determining its cause. Often the expected standards and ideals of performance are unclear or confusing, or the roles and norms in one organizational unit may be confusing while in another they are clear.[8] Sometimes the public or special groups receiving services do not know exactly what they want the agency to accomplish. Or managers and employees may not know just what should be done and how to do it. Even if the standards or ideals are clear, deviations may occur that cannot always be precisely identified, located, or even described. The causes of deviations from established norms may be subtle or completely hidden from view or analysis. Even if the problem is clear, the persons involved may disagree about the principal cause. The manager's perspective determines in large measure just how he views the cause or causes of a problem. A manager with vast investigative experience may see the cause of a serious crime wave as ineffective investigation, while a manager who has spent much time patrolling may blame laxity in that area.

Information is a problem simply because it is difficult to obtain. Money, time, and effort are required to collect and comprehend the data that result from analyzing information, and money, time, and effort are in short supply in any agency. Furthermore, even if information is at hand, there is no guarantee that it is factual. The problems of data collection, analysis, and comprehension are many, even in this era of computers.[9] And despite the claims of the advocates of computers, they are only as good as the information that goes into them and their programs of analysis.

A decision-maker is not always able to choose the best alternative even if he is able to think of every possible course of action. The best alternative may be expensive or beyond the means of the agency. Or the alternative may raise costs in other departments or agencies. If the manager does not fully understand the cause-and-effect relationship between the problem at hand and the solution he has in mind, he may be reluctant to commit the resources of the agency. The decision-maker's perspective also may provide the solution in only one functional area while curtailing activities elsewhere in the agency. Hopefully, the decision-maker can see that such problems exist. However, the best solution may be ignored if the public has little regard for the decision-maker. For example, the open campus policy of many high schools may be one cause of increased daylight residential burglaries. Yet police officials may find the alternative of reversing this policy frustrated by the school officials' regard for the police and their analysis of the problem. They may even be openly hostile.

Once the decision is made, the manager must implement it. The decision must be "sold," since everyone will not accept the decision and implement it as it was intended. The manager decides, but so must those who will execute the decision.[10] The acceptance of any plan, decision, or policy depends on power. The manager's power has a variety of forms. First, he has his rank and the job of making decisions, and many people will follow his orders or directives simply for that reason. Second, he can reward individuals for conformity and punish them for noncompliance. Employees will tend to follow his orders both because of his rank and because he is considered to be an expert who possesses information that they do not have or who has extensive experience in the matter at hand. Whenever decisions are made, there is a wide range of responses, from full compliance to misunderstanding and even disobedience.

Last, the decision-maker has problems of feedback and alterations after the decision has been implemented. He must establish indicators that will assist him in determining whether the organization is, in fact, achieving the objectives that were established. He must discover deviations and determine their exact nature. (This area is covered in greater detail in Chapter 10.)

This examination of the problems encountered in applying the rational/normative decision-making model indicates that this model is somewhat incomplete for the police manager. The police manager should use the rational model but must be aware of its deficiencies. The recognition of these inadequacies does point out the need for some additional guidelines, even oversimplified ones. These simple guidelines are suggested below:

1. Be flexible. As in planning, expect problems. Train all personnel to point out deficiencies if they encounter them. Be prepared to make changes when necessary. A manager has to make decisions even when hazards are present, but he need not pursue a mistake in the face of evidence that he was wrong.

2. Admit mistakes; managers are bound to make them. If your organization has an atmosphere in which mistakes, when recognized, are corrected, you will be on the way toward a healthy administration. An honest administration is bound to have a good batting average after a while.

3. Be inquisitive; constantly ask questions about your operations. The good patrol officer is the one who knows his beat. The same is true of managers. Check constantly on operations, even if they are not in your unit. Find out the other person's perspec-

tive. The manager should become his own computer by gathering information with questions.

4. Encourage discussion. Do not overlook the importance of seeking information about your department from others—police and citizens. Let others know how you view situations and problems. This will allow you a chance to see whether your information sources and perspectives are valid. Openness will also allow subordinates to bring forward ideas for improvement of the agency and allow the manager's thoughts to be aired and tested.

5. Avoid identifying decisions with personalities. Nothing will create internal friction faster than linking policies, decisions, and programs with individuals, particularly in a sarcastic or demeaning fashion. Give every idea or alternative a chance for a hearing. Often ideas become known in a department as "the Jones plan," "the Smith policy," and so on. If a previous idea from Jones or Smith didn't happen to work out, a perfectly operable suggestion from the same person may be unacceptable and may fail simply because people expect it to. On the other hand, Jones' or Smith's reputation as a decision-maker is at stake if an idea is identified with him, and it may take longer to discard a poor plan for this reason.

6. Analyze action; criticize and amend. The military technique of debriefing should be standard practice for normal daily operation, unique experiences, and special programs. People learn by doing, and hopefully the agency can benefit from unique experiences as well as from routine ones. Whether a certain action turned out to be a success or a failure, the purpose of debriefing is to learn and improve operations.

Only through conscious inquiry will a manager move his organization toward the rational/normative model of decision-making. Only through an inquiring atmosphere will the personnel in the agency fully understand its present inadequacies and be able to overcome them. Full knowledge of the not-so-rational/normative model is a prerequisite to achieving the ideal model.

Policies and Policy Formulation

The term *policy* has several meanings for personnel in police agencies. At the patrol, jail, and investigative levels, a *policy* means a set of guidelines designed to standardize the behavior of personnel. Some of the common policy definitions for these levels are provided below:

> Policy consists of principles and values which guide the performance of a Department activity. Policy is not a statement of what must be done in a particular situation; rather, it is a statement of guiding principles which should be followed in activities which are directed toward the attainment of Department objectives. [Los Angeles Police Department, *Policy Manual*, 1972, paragraph 010.]

> ... policy can be defined to mean a guideline for carrying out even the most detailed action, the term usually refers to the broad statement of principle. [O. W. Wilson and Roy C. McLaren, *Police Administration*, 3rd ed. (New York: McGraw-Hill, 1972).]

> In private management literature ... "policy" often means either (a) any general rule that has been laid down in an organization to limit the discretion of subordinates (e.g., it is "policy" in B department to file a carbon of all letters by subject), or (b) at least the more important of these rules, promulgated by top management (e.g., an employee is allowed two weeks' sick leave per year). [Herbert A. Simon, *Administrative Behavior* (New York: Free Press, 1957).]

> They are general statements, or understandings, which guide or channel the thinking and action of subordinates in an enterprise or one of its departments. [David W. Ewing, *Long-Range Planning for Management*, rev. ed. (New York: Harper & Row, 1964).]

> Policies represent the totality of standards or norms that govern the conduct of people in the organization. [Henry H. Albers, *Organized Executive Action* (New York: John Wiley, 1961).]

At the middle-management level and above, *policy* often has a meaning different from that at the operational levels. Policy at the highest levels is generally similar to the objectives of the agency, the thrust or direction of the leadership of the organization, the allocation of public resources, the services that are to be delivered and, sometimes, the way those services will be delivered. Definitions of policy at the top of the organizational hierarchy are provided below:

> Policy is concerned with future activity and must frequently be directed toward changing goals. ... Goals are an important concern of

politics. [John M. Nickerson et al., eds., *A Study of Policymaking* (Berkeley, Calif.: McCutchan, 1971).]

When we speak of policy we usually mean a principle, plan, or course of action . . . without policy there can be no administration . . . what is to be done determines, in part, how it is to be done. [Charles E. Jacob, *Policy and Bureaucracy* (Princeton: Van Nostrand, 1966).]

A policy can briefly be defined as a course of action followed by an actor or group of actors on a given subject. A common-sense definition of a public policy is one made by government officials or agencies. . . . Defined as a course of action, a public policy is more than a decision or a series of decisions that something shall be done or not done; it also includes the action undertaken to implement the decision(s). Policy includes not only what is supposed to be done but also what is actually done. [James E. Anderson, *Politics and the Economy* (Boston: Little, Brown, 1966).]

A definition of policy . . . is the important activity of government. An activity is "important" if it involves large amounts of resources or it is relevant to the interest of many people. [Ira Sharkansky, *Public Administration: Policy-Making in Government Agencies* (Chicago: Markham, 1970).]

Policy for Operating Units

One of the major reasons for developing policies for patrolmen and deputies is to provide guidelines or norms for behavior. By providing operational principles the values or ideals of the organization can be implemented.

Policies also provide consistency, continuity, and uniformity. The major problem for the manager is, of course, to have operating personnel all behaving in a similar fashion that is consistent with the values or ideals held by the organizational hierarchy or top management.

Once policy is decided, several problems can be encountered in its implementation. Like the planning and decision-making associated with policy development, a policy must be "sold" to the personnel. If employees understand and accept the rationale for a policy, they will carry it out much more willingly. At times, however, policies must be carried out even when they are not universally accepted. In such cases, positive supervision can help assure that the guidelines are being followed, as can employee participation in policy development.

Some operational policies are generally accepted inside the department but not by those outside. For example, police officers understand the need for handcuffing most, if not all, arrested persons. Yet such an operational policy may not be understood by the public at large. Police managers should see that such policies are explained to the public. Citizens should be aware that although the arrested party may come along peacefully and have no intent to injure the arresting or transporting officer, the handcuffing practice arose from experiences of injuries and even deaths to police officers by those who appeared unthreatening. The public as well as agency employees may need to be "sold." It is important for the public to be aware of the reasons for police operational policies.

Policy in the Organizational Hierarchy

Policy also applies to the development of guidelines for dealing with other agencies in the environment in which the agency functions. The concept of the agency's environment was discussed in the introductory chapter. Briefly, in order to understand policy and its formulation, the manager must view the agency as part of a system. This system, the criminal justice system, has a myriad of parts and pieces that are interdependent and interact with one another. Every manager must understand this system and the environment if the agency is to be effective.

The policy arena for top police management is political. The police represent only one of many community organizations that are part of the public services sector. In this sector, values and interests complement one another one moment and clash the next. These clashes, and limited resources, result in compromises —the balancing of issues. Because of this environmental interaction, policy concerning overall guidelines and objectives is often politically determined rather than based on a rational/normative model.

The wise manager will study and understand this arena to learn the realistic limitations on the attainment of desired organizational goals. The manager's knowledge of the arena will also assist in the improvement of those aspects of the policy formulation process that fall outside the immediate arena and frustrate the attainment of the formal, normative, and rational model sought for planning and decision-making. Reality, awareness, and understanding help the policy formulation process.

Policy Formulation and Modifications

The rational/normative model used in planning and decision-making is also described in much of the police management literature. The problems discussed concerning the rational/normative model should be reviewed when considering models for policy formulation. The attempts at reformulation of the ideal model and suggestions of others, such as Charles Lindblom and Agger, Goldrich, and Swanson, should also be reviewed to better understand the attempt to account for reality. What follows will be an examination of two other modifiers of the rational/normative model—internal and external politics.

Internal Politics. The politics within the agency has already been mentioned in the sense that the guidelines chosen by top management need to be accepted and internalized by employees if the policy is to be a true guideline for actual behavior. The assumption is that top management is in full agreement on policy guidelines. Often this is not the case. Many policies do not, for whatever reason, have the full and complete backing of all those in the organizational hierarchy. Several writers from the business and public administration areas have developed models that can be used to analyze such internal divisions.

In essence, the writers suggest two examples of internal politics.[11] First, many organizations contain subgroups. These groups may actually be dysfunctional in that they may be more concerned with their own particular subgoals than with those of the entire organization.[12] These subgoals may even concern means rather than organizational ends. Often, top management cannot resolve problems and may even avoid them, because greater internal conflict would result if an issue were confronted by the organization. Questions of resource allocation often bring subgroups into the open.

The second example of internal politics is the formation of coalitions. For example, a decision-maker might consider eliminating a traffic unit and transferring resources to an investigative division. Faced with this possibility, the traffic *and* patrol hierarchies, who may have been at odds in the past, may very well unite over the issue of *uniformed* personnel being shifted elsewhere. Such temporary coalitions may form and then dissipate as the initiating issue fades.

The organization can overcome such problems, of course, by recognizing and accepting mutual interdependence in achieving the goals that all departments are striving to obtain. No organization should demand blind obedience. Participation and an honest understanding of the values present in the conflict are necessary, but personnel must be willing to abide by policies even if they appear to harm individuals' own positions. No decision is really ever final, and if a decision was incorrect, reconsideration is always possible.

External Politics. The environment outside the agency also affects the formulation of policies by the police agency. Society is composed of many subgroups, often with differing values and goals. The ideas of many of the theorists discussed so far, whether regarding planning or decision-making, apply as well to policy formulation in the wider arena. The theories all have certain common elements—they assume that the decision-maker plans to achieve his ends and that he attempts to coordinate activities so as to assure the completion of his mission.

Norton E. Long, however, argues that many of the policies and decisions in the public sector are often made by accident.[13] These accidents come from the uncoordinated and unplanned activities of the various subgroups operating in the environment. Some policies develop from the interaction of these subgroups, and the policies that result may not be what was expected. Long explains that man is a "game-playing" and "game-creating" creature. The game-playing gives him a sense of significance and gives meaning to his life. Among the interaction games man engages in are the highway game and the police game. The actors in one game often use others. Occasionally, the public is mobilized, but it is fickle and often confused. From out of this arena the politicians and agency representatives orchestrate the game players to develop the general thrust of the organization. It may be that some policies develop purely by accident. Whatever the policy, or however it is developed, the external environment and its various and often conflicting subgroups have an impact on agency policy formulation.

Summary

The purpose of this chapter has been to describe the traditional rational/normative model of decision-making and policy formulation and show how the model is modified in actual practice. The rational/normative ideal should be followed by the manager if possible, but the manager must also be aware of resources and political and organizational realities. The degree to which the manager can use the model and make it fit his organization is a matter of individual capability and the particular environment within each organization. Most managers are too eager to accept the "realities" and "shoot from the hip" in policy formulation and decision-making, just as most academicians are too eager to apply the rational/normative model. Somewhere in between is the middle ground, the reasonable compromise that will improve organizational performance.

Suggested
Reading

Abrahamson, Mark. *The Professional in the Organization.* Chicago: Rand McNally, 1967.

Alexis, Marcus, and Wilson, Charles Z. *Organizational Decision Making.* Englewood Cliffs, N.J.: Prentice-Hall, 1967.

Allaire, Jerrold R. *Policy Statements: Guides to Decision-Making.* Chicago: American Society of Planning Officials, 1961.

Babcock, Richard F. *The Zoning Game: Municipal Practices and Policies.* Madison: University of Wisconsin Press, 1969.

Bauer, R. A., and Gergen, K. J., eds. *Study of Policy Formation.* New York: Free Press, 1971.

Davis, James W., ed. *Politics, Programs and Budgets.* Englewood Cliffs, N.J.: Prentice-Hall, 1969.

Davis, M., and Weinbaum, M. *Metropolitan Decision Processes.* Chicago: Rand McNally, 1969.

Downs, Anthony. *Bureaucratic Structure and Decision-Making.* Santa Monica, Calif.: Rand Corporation, 1966.

Dror, Y. *Ventures in Policy Sciences.* New York: American Elsevier, 1971.

143

————. *Design for Policy Sciences.* New York: American Elsevier, 1971.

Elder, Robert E. *The Policy Machine.* Syracuse, N.Y.: Syracuse University Press, 1960.

Eulau, Heinz. *Policy Making in American Cities.* Morristown, N.J.: General Learning Corporation, 1972.

Freeman, L. C., et al. *Metropolitan Decision-Making.* Syracuse, N.Y.: University Press, 1962.

Gore, William J. *Administrative Decision-Making: Heuristic Model.* New York: John Wiley, 1964.

Held, Virginia. *The Public Interest and Individual Interests.* New York: Basic Books, 1970.

Kepner, C. H., and Tregoe, B. B. *The Rational Manager.* New York: McGraw-Hill, 1965.

Kuenzlen, Martin. *Playing Urban Games.* New York: George Braziller, n.d.

Miller, D. W., and Starr, M. K. *Structure of Human Decisions.* Englewood Cliffs, N.J.: Prentice-Hall, 1969.

Odiorne, George S. *Management Decisions by Objectives.* Englewood Cliffs, N.J.: Prentice-Hall, 1969.

Reagan, Michael, ed. *The Administration of Public Policy.* Glenview, Ill.: Scott, Foresman, 1969.

Rehfuss, John. *Public Administration as Political Process.* New York: Charles Scribner's Sons, 1973.

Ulmer, S. S., ed. *Political Decision Making.* New York: Van Nostrand Reinhold, 1971.

White, D. L. *Decision Theory.* Chicago: Aldine, 1970.

Wilson, C. Z. *Organizational Decision Making.* Englewood Cliffs, N.J.: Prentice-Hall, 1972.

CHAPTER 6

Manpower
Determination
and Allocation

The purpose of this chapter is to analyze and discuss alternative
methods of determining police manpower needs and allocating
manpower resources. The discussion will be general in nature
rather than describing specific systems. If the manager has a firm
grasp of the important factors involved, manpower problems can
be resolved more easily than by attempting the use of a specific
system. This approach to manpower planning is innovative and
provides considerable flexibility.

For police managers, the most important resource is manpower. Regardless of how measured—in man-hours, man-weeks,
man-months, or man-years—the basic resource for investment

Most of the material for the section "Manpower Determination Models" is taken
from Jack L. Kuykendall, "Alternative Models for Determining Police Manpower,"
Journal of California Law Enforcement 7 (April, 1973): 169–174. Permission to reprint
has been granted.

by the manager is people. Consequently, the issue of the number of employees a police agency should have and how they should be allocated are most important. If human resources are insufficient, or if they are not directed at "problems"—that is, the work of the police agency—then the agency will not be as effective as it could be.

This chapter is divided into two major sections. The first describes models of determining manpower needs, although the body of knowledge available in this area is limited. The second discusses and analyzes the principal factors for consideration in allocating manpower. Considerable information exists in this area, but it is often confusing, and suggested allocation systems are often based on unproven assumptions. The manager is better served if he becomes aware of the issues and develops his own system for allocating manpower.

Manpower Determination Models

We will consider four models—the *intuitive model*, the *comparative model*, the *workload-functional model*, and the *workload-strategic model*.

Intuitive Model

The intuitive model includes three components: police and management knowledge, experience, and the unspecified reasoning process employed by the manager. Expressed another way, this model involves "guessing" that is more or less "educated" depending on the quality of the components in the model. In terms of a police agency, the manager guesses how many men he needs. The more "educated" the intuitive decision, the more likely it is that "guessing" will be called "judgment."

This model is, of course, used in all areas of human endeavor. In making manpower determination decisions, the model is more useful in small police agencies where any decision about needed manpower is inherently limited. Used in increasingly larger organizations, the model's predicting power declines even when the three components are of the highest quality. In other words, use of this model becomes less and less useful in assuring that the desired objectives will be met through applying the model.

Comparative Model

The comparative model has two components: a specific kind of knowledge and a specific kind of reasoning process. The knowledge in question is the ratio of police employees (sworn and/or nonsworn) per 1,000 population units in a community, along with the same knowledge about other communities or groups of communities. The reasoning process is a comparison of the ratios to determine the manpower disparity.

The comparative model can be used as follows if the data are available. The manager subtracts the ratio of police employees (or sworn personnel) per 1,000 population in his community from the same ratio of the community with which he wants a comparison. He then multiplies the result by the number of units of 1,000 population in his community to determine the positive or negative disparity that exists. For example, a community with a population of 30,000 has 30 units of 1,000 population. If the police organization has 60 employees (sworn or nonsworn personnel or both) the ratio per 1,000 population is 2.0 ($60 \div 30 = 2.0$). Assume that the community or communities used for comparison have a ratio of 2.5 police employees per 1,000 population. To determine the manpower disparity for the original community the ratio of that community must be subtracted from the comparison community or group ($2.5 - 2.0 = .5$). The resulting figure (.5) is then multiplied by the number of units of 1,000 population in the original community ($30 \times .5 = 15$) to determine the manpower disparity. In this case, 15 new persons would be required by the original community to have a force comparable to that of the other community or communities.

An important consideration in using the comparative model is the community or group of communities to be used for comparison. Possible comparison groups are (1) a city or cities with similar populations, (2) a city or cities with similar crime rates, (3) a city or cities with similar population compositions, and (4) a city or cities in the same geographical area.

Information concerning police employee ratios per 1,000

population is available in *Crime in the United States (Uniform Crime Reports)* from the Department of Justice (Federal Bureau of Investigation). Data from *UCR* permit comparison by city size, crime rate, and rather large geographical areas. Population composition data can be obtained from census reports or local planning units. Ideally, all these factors—population, crime rate, population composition, and geographical area—would be considered in using the comparative model.

Several important factors are not properly considered by the comparative model, however. Some of these include political and social development of the community, geographical size, police services performed, the delivery system of police services (that is, policy, procedures, man-machine combinations, and so on), availability of police reserves, competency of personnel, motivation, the administrative system of the organization, and whether total number of employees or only the number of sworn personnel is used. The last factor has questionable significance, however, because it is more important to identify differences in activities performed than to distinguish between the position classifications of those performing the activities.

Workload-Functional Model

The workload-functional model has three components: knowledge of the time required for police activities, knowledge of the number of time-consuming activities, and a "working man" time period—often a working man-year. If a manager knows how much time each activity takes, how many activities are performed, and how many hours each man puts in, he can determine how many men he needs. The functional dimension of the model concerns how the workload approach is applied. The term *functional* refers to the organizational structure in terms of the jobs or functions it performs. For example, functional units are patrol, traffic, investigations, and so on.

There are three variations of the workload-functional model— the *systems variation*, the *sample variation*, and the *modified variation*. In the systems variation, an information system records, analyzes, and computes all time-consuming activities in a variety of categories. It is a simple matter, once the system is established, to divide the computed totals by a working man-year to determine needed manpower. And, of course, historical trends can be used to project needed increases. In the sample variation, no information system for ongoing recording of data exists, so random sampling techniques must be used to determine mean times for each category of activity. From these, time estimates can be developed and divided by the working man-year to determine manpower needs.

The modified variation of the model is somewhat more complex. In certain uniformed functional units such as patrol and traffic, a visibility strategy is employed in hopes of limiting the opportunity or influencing the motive to commit crime. Therefore, the manager must determine what portion of the working man-year should be devoted to visibility. To adjust his manpower determination calculations, he can either subtract that portion of time to be given to visibility from the working man-year, or he can count desired visibility time as a category of activity. (See the next subsection on the workload-strategic model.)

The workload-functional model need not be used for all functional activities; rather, it can be applied to selected units, such as patrol.[1] Extensions from the workload analysis of patrol to other functions can be intuitive, comparative, or even perhaps determining manpower for other units on a "percentage of patrol" basis.[2]

In other words, the manager may employ the workload-functional model for patrol and determine that 100 personnel are needed. From this, he may decide simply to guess, or use the intuitive method, to determine the number of needed investigators, clerks, supervisors, and so on. Or perhaps the manager can determine the number of personnel needed in those positions by comparing his department to others with approximately 100 personnel. Or the manager may want to establish a certain percentage or ratio of other positions to patrol officers. A percentage or ratio used at times is 10 percent, or 1 investigator for every 10 patrolmen. Systematic justification for such a percentage or ratio is lacking, however.

The percentage or ratio approach can also be used for other positions. This method of determining personnel needs usually is based on managerial experience as to estimated workloads for various positions, and, in the case of number of supervisors—spans of management and managerial philosophy. Intuition and ratios, however, are not always adequate substitutes for the more systematic approach suggested by the workload-functional model.

If the workload-functional model is employed, a method must be developed to gather and analyze information about activities and time consumed.[3] This can be done in a variety of ways. One very important consideration in computing time consumed is that of multiple policing units. A two-man patrol unit that works one hour investigating a crime has consumed two man-hours of time.

The actual time in a "working man-year" depends on several factors: (1) what is counted as working, (2) the hours per week or day normally worked, and (3) nonworking activities to be subtracted (court time, training time, sick time). This determination is discussed in more detail in the section on allocation. Once the decision is made as to what is considered "working time," a method to gather and analyze "nonworking" time needs to be developed.

When this model is applied to functions investing time in visibility, the manager must decide how much time to devote to that strategy. Suggestions range from 25 to 67 percent.[4] The assumption, of course, is that visibility has an impact on crime and that the patrolling units, if properly allocated, will be available to respond rapidly to calls. Although visibility has evolved as a major police strategy, no one knows exactly how effective it is. Systematic effort needs to be devoted to discovering the relationship between visibility time and frequency of coverage in a given area and in turn between those factors and a change in deviant activities. Elliott has moved in this direction,[5] but more work is required before the predicting power of visibility time is precisely determined.

Workload-Strategic Model

The workload-strategic model is essentially the same as the workload-functional model except that the strategic model determines the manpower needed for the various *resource investment strategies* rather than for the functional units of the organization. A resource investment strategy is a general activity in which police engage and that is assumed to have predicting power in accomplishing the overall police mission.

The primary resource investment strategies of community police agencies are the following:

1. *Visibility*—all time-consuming activities related to being seen in order to reduce the opportunity and/or motive to engage in deviant acts. This includes saturation, an extreme form of visibility. (This strategy might be called *deterrence*, but that word suggests the desired result of the strategy rather than the strategy itself.)

2. *Apprehension*—all time-consuming activities related to investigating and processing individuals suspected of deviant acts. (This strategy might be called *prevention*, but again that word suggests results.)

3. *Education*—all time-consuming activities related to telling citizens how to protect themselves and their property in order to reduce the opportunity and/or motive to engage in deviant acts.

4. *Counseling*—all time-consuming activities related to efforts to influence behavior of individuals in which arrests are not made or in which prosecution is not undertaken. This includes mediation—crisis intervention referrals, diversions, and so on. (The word *counseling* should not be interpreted to mean that policemen are skilled therapists. Yet police officers do "counsel" many individuals in a direct attempt to influence behavior short of arrest and/or prosecution.)

5. *Service*—all time-consuming activities relating to other noncriminal matters.

Police agencies also have other strategies, but these are related to supporting the operational strategies (records, communications) and management (planning, training). Police managers may prefer to conceptualize their strategies in a somewhat different way, but they should attempt to move toward structuring their thinking along these lines.

The workload-strategic model helps the manager identify needed manpower resources based on strategies used by police agencies. Ideally, the relative predicting power of each strategy would be known singly and in a variety of combinations. Presently, however, limited knowledge exists in this area. Once systematic data are obtained concerning the effectiveness of alternative strategies, however conceptualized, and once the manpower needed for each strategy is determined, this model of manpower determination may be more applicable. Methods of implementation and limitations in the use of this model are similar to those of the workload-functional model.

Model Combinations

It is possible to use these models in various combinations. The comparative model can be used to determine total personnel needs, and the workload-functional model can be used on a proportional basis for each functional unit. The workload-functional model also can be applied to only one functional unit, and manpower for other functional units can be determined by the comparative model or modifications of it. And, of course, the intuitive model is always available.

Constraints on the Use of Models

Several factors must be considered in using any of the models described. First, government resources are always limited. A police manager may attempt to determine manpower requirements objectively yet not be able to obtain such manpower because of scarce funds.

Second, an important factor in use of the workload-strategic model is community expectations about police services. For example, it might sometime be shown that such traditional strategies as visibility and investigations are only minimally effective. However, if citizens are conditioned to expect to have crimes investigated (even the ones that cannot be solved) and to see visible police units, they may demand that these strategies be maintained. Because of community expectations, police managers often measure their effectiveness by the rapidity with which their agencies respond to unsolvable problems.

Two other important possible constraints in using models concern police managerial perspectives. Once a manager determines that additional manpower is needed, he may think only in terms of adding more personnel. Alternatives are to gain manpower through internal rearrangements and modifications of delivery systems, increased skills, and improved motivation. In addition, police managers may view the increasing of personnel as possible only through the existing occupational structure. Normally, manpower resources are computed in a total dollar figure. More manpower resources can often be obtained, however, through use of police assistants, cadets, and civilians. In sum, police managers should think of manpower resources apart from the existing organizational structure. The structure is a tool by which resources are directed at police problems, and it should be viewed as flexible.

The four models described in this chapter are useful in conceptualizing the problems related to deciding how many employees a community police agency should have, and they are intended to assist the police manager in structuring the manner in which manpower decisions are perceived and made.

Any application of the last three models requires development of a system to gather data to feed into the major components of each model. The necessary data for the use of the workload-strategic model will be available only after massive research.

Once the number of personnel needed for a police agency is determined, it is necessary to consider their allocation. To a considerable degree, determination and allocation are interrelated. For example, in the workload-functional model of determination, the total amount of work is established; in allocation, the manpower is "divided up" and invested in the most effective manner by time and area to achieve agency goals and objectives.

Allocation of Manpower

This section does not recommend a specific system of manpower allocation; rather, it discusses the major factors for consideration in manpower allocation decisions. While the discussion will be limited primarily to the operational, or line, activities of a police agency (patrol, traffic, investigations, and so on), the general ideas are applicable to all types of police manpower allocation decisions.

Figure 13 depicts the relationship between manpower determination and manpower allocation. The models useful in considering determination problems were discussed in the previous section; the allocation concerns, and major factors for consideration in decision-making, are time, geographical area, and police strategies. Each of these is discussed below.

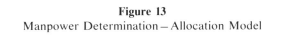

Figure 13
Manpower Determination — Allocation Model

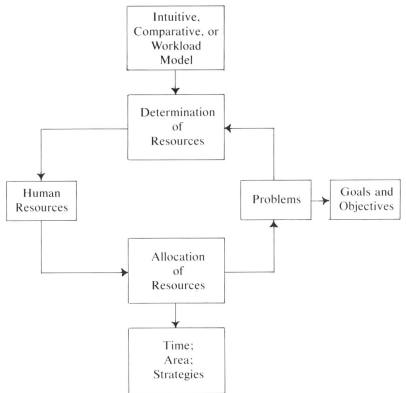

Time Considerations

Several important dimensions of time enter into allocation decisions: (1) time-framework, (2) time-specific, (3) time-problem, (4) time-response, (5) time-resource, and (6) time-mobility.

Time-Framework. The *time-framework* dimension is concerned with the continuous time frame within which almost all police agencies operate. Community police agencies have ongoing time frames in that they normally operate 24 hours per day, 365 days per year. It is within this continuous time frame that police agencies must function and managers must allocate resources directed at police problems.

Time-specific. The *time-specific* dimension encompasses the specific times at which various police problems occur. Within the continuous time frame, knowledge of the specific time of a crime, a call for service, or a car stop is important because it is the basis for the allocation of manpower to police problems in proportion to their frequency.

The specific time of each police problem should be recorded by time of day, day of the week, week of the month, and month of the year to establish patterns. Problems should be divided into categories so that the police manager will know what kind of problem exists. Categories can be types of crime (murder, robbery, assault), city ordinance categories, or nonenforcement categories (information, assistance, lunch, "breaks," court appearances). For certain police activities such as patrolling, or visibility, a separate category is necessary.

Time-Problem. Police problems are related not only to time of occurrence but also to the amount of time it takes the police to handle the problem. The time-specific dimension concerns when the crime or activity occurs; the *time-problem* dimension concerns how long it takes to resolve the problem to the point at which police are no longer involved. Knowing when certain crimes or events are likely to occur, and in what volume, permits the police manager to assign the officers within the time frame; knowing the amount of time it takes to perform the activity related to the crime or event permits the police manager to assign an appropriate quantity of manpower.

Time-Response. *Time-response* is related to time-problem. The quantity of manpower to be invested in a problem is influenced not only by the frequency of the problem and the amount of time it takes to handle it, but also by the time it takes the police officer to respond to the problem. The time consumed in handling a problem or event should include the response time, but response time should be recorded in a separate category because it is one criterion to use in determining both the quantity of police resources to be invested during a given time period and the geographical layouts of the beats. Time-response has three general parts: (1) the time between occurrence of the crime and the report to police, (2) the time between the report to police (if to a central location) and dispatch of a unit to the scene of the crime, and (3) the time between the dispatch and the unit's arrival at the scene. The police have the strongest influence on parts 2 and 3, but they can also educate citizens to reduce part 1.

Time-Resource. All the time dimensions discussed so far are useful in perceiving and structuring the problems with which the police are confronted. The next time dimension, *time-resource*, concerns the measurement of the manpower resources available to the police manager for investment in attempting to cope with police problems. A typical unit of measurement in the resource dimension is the man-hour—that is, one man working one hour. While the time frame for police agencies is continuous, it is not continuous for the individual. This means that the number of man-hours available to the police manager must be invested within a time frame of 24 hours a day, 365 days a year. Over a year there are 8,760 hours (24 × 365). For a police agency to place one police officer on the street 24 hours a day, 365 days a year, the agency must employ four or more individuals. The number of hours one man works in a year can be determined in various ways. One such method is described below.

1. Determine the number of hours worked per day. Normally policemen work 8 hours a day, but in some cases they may work as many as 10 or as few as 7 or 7½.

2. Determine the number of days worked per year. This is difficult to determine because of the differences in how "working" is defined. Assume that the average workday is 8 hours, with a 40-hour, or 5-day, week. This means that 2 days a week for the 52 weeks in the year would be weekends or days off, so deduct weekends from the 365 days in the year (365 − 104 = 261). Then deduct vacation days. The number can vary considerably.

If possible, deduct the actual number of vacation days per man. If not, use the average number of days per man. Assuming the average is 10 vacation days, 261 − 10 = 251 working days.

3. After deducting vacation time, other possible deductions include the following:

   a. Absence due to illness based on average per man per year. Assume 3 days, so 251 − 3 = 248 working days.

   b. Absence due to military leave based on average per man per year. Assume 2 days, so 248 − 2 = 246 working days.

   c. Absence due to training time based on average per man per year. Assume 5 days, so 246 − 5 = 241 working days. (Some police agencies may consider this "working time," while others do not. If a strict definition of working time is used, then training would be excluded.)

   d. Absence due to court appearances based on average per man per year. Assume 5 days, so 241 − 5 = 236 working days. (Once again, a strict definition of "working time" would exclude court appearances. Some agencies count court appearances, or time in court, as working time.)

   e. Other deductions are also possible. However, as noted in c and d above, the definition of what constitutes "working time" is most important. A strict definition would hold that all activity not directly related to responding to calls, initiating crime-related or service-related activities, conducting investigations, patrolling, and writing reports is *not* working time. Coffee breaks, lunch breaks, and personal convenience stops would also be excluded in this definition. Assuming that a police officer averages 1 hour a day on such activities, then 236 hours (for the 236 working days left) is equal to approximately 30 8-hour working days, so 236 − 30 = 206 days.

4. Overtime can add hours to "working time," so it is important to consider the average amount of overtime per man. Remember that if a strict definition of working time is used, then only overtime in which work is done can be counted. Court appearances, training, and so on would not count. It is also im-

portant to remember that if overtime is compensated for in like man-hours, *nothing is gained* over a year, because the officer usually takes such time off. If "time and a half" is given in man-hours, then one-third the number of hours of overtime worked must be subtracted from normal working time because for every hour worked, the police officer will take one and one-half hours off. If the overtime is compensated for in money, then the time can be counted. For the purposes of this illustration, it will be assumed that overtime is paid and that the average number of overtime hours per man per year is 32, or 4 working days. This means that 4 would be added to 206 (the number of working days left) for a total of 210.

5. Returning now to the original problem, the number of hours in a year is 8,760. The number of hours per year one man works in this problem is 1,680 (210 days $\times$ 8 hours). The number of individuals to be employed to cover the entire 8,760 hours is 5.21 (8,760 $\div$ 1,680), or 5 men. If the above police agency wants to have an average of 3 officers working on the streets 24 hours a day, 365 days a year, the agency will have to employ approximately 15 police officers (3 8-hour shifts per 24 hours $\times$ 5 men).

This example illustrates some considerations in determining the number of men needed for 24-hour coverage. Most departments need between 4.5 and 5.5 officers for one-man, around-the-clock coverage. The number is determined by the manner in which working time is defined and the number of deductions from the basic working time. Each police manager should be aware of the amount of working time of his individual officers and of his entire organization.

In allocating manpower, the manager must take into account the use of 2-man cars or other multiple units. He should define a man-hour in terms of *individuals* working 1 hour rather than in terms of numbers of units. Assume that the police manager wanted 15 men for an average of 3-man coverage 24 hours a day. Further, assume that he intends to place the men in 3 beats in the community. But what if the manager decides he wants one 2-man car and two 1-man cars? Obviously, 15 men would be insufficient, because while the manager would have 3 beat units, he would need 4 police officers. To get 3 beat units 24 hours a day, one with 2 men, would require the employment of 20 men and not 15, because the second man in the 2-man unit represents 5 persons to be employed for 24-hour coverage. If the manager's determination of manpower is based on the amount of the workload, then one 2-man car working 1 hour on a case requires 2 man-hours of resources.

Once the police manager has some indication of the manpower resources that are available, he should consider the restrictions that affect the assignment of personnel within the continuous time frame. First, he must be aware of the energy of the individual. Employees get tired working long hours. This fact has led to the 8-hour day, though some police departments have a 10-hour day and a 4-day week instead of an 8-hour day and a 5-day week. Second, he must be aware of limits on the number of consecutive days an employee can work without days off. This varies from 4 to 9 or 10 in some police agencies. The most typical pattern is 5 days working, 2 days not working, or 4 days working, 3 days off.

It is important for the manager to remain flexible in considering the use of man-hours. The limits presently imposed are those generally expected by society and employees. The most rational allocation, however, is to invest the man-hours where needed while insuring that the employee has the energy to perform at a desirable level. The 8-hour day and 5-day week have become the 10-hour day and 4-day week in some police agencies. Perhaps the 13-hour day and 3-day week will be next, or perhaps people will prove to be most effective working 6, 10, 15, or even 20 days and then having more than 2 or 3 consecutive days off. The manager should be receptive to all these possible options.

It is the manager's responsibility to attempt to allocate the man-hours available in proportion to the problems that require attention within the continuous time frame of the police agency. The limits placed on the hours worked per day is a manpower allocation decision. For example, a decision to work an 8-hour shift can result in three 8-hour shifts in 24 hours in which available resources are allocated by a threefold division. However, if most of the police problems occur in only one or two hours of the 8-hour shift, man-hours are usually wasted during part of the shift and can be inadequate during the busy hours. Responses to such problems have led to overlapping shifts and the 10-hour day to permit more flexibility in assigning resources. It is important for the police manager to remember that the allocation of resources is concerned with investing the man-hours available *when* the problems occur.

Time-Mobility. Although geographical considerations in manpower allocation will be discussed later, geography enters into the remaining time consideration. *Time-mobility* is related to the speed, or rate, of coverage of a specified geographical area. The degree of mobility of police is related to the energy used. Historically, police have relied on three sources of energy: human, animal, and motorized. Human energy has manifested itself in two forms of police mobility—walking and bicycling. (There may be some policemen who have used roller skates, but the authors are not aware of them!) Animal energy has primarily been in the form of horses, but in some areas, such as Alaska, dogs have been used to pull sleds. Motorized police mobility has taken the form of cycles, cars, snowmobiles, helicopters, and planes. The advantages of motorized energy appear obvious; police can go farther and faster. In some instances, police may have little choice in the method of mobility selected, but whichever one is used, the police manager both gains and loses some desirable advantages.

Four important factors in determining the method of police mobility are access, density, tradition, and community expectations. Access is the ability to get to a certain location. For example, if there are no roads, cars may be rejected in favor of horses or helicopters. Walking even may be considered unless the distance is great. Access problems in cities involve streets, alleys, entrances to buildings, and so on. In each case, one form of mobility may be more desirable than another.

Density is related to access in urban areas. Density refers to the number of people, buildings, cars, and so on in a given geographical area. In highly dense areas, police cars may lose their maneuverability. In such a case, walking, horses, or perhaps motorscooters or motorcycles could be employed.

Tradition plays an important role in determining the method of police mobility. Police agencies that were well developed prior to the 1920s and 1930s had long relied on walking and, in some cases, horses. The very problem of mobility for citizens en-couraged building towns and cities with businesses and homes close together. When motor-driven vehicles began to be used, some police agencies were slow to adopt them because of the traditional methods used and, of course, the expense. Newer cities created during the motor era, however, were spread out, and policing styles had to adjust to meet the needs of citizens. These expectations of the community's citizens play an impor-tant role in determining methods of police mobility. In cities that had, and have, walking beats, community expectations are relat-ed to the citizens' determination to maintain those beats. The reverse may be true for cities where motor-driven, visible patrol units are used.

When the police manager considers density, access, tradition, and expectations in his decision-making, the result is not always the most rational decision concerning the best method of police mobility; more often it is a compromise and balance. In balancing mobility alternatives, the manager must also consider other fac-tors. As noted earlier, it may appear that motor-driven vehicles are the most effective because of the great area covered in the time available. While speed is important, however, usually as the speed of the method increases, so does the isolation of the police officer from the citizen. Walking is the most personal form of policing; helicopters and airplanes are the least personal form and are often the most resented. Yet in terms of coverage, or area traversed in a given time, the plane or helicopter is the most effective. On the other hand, however, as mobility increases, close observation of people and buildings decreases. But then a helicopter can provide a bird's-eye view and therefore reveal things other policing units cannot see at all.

Each kind of mobility has its own advantages and disadvan-tages, and its effectiveness can be continually debated. Unfortu-nately, most police managers cannot select the most desirable combination of methods. Rather, the manager must take the resources that exist, analyze the workload, and then, in the case of patrol, attempt to allocate the manpower to geographical areas of approximately equal workload. In the case of investigations, he must attempt to assign policemen by type and number of cases. In patrol, the method of mobility is important, because, along with workload, it determines the size of the area that can be covered and the kind of patrolling that will exist when the police officer is responding to calls or initiating activity.

If the area to be covered is very large and/or the desired frequency of coverage in all or selected locations is extensive, then police must use a highly mobile method such as the car. If density, access, tradition, or expectations call for a slower form of mobility, such as walking, the area covered will of necessity be smaller. The exact dimension of beat size for coverage is a function of all these factors. The police manager must assess his resources, determine the time dimensions of police problems, and match up the allocation and mobility method with the workload in a given area as determined by desired frequency of coverage, density, access, tradition, and expectations. He must consider the trade-offs in observation and isolation that each means of transportation creates and, when possible, use methods that increase both observation and personal contact. Having officers walk all or part of the time or sponsoring special programs or group meetings for police officers and citizens are useful accommodations to problems of isolation. The police manager's imagination can often overcome problems imposed by limited resources or a heavy workload.

Geographical Considerations

In addition to all the time considerations just described, the police manager must know *where* police activity occurs. The parameters of the community are determined by the jurisdictional boundaries, or the limits posed by incorporation. Within these boundaries there are numerous ways to view the geographical area: (1) location by street and/or house number, (2) location by a community block designation, (3) location by census tract, (4) location by an area designation, and (5) vertical location in areas of tall buildings.

Most communities have some system to designate the locations of streets, houses, businesses, and so on, and this may be the most convenient method for police to use in noting specific locations. Sometimes, however, a police agency develops its own system for designating locations. Community systems normally involve a street, road, or highway and a number. Police agencies may want to consider developing a more systematic method to identify locations, for many street and numbering patterns are far from consistent.

Usually police agencies also need to designate areas in which to group police activity by category. This area designation can be by block, census tract, or some special area designation developed by the police agency. Area designations usually are called *beats, sectors, divisions, reporting districts,* or *areas.* The basis for establishing such an area—whatever name is used—can be the workload that one officer or unit can perform, sophistication in analysis of the location of problems (for example, small reporting districts permit rapid adjustment of beat size as the workload changes over time), and man-made and geographical constraints (highways, railroads, bridges, mountains).

In some areas, the vertical aspect of a geographical area is as important as the horizontal. Buildings are both horizontal and vertical. More and more new buildings have much more floor space on upper levels than horizontal space at street level. Police agencies seldom have the responsibility for policing the floors of buildings, but at times it may be necessary to provide such a service. A multiple-story building can have as much space on all its floors as does a beat on the ground.

Another important consideration for police managers in determining beat or area size in relation to response time is the time it takes to traverse the area itself. For example, if a police manager wants his patrol officers to respond to every emergency call for service in five minutes or less, then they must be able to traverse the beat in five minutes, or some system needs to be developed to place patrol units within five minutes of every part of the community. If the beat takes ten minutes or more to traverse and there are no other patrol units available, the five-minute response time will not always be possible. Of course, bridges and major highways may be barriers that can slow patrol units down, and the speed of travel or coverage in the area may be hindered by traffic. The time it takes to cover a given area is a function of mobility; what police do to respond to police problems is another matter.

Strategy, Method, and Function Considerations

Once the police manager determines what manpower is available and the extent and location of the police problem, he must concern himself with police strategies, methods, and functions. As defined in the section on manpower determination, police strategies are the major time-consuming activities in which police engage and that are assumed to have predicting power in achieving the overall police mission. These strategies usually are believed to have an impact on the opportunity or motive to commit a deviant act or are responses to requests for services. The five major operational, or line, strategies of community police agencies are (1) visibility, (2) apprehension, (3) education, (4) counseling, and (5) service—all defined in the first section of this chapter. The other major strategies of police organizations are *administration* (finance, personnel, training) and *support activities* (records, communications). These two will not be addressed directly in this chapter; rather, the emphasis will be on operational strategies and important factors in their use.

Police strategies and methods should not be confused, although at times they are closely related.

Perhaps a useful way for the manager to think of the difference between strategies and methods is to consider the differences between policies and procedures. Policies are broad statements of purpose that provide direction and guidance. Procedures are more specific means to implement or carry out policies. Police agencies may emphasize a policy of increased visibility in responding to a rising crime rate. Since this policy also deals with manpower allocation, it can be considered as a resource strategy. Methods of implementing this visibility strategy could include increased marked vehicles, more walking beats, use of helicopters, and so on. In this respect, these visibility methods help implement the strategy of visibility in the same way procedures help implement a policy.

Functions, or specializations, on the other hand, are determined by the organization of the police agency. A typical police department of moderate size has a patrol, an investigative, and perhaps a traffic function. However, in patrol *all strategies are used.* Patrol officers are visible; they apprehend; they educate at times; and they frequently counsel people and provide services. The investigative function, of course, includes apprehension and can include counseling, especially with juveniles, and often education. Traffic is similar to patrol in that it includes all strategies.

Visibility. The visibility strategy is often called deterrence or prevention. The rationale of the visibility strategy is that if policemen can be seen, the opportunity and/or motive to deviate will be deterred or prevented. Visibility is accomplished by wearing uniforms, driving marked police vehicles, or flying marked helicopters or planes.

The amount of visibility is usually related to the time per shift a patrol unit should have to patrol a beat or area. As previously noted, estimates range from 25 to 67 percent for visibility, or preventive patrol, for each patrol unit per shift. More research is needed to determine whether visibility does deter deviant behavior and, if it does, whether it is the most effective of the available strategies. The authors are inclined to believe that it does, but the relationship is difficult to establish given the problems of reporting crime (a substantial amount of crime that occurs is not reported to police) and the mobility and abilities of the prospective deviant. In addition, police managers are always limited by the amount of preventive patrol that can be given to an area. Perhaps if more resources were available, preventive patrol would reduce some types of crime. Police patrol, if it has a meaningful impact on crime, probably only affects crimes that the police are likely to see or can deduce from visible signs. Some robberies, burglaries, and street assaults may be deterrable, but murder probably is not, nor is an assault by a man on his wife in their home. The measurement of the relationship between police patrol and crime is very complex, and available studies with which the authors are familiar are certainly not conclusive, or even very helpful, in this regard.

A more precise measure than time per shift in patrol is frequency of coverage. For example, if a patrol unit could be seen at every point in a given area every ten minutes, what would be the impact on deterrable crimes? J. F. Elliot suggests consideration of frequency of coverage in determining police patrol,[6] and certainly this is a more precise measure than the amount of time per shift. Police managers should consider allocating police patrol on a "frequency of desirable coverage" factor. As the frequency of coverage increases, the police strategy of visibility moves close to the saturation level. There appears to be no available information on the relationship between frequency of coverage and deterrable crimes, so the police manager will have to experiment with this concept. And, as previously noted, attempts to establish a consistent and measurable relationship between patrol and crime are extremely complex, if not in fact impossible. The police manager should seek expert assistance in studying such a relationship.

Pattern of coverage is a relatively unexplored area in police patrol. A pattern of coverage is the systematic patrolling of a given geographical area by one or more police units. A pattern can involve patrolling in an increasingly larger or smaller pattern, or it can involve two patrol cars on parallel streets turning at predetermined intersections, crisscrossing, and so on. There may be some merit in police managers' attempting to develop different patterns of coverage for a given area. Such methods could be implemented by one or more patrol units using patterns designed to be as systematic and complete in coverage as possible. Examples of patterns for use could be drawn from naval ship patterns of movement or airplane search patterns or could be of the agency's own design. It is important for the manager to remember that patterns are a tool to systematize coverage and should not become predictable patterns of patrolling.

Apprehension. The second strategy, apprehension, involves all time-consuming activities related to investigating and processing individuals suspected of deviant acts. The processing of suspects involves booking, writing reports, attorney consultations, and court appearances. These will not be discussed here; rather, the emphasis will be on apprehension activities related to investigations. Although there are many investigative techniques, the two basic approaches are to apply investigative methods (1) by case or (2) by individual or group. In other words, investigations are pursued through following up on a specific crime or by following up on a person or a group of persons suspected of ongoing involvement in criminal activities. Many police departments wisely rely on both kinds of investigation. Many types of crime (burglary, auto theft, larceny, and some robberies) are very difficult to resolve by arrest, so the manager may obtain better results if he invests resources in studying individuals or groups believed to be involved.

Education. The third strategy, education, involves all time-consuming activities related to giving the citizens in a community the knowledge and/or skills to protect themselves and their property. The education strategy usually has two forms: (1) information designed to influence attitudes and behavior and (2) information designed to assist persons in protecting their property. The former is often applied in such efforts as traffic safety information programs and drug education programs. These are designed to influence the citizen to drive safely or not to use drugs. The latter is usually information for owners of homes and businesses in terms of locks, location of valuables, marking property, lighting, and other issues related to crime prevention. (This is called "target hardening," or making a person less likely to become a target of a crime.) In some cases, education is aimed at preventing crimes against individuals. For example, posters or advertisements can warn women about rape, telling them what places and hours are most dangerous and suggesting that they carry some protective device. Such efforts are designed to influence women's behavior. Educational strategies, or crime-prevention efforts, as they are currently called, have great potential for use by police managers. Not only can they have a significant impact on crime, but they and their various methods are positive in that they place the police in a supporting relationship with the community. Education helps accomplish both major goals of police—controlling crime and maintaining community trust and support. The next strategy also falls in this category.

Counseling. The fourth major strategy involves all major time-consuming activities related to efforts to influence behavior of individuals when arrests are not made and prosecution is not undertaken. Counseling occurs when a policeman discusses a traffic infraction with a violator but does not issue a ticket; it occurs at family fights, with juveniles, and in many cases in which a violation of the law is involved and the officer discusses the matter with the suspect or suspects but does not arrest anyone. Increasingly, policemen are receiving specialized training in certain facets of counseling, such as crisis intervention, violence prevention, and juvenile problems. This training is designed to provide counseling skills for situations that involve conflict and that have the potential for escalating into violence. Increasingly, counseling is being supplemented by other community resources and groups to provide more intensive efforts to deal with behavioral problems. Many police agencies now have referral or diversion programs in which many juveniles and some adults are diverted, or referred, to community agencies for assistance rather than being arrested and going through the judicial process. Most referrals do not involve serious crimes, and the police and community, working together, may be able to prevent the individual from engaging in deviant behavior in the future.

Service. The fifth, and final, major strategy is *service* and involves all time-consuming activities related to all other non-criminal matters (changing tires, providing directions, caring for lost children, and so on). The police manager should remember that while services provided for the community are often well received, the time invested in such activities diverts the available resources. The manager should establish priorities in the use of resources to be devoted to activities in each strategy in relation to its impact on organizational goals. Since resources are almost always limited, the manager must consider carefully which strategies to employ and how much time should be invested in each one.

Manpower Allocation Process

The following is a systematic process that a manager can use to make decisions in allocating manpower. The decisions are difficult because of the lack of adequate information concerning what police do in relation to crime and citizen attitudes. However, this should not prevent the manager from attempting to make the most effective decisions possible with the data available. And, if systematic consideration is given to evaluating each phase of the police operation, the information available will increase in quantity and improve in quality over time.

1. As discussed in Chapter 3, establish goals and agency-level

objectives supportive of those goals. These goals and objectives should reflect legal, community, and departmental expectations.

2. Determine the human resources available for use, considering the working time per man and the working time for the entire organization. Consider *all* the available human resources at this stage, and do not exclude administrative or support personnel.

3. Develop the strategies and methods available to police to address the problems associated with the goals. For example, in the goal of crime control the problem is crime and its reduction; for a goal related to citizen attitudes, the problem is to change or improve those attitudes. This is essentially a creative process for the manager and others in the organization. The tendency is to rely too heavily on the strategies and methods traditionally employed or used by others. This is a phase in which innovation should play an important role.

4. Consider the relative effectiveness of each operational strategy and method and the number of resources to be given to administration (management) and support. Since organizational goals and agency-level objectives are normally operationally oriented, the major concern of the police manager at this stage is to determine the effectiveness of each operational strategy. This is most difficult to do, and, as suggested earlier, the manager should solicit expert assistance in gathering the information that will make it possible.

5. Determine how many resources will be invested in what strategy and method. This stage, along with stage 6, is both proactive and reactive. It is reactive in that the manager will have no choice concerning how part of the resources will be invested. For example, some calls *must* be answered and some cases *must* be investigated. For the resources that remain after required investments, however, the manager can take a proactive posture; he can attempt to invest these resources in the most effective of the strategies and/or methods available. (At this point, organizational structuring considerations are important, but these will be discussed in a later chapter.)

6. Assess the police problem relative to time-specific and time-problem. This stage and stage 5 of the process can be undertaken at the same time. In other words, determine when the police problems (calls for service, crimes) are occurring and how

long it takes to provide the required services. Again, part of the police problem will be reactive and part will be proactive. In this stage, consider the allocation of manpower within a time frame.

7. Consider manpower by area. Strategies and methods have been determined; the problem has been assessed in relation to time; and now the location of the activity must be considered in allocation of manpower. Consider all the factors described under time-mobility, time-response, and geographical area.

8. Develop an evaluation system to assess the new system of manpower allocation. The system should focus on establishing relationships between strategy and methods by type of crime and citizen attitudes, the amount of time it takes to perform activities, the relationship of response time to a crime's solution by type of crime, and the relationship of existing manpower to changing workload.

Summary

This chapter is concluded with some serious misgivings. Manpower determination and allocation are among the most important considerations of police managers. One chapter on the subject is certainly inadequate to cover all the needed concepts and ideas, so the reader is strongly encouraged to review some of the suggested readings. To fully understand and apply manpower determination and allocation models, such a review is essential.

Perhaps the most important concepts in this chapter are (1) that manpower should be allocated to police activities (strategies and methods) that have proven most effective in resolving problems related to goals, and (2) that the determination of manpower needs should be based on the amount of resources needed to be effective in solving problems. Many factors must be considered in applying each of these concepts, and the tools used to consider them range in sophistication from intuition to use of mathematical computer models. In small agencies with limited manpower and police problems, decisions may be based on minimal analysis of information, but in larger police agencies the police manager should learn to apply sophisticated methods of analysis to manpower determination and allocation problems.

Suggested
Reading

Butts, Orville. "Determining Police Manpower Needs." Master's thesis, California State University, San Jose, 1972.

Carlin, Jerry L., and Moodie, Colin L. "An Evaluation of Some Patrol Allocation Methods." *Police* 15 (September 1971): 56–60.

Eastman, George D., and Eastman, Esther M., eds. *Municipal Police Administration*. 6th ed. Washington, D.C.: International City Management Association, 1969.

Gourley, Douglas, and Bristow, Allen. *Patrol Administration*. 4th ptg. Springfield, Ill.: Charles C. Thomas, 1968.

Grertz, J. Fred. *An Economic Analysis of the Distribution of Police Patrol Forces*. Washington, D.C.: National Technical Information Service of the U.S. Department of Commerce, 1970.

Heller, Nelson B., and Markland, Robert E. "A Climatological Model for Forecasting the Demand for Police Services." *Journal of Research in Crime and Delinquency* 7 (July 1970): 167–176.

Kenney, John P. *Police Administration*. Springfield, Ill.: Charles C. Thomas, 1972.

Kreutzer, Walter E. "A Simplified Method of Patrol Distribution." *The Police Chief* 35 (July 1968): 32–41.

Larson, Richard. "On Quantitative Approaches to Urban Police Patrol Problems." *Journal of Research in Crime and Delinquency* 7 (July 1970): 157–166.

——. *Urban Police Patrol Analysis.* Cambridge: Massachusetts Institute of Technology Press, 1972.

Law Enforcement Assistance Administration. *Allocation of Patrol Manpower Resources in the St. Louis Police Department.* 2 vols. Washington, D.C.: U.S. Government Printing Office, 1966.

President's Commission on Law Enforcement and Administration of Justice. *Task Force Report: Science and Technology.* Washington, D.C.: U.S. Government Printing Office, 1967.

U.S. Department of Justice, Law Enforcement Assistance Administration, National Institute of Law Enforcement and Criminal Justice. *The Use of Probability Theory in the Assignment of Police Patrol Areas.* Washington, D.C.: U.S. Government Printing Office, 1970.

Wilson, O. W., and MacLaren, Roy. *Police Administration.* 3rd ed. New York: McGraw-Hill, 1972.

CHAPTER 7

Budgets and Budgeting

In medieval Europe the word *budget* meant a container for valuables and money. Today, the word still refers to money. For the police manager, the budget is the document that explains just how the agency intends to accomplish its goals and objectives in terms of dollars and cents. By carefully determining and utilizing the funds allocated from the community's resources, the department spells out in reasonably exact monetary terms just what it is going to do between the time the budget is adopted and the time it runs out. Like a plan, the budget indicates in financial terms who will be doing what, when, where, and why.

The budget, documenting the agency's planned activities, is most commonly made on an annual basis. Management literature defines the budget as being a plan within some time framework. It may, in fact, be a series of plans and can be thought of in a series of varying time frames. For instance, a sheriff's department may have three budget plans in operation at one time. First, it may have an operating budget that covers the department's normal activities for the fiscal year. Second, it may have a budget for a special project funded from revenue sharing, state planning agency grants, or "earmarked" funds (such budgets may be operating concurrently and over varying periods). Last, the department may have a capital budget for a new jail being constructed (a budget of this kind may exist until the bonds for the construction are finally paid). Regardless of the kind or source of funding, the budget is a written plan or document and has a specific time frame for its life. Here are several budget definitions:

The budget is nothing more than the work program of the department stated in terms of the money needed to carry it out. [O. W. Wilson and Roy C. McLaren, *Police Administration*, 3rd ed. (New York: McGraw-Hill, 1972), p. 178.]

[Budget] . . . is really only a document in which is recorded the plans and proposals necessary to establish a sound program of police work and which itemizes the funds required for effective operation of the department for a specified period of time. [George L. Lumpkin, "Preparation and Presentation of the Police Budget," in Southwestern Law Enforcement Institute, *Police Management for Supervisory and Administrative Personnel* (Springfield, Ill.: Charles C. Thomas, 1963), p. 81.]

The budget . . . should itemize the revenue or income sources . . . establish a legal basis for expenditures . . . communication between city officials and citizens . . . basic tool for fiscal control . . . guide for review of past, present and future programs and services . . . [and] analysis and evaluation of city programs with respect to need, adequacy and efficiency. [Glenn W. Nichols et al., *Handbook for City Finance Officers in Idaho* (Moscow: Bureau of Public Affairs Research, University of Idaho, 1969), pp. 1–5.]

A Budget is, in effect, a comprehensive plan expressed in financial terms by which an operating program becomes effective for a given period of time. [John P. Kenney, *Police Management Planning* (Springfield, Ill.: Charles C. Thomas, 1959), pp. 91–92.]

. . . "budget" is most commonly associated with a document that expresses the anticipated revenues and expenditures of government for a specified period of time. [Robert D. Lee, Jr., and Ronald W.

Johnson, *Public Budgeting Systems* (Baltimore: University Park Press, 1973), p. 17.]

The Budget and the Community

In its origin and purpose, the budget is based on the community or jurisdiction. Aside from the dollars that can come from federal or state sources, the money on which the police will function is derived from the community that the agency serves. The bulk of this revenue comes directly from the property tax (some 87 percent in 1966) and from various charges, fees, fines, and other general revenue.[1] Law enforcement agencies are somewhat involved in the generation of local revenues, since some services have charges (serving papers, for example), and many fines are retained by the jurisdiction in whole or in part. Some law enforcement officials have attempted to modify police operations in the parking and traffic sectors only to discover how "addicted" the city administration has become to fines as a source of revenue. Generally, however, the property tax dollar has been the primary source of monies for police agencies.

The community will also determine in large measure just how those dollars are spent by their demands for services, both serious and trivial. In one city, assaults on the municipal railway caused a large expenditure to be made for personnel to patrol the transit system. In another, complaints about stray dogs forced the police to apply scarce funds to animal control. Regardless of how the management views the problems, the public may determine how the resources will be used.[2] In short, law enforcement usually has restricted funds and limited freedom to decide how they will be spent.

Few writers have considered the impact of the local budget on the local community. Many studies have examined the impact of federal (such as military) spending on the local economy, but not one has looked at the impact of law enforcement spending on cities and counties. The police department puts a substantial amount of money into the local economy with the purchase of patrol vehicles and other items. The largest segment of the police or sheriff's budget is the wages and benefits paid to departmental personnel. These salaries, spent in the jurisdiction, create other jobs and goods and services. Some counties use prisoners from honor farms to help maintain local parks, conservation projects, and other community developments that are quite beneficial to the area. In addition to keeping expenditures low, the use of prison labor may enable a town to complete projects for which funds would not otherwise have been available. The resulting parks and projects can help make the community attractive to new residents and businesses.

Some police agencies create jobs during periods of unemployment. In a small town of 3,500 people, one resourceful chief of police created jobs for the unemployed young people by establishing a Community Action Corps through the Neighborhood Youth Corps (NYC). Corps members opened a day care center, maintained parks, painted schools, and even filled some cadet jobs in the police department. Federal programs were utilized to train personnel in police communications. By the wise use of local and federal funds, the agency had an impact on the community's economy.[3]

The Revenue Aspect of Government Budgeting

As mentioned previously, the bulk of the revenue for local government comes from property taxes. Each state's subdivisions rely on the property tax differently; for example, Montana has a higher dependence than Alabama (78 percent versus 28 percent) at the county level,[4] and there can be little doubt about that dependency. Many property owners are acutely aware of their tax burden and feel it should be distributed differently throughout the community. At the same time, they are concerned with the value of their property. The assessment of value depends on the judgment of local assessors, and it is influenced by police protection. Often property depreciates as it gets older —a real problem, since decaying neighborhoods often breed increasing crime while their capability to generate revenue is declining. Even if a piece of property is located in a vital and thriving area, the state may have ceilings imposed on property tax rates. This tax is under severe criticism as a generator of revenue, for the influence of police services on the community can increase the value of property past the point where revenues are increased.

Other important sources of revenue are intergovernmental. Federal revenue sharing, called everything from a boon to a boondoggle, has had its impact. Announcements of the revenue to be shared have unearthed many schemes for use of the money. In some police and sheriff's departments, chief executives have been literally buried with proposals by subunits, ranging from the hiring of additional personnel to the purchase of exotic hardware. A manager should keep in mind, however, that unless his government has a firmly established tradition of revenue sharing, such funds should be treated initially as essentially short-term and as being subject to a multitude of new demands (reports, compliances) competing for his attention.[5] More established and dependable is the revenue received by local governments from their own states. These revenues are normally specified grants-in-aid or are established shares of designated funds from specified taxes collected by the state. Grants-in-aid are allocated amounts of funds given to the local government based on certain criteria, such as population. Shared or designated funds are not fixed but are usually a certain percentage of state tax dollars collected in the locale. One tax that is often shared is the gasoline tax, and the town or county receives a percentage of every cent collected in state gas taxes in that local area. Usually the local share of gasoline taxes is legally required to go for such purposes as highways and highway safety. Occasionally one finds a traffic bureau affiliated with a police department but having a separate budget. The officers are sworn personnel, but their prime responsibility is traffic and accident investigation. In such a situation, the manager has taken advantage of legislative intent to utilize designated funds to develop a specialized traffic unit within the police department in order to qualify for traffic safety funds.

In some jurisdictions, the state shares the taxes generated from beer, wine, and liquor sales. Often these monies go into the general fund, but a case could be made for designating some of them for law enforcement, since some police problems are related to alcohol. This is especially true of "border towns" along state lines. When the two states have different drinking ages or different hours during which liquor can be sold, towns near the border in the more liberal state will attract people who want to buy alcoholic beverages.

Some police managers are seriously considering the possibility of generating revenues for specialized services provided to only a few people. Publicly owned utilities and services are well established and charge rates according to the services performed, but police officials have been reluctant to think of themselves as "selling" their services. Except for agencies in metropolitan areas, many agencies provide central alarm station services without charging for them. Constantly plagued by false alarms and the "take-it-for granted" attitude of many individual businessmen, some jurisdictions have begun to charge monthly rates for this service and, particularly, to charge for the time spent answering the countless false alarms and awaiting the resetting of the systems. Uniformed officers are expensive, and requiring them to waste time because of a negligent clerk or a cheap alarm system denies the city or county the services of those officers. If a service is provided for a select few, then those few should be expected to pay a reasonable fee. Some departments charge a fee for checking homes while people are away and turn this responsibility over to their reserve or auxiliary program. The fees then go into the auxiliary budget to defray its costs. This same service could be used by realtors when homes are vacant and vandalism can influence possible future sales. Specialized calls for individual attention that consume time and money should be financed by those receiving the attention. With increasing costs and declining sources of revenue, police departments should seek new sources of income.

The police manager today needs to know where his funds come from and particularly where they will come from in the future. Without a knowledge of revenue generation, the best-laid plans will be little more than guesswork. Dollars make things happen, and without a thorough knowledge of what the community is capable of supporting, planning will not be effective. This is especially true of long-range plans.

The Budgeting Process

As a process that involves the choice of ends and means of the community, budgeting is a cycle that has several decision points.

Like the decision-making process described earlier, the budgeting process has a standard format that is fairly universal and is practical for almost all political entities whether they be cities, villages, counties, or larger units of government. The reader should bear in mind, however, that many of the difficulties related to decision-making also apply to budgeting. The budgeting process is generally considered to have an annual, or one-year, life. In fact, however, the cycle is ongoing and ends only when the funds are expended or the accounts closed. Figure 14 shows the steps in the process or cycle: preparation, submission, approval, execution, and auditing. Figure 15 shows the approximate timetable. Here is an explanation of the process.[6]

Figure 14
Budgeting Process or Cycle

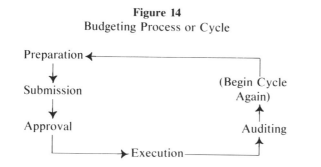

The Budget Path (Example from a Sheriff's Department)

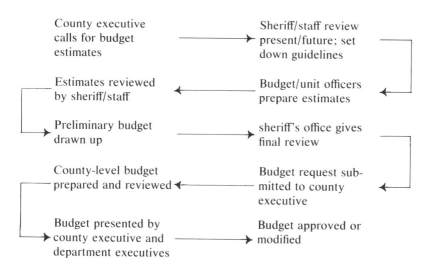

Preparation

The preparation phase normally begins well in advance of the year for which the budget is to be used. It begins formally or informally when the city or county manager sends out a budget directive and budget work sheets to the various agency or department heads. Each agency head assesses his ongoing programs and operations, looks over the plans he has approved for the forthcoming period, and informally inquires into the resources potentially available for the period in question. He in turn may do exactly what the city management has done. For instance, the agency manager may distribute his work sheets and allow the heads of the various units (communications, jail, patrol, and so on) to develop a tentative prospective budget. Eventually, all the working papers are combined and integrated into a departmental budget estimate for the fiscal year. Some organizations have a budget officer who completes the work sheets for the department and then, in conjunction with management, develops the budget estimates.

In the traditional and most common format employed—the line item budget—the estimated budget of the agency will be made up of several forms. The package may include capital projects, workload indicators, salary details, and maintenance and operations summaries. If increases are anticipated, the agency prepares to justify them so that those who will make the decision will know exactly why each increase is needed and just what they can expect for the dollars expended.

Writing justifications for budgets has been described as an art. Forms often lack sufficient space for the budget officer to present a case fully, so the budget officer, in conjunction with heads of other subunits in the organization and other departments in the government, must either prepare the justification in the form of a study or carry the details in his head for a later presentation to the manager and council. Information, for example, may indicate a large number of complaints about speeding motorists and an inordinate number of accidents in which excessive speed was a causal factor. After data are gathered concerning the problem and possible solutions, it may be that signal lights or arterial stops are out of the question. The agency then may request a speedgun

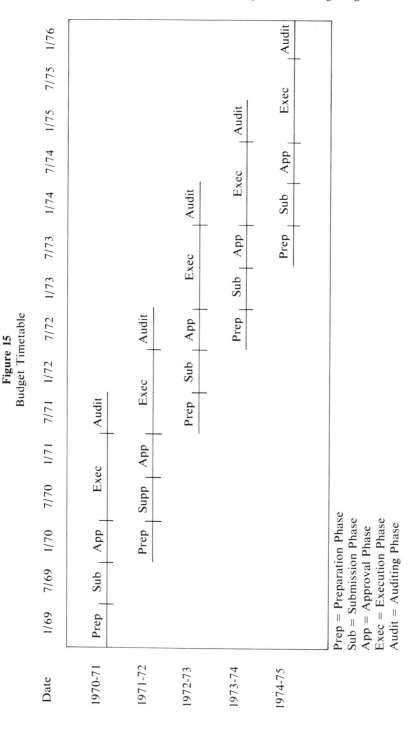

Figure 15
Budget Timetable

Prep = Preparation Phase
Sub = Submission Phase
App = Approval Phase
Exec = Execution Phase
Audit = Auditing Phase

radar unit. In attempting to predict the effect of this equipment, the budget officer can compute how the speedgun radar unit will increase the rapidity with which violators are identified in comparison with traditional deployment of marked patrol vehicles for longer periods. He must also suggest how the equipment will impact on the target and just what benefits will accrue to the community (savings in vehicle damages and human lives, saved "down time" investigating accidents). The issue is a choice of strategies and their costs. It is assumed that both strategies will deter speeding, but the budget-makers want the highest possible level of deterrence for their money.

Again, all this may be in a justification study or in the budget officer's head (a practice *not* recommended by the authors). It will be necessary to condense the justification to fit the form, but the essence should be explained. The officer can make the full justification available for study by the manager, council, commissioners, and public. The studies also should be available when the budget is being presented in order to answer adequately any question asked of the police manager and/or budget officer.

Submission

Once the department is satisfied with the document, then the tentative or preliminary budget is submitted to the city or county executive or his budget officer. Ideally, contact and interaction about the budget will have been an ongoing process so the submitted form is the final format that can then be submitted to the political decision-makers. The department that has been realistic in terms of what is available and what the plans of other functions of government are calling for, that has been careful in all its analyses and presentations, and that has a history of budgetary care should encounter few problems in the submission phase of the process.

The county or city executive or his budget officer must review all departmental demands and put them together into the total budget for the jurisdiction. It is rare that departmental monetary requests total less than the resources available.

When submitting a budget, a manager should request only what he actually needs and have proper justification for his needs. Some have advocated padding both the departmental and jurisdictional budgets to satisfy some psychological need of executives and politicians to cut budgets. If sufficient "fat" is included, the subsequent cutting supposedly satisfies this need while leaving intact the essence of what the department or jurisdiction actually desires. This practice is easy to condemn, but it often is encouraged by the actions of some executives and politicians. The submitted budget, however, should be carefully researched and developed and be as accurate a financial plan as possible.

Approval

After all the departments in the jurisdiction have arrived at acceptable projections of what they will need in the way of resources, the budget is submitted to the political decision-making body for its approval. Budgets for state agencies are submitted in the governor's budget to the legislature. In the case of cities and counties, the approving body is usually a city council or a county board of supervisors or commissioners. The budget may be directed to the entire body, or it may go to a select committee that has expertise in financial matters.

Budget hearings are held either by the political decision-making body as a whole or through its committee. Usually the police agency head and perhaps a chief budget officer explain their general operations and any special or new plans they have developed in the proposed budget. The political body or any of its members ask whatever questions they want about the agency's plans and the resources needed to carry out those plans. "Friends" of the requesting agency may ask questions designed to educate the decision-makers about the agency's needs; "enemies" may attempt to embarrass the agency by showing that it has not done its homework, that it is frivolous in its handling of money, or perhaps that it is administered by incompetents. In the budget presentation and hearings, the police manager must be thoroughly prepared and competent in presenting the agency's case before the politicians and the segments of the public present at such meetings.

In local governments that employ such executives as city or

county managers, the politicians are highly dependent on these professional managers. It may be that the council or board simply conducts hearings as a matter of form and adopts whatever the manager suggests. Often the political decision-makers do not have expertise concerning items requested. A humorous story that illustrates this point is a case of a city council that did not comprehend the use or significance of some computers requested in a police department budget. Armed with in-depth studies, audio-visual materials, and experts to support the wisdom of certain computer purchases in the proposed budget, the police chief expected a multitude of questions about these exotic machines and their frightening price tags. Instead of the major expenditure, the council concentrated on a budget item that called for a stapler. For over an hour, the council discussed the stapler, and, for the sake of economy, did not approve it. Unsure of their ground in talking computers (which they finally approved), the council zeroed in on what they knew about! In budget presentations, attention can be diverted from key expenditures, and the presentation team must be prepared to field any question even when the manager has "sold" the underlying concepts already.

Authorization for the budget normally occurs when the politicians have voted to accept the budget in its final form. In some jurisdictions the council or board votes on each budget from the various departments and then accepts the total budget. Occasionally certain expenditures are reduced or deleted. At other times, allotments may be increased or new items added. The police manager should have a member of his staff immediately available to ascertain the potential impact of any change in order to adjust plans. Budgetary changes generally involve reductions, but if an increase is granted or perhaps a new responsibility funded, the manager should provide the approving body with an outline of just how the agency plans to use the increased funds.

Execution

Generally the execution of a budget begins either January 1 or July 1 and lasts for a one-year period. The year covered by a budget is called the *fiscal year.* Some local governments use a *quarter system* in which the budget and its anticipated expenditures are broken down in terms of expenses in each three-month period. The approved expenditures are then allotted on a quarterly basis. Because revenue is collected throughout the entire year, any adjustments that may be required can be made more easily if the money is allotted quarterly. New priorities can also appear, and the jurisdiction's executive can informally veto certain quarterly allotments and shift them to new priorities or emergencies.

In the quarter system, the police manager normally submits his schedule of quarterly allotments to the departmental budget officer based on what he anticipates he will need during each quarter. The schedule is then provided to the jurisdiction. Each unit within the agency is then assigned the funds it will need to operate. Should actual needs or expenditures be greater than anticipated, the unit or agency can request the council or board of commissioners to shift funds from one account to another or to authorize additional funds from a contingency account. (Contingency funds are often maintained in reserve to cover items that were unforeseen when the budget was drafted—excessive overtime pay, an unexpected influx of prisoners in the jail, and so on.)

Another problem in the execution of a budget is the practice in some jurisdictions of "freezing" funds. In order to reduce expenditures and to carry funds over to another time period, the manager or executive may place a freeze, ordering drastic curtailment in the expenditure of allocated funds. Such action can stimulate a wild purchasing spree prior to the freeze date or rapid expenditure in anticipation of a freeze order. Even if the jurisdiction does not face a freeze, the agency and its units may spend their funds rapidly simply to avoid showing that they had estimated too high and to avoid being allocated less in the future.

Auditing

When the agency begins to spend its funds, the auditing phase begins. Many agencies require submission of a requisition before purchases of expensive or unique items. The auditing body, usually the finance department, checks the requisition against the goals or objectives of the account and against the budget in order to assure that the requisition conforms with the financial plan.

Once the purchase is approved, the agency or unit usually orders what it needs and notifies the finance department on receipt so that payment can be made. Or the agency draws a check and notifies the finance department of the expenditure and the circumstances surrounding the purchase. Minor or routine purchases are usually made without the finance department's checking the expenditure against the goals and objectives of the account until the entire account is examined to assure that expenditures were in conformity with the intent of the city council or board of commissioners. Occasional spot-checks may be made to assure that expenditures are consistent with purposes.

The primary purpose of auditing is to assure that the agency does what it said it was going to do with the money and what the council or board authorized it to do. Although spot-checks are used and large expenditures are audited when money is dispensed, the auditing function is normally performed sometime after the fiscal period in question is completed.

The audit may also be applied to material purchased in an earlier fiscal period. Normally called *inventory control* when performed as part of the budget audit, this provides the budgeting personnel with feedback useful for planning purposes. These and other auditing controls provide the data necessary to determine the practicality of current financial management and to develop future practices.

Types of Budgets

Police agencies can use several kinds of budgets. Among them are the *line item budget,* the *performance budget,* and the *Program Planning Budget System (PPBS).*

The Line Item Budget

Many police agencies still use the traditional line item budget (see Figure 16). This budget, simple in form, is the most easily developed and suits the needs of many small agencies throughout the country. Resembling a shopping list, the budget simply lists the various personnel, equipment, repairs, and structures it will require to function during the fiscal period under consideration.

The needs are usually categorized into parts or classifications, such as salaries, maintenance/operations, capital outlay, and capital improvements. Dollar figures indicate the cost of each particular item as well as the current financial status and the record of the past few years, so the political decision-makers will be able to view past as well as projected expenditures.

While excellent for the small department or for a jurisdiction with little impetus for future planning, the line item budget has come under criticism in the past few years. It has been criticized mainly for failure to provide a sense of direction. The line item budget says little about what the agency's goals or objectives are, how it plans to accomplish them, and how each expenditure is coordinated with the achievement of the goals and objectives. For this reason, other forms of budgeting have been demanded by politicians as well as administrators.

Another major problem with the line item budget is the "traditional" slashing of the budget by the council or board. Many Americans complain of excessive taxation and wild government spending. Responding to these complaints, politicians often cut item after item from governmental budgets in order to keep spending within bounds. These cuts normally are made without full knowledge of their consequences. Chiefs of police and sheriffs are told to make do with what is left, but they get no guidelines, in the sense of services and programs, as to where the savings are to be accomplished. Thus, the chief or sheriff, using his discretion, abides by the cuts. Later, when the public complains about the quality of jail food, or the frequency of patrol, or some other service, the police manager may be accused of having curtailed or cut in the wrong category. Increasingly, agencies are adopting other forms of budget designed to overcome such problems.[7]

The Performance Budget

Unlike the line item budget, the performance budget focuses on the work units that can be accomplished for the dollar expended. It usually concentrates on the line functions such as cases investigated, service calls answered, and proactive patrol time. By seeing the funds in the context of units of work, the decision-

Figure 16
Sample Line Item Budget
Personnel Salaries and Wages Section

Salaries and Wages	Amounts Expended			Estimated Expenditure Remainder FY 72–73	Estimated Expenditure FY 72–73	Estimated Approximate Balance for 1972	Departmental Request for 1973
	FY 1970	FY 1971	To 2nd Monday Dec. 1972				
Sheriff	13,500	13,750	7,000	7,000	14,000	0	15,000
Chief Deputy	12,000	12,200	6,250	6,250	12,500	0	13,000
3 Deputies III¹	30,000	30,600	15,750	15,750	31,500	0	33,000
8 Deputies II	72,000	73,600	38,000	38,000	76,000	0	80,000
17 Deputies I	136,000	139,400	70,036	68,000	144,500	6,464	148,750
6 Deputies I (new position)	—	—	—	—	—	—	52,500
1 Corrections II	10,000	10,500	5,375	5,375	10,750	0	11,000
6 Corrections I	48,000	51,000	26,250	26,250	52,500	0	54,000
2 Matrons	16,000	17,000	8,750	8,750	17,500	0	18,000
1 Cook	8,000	8,250	4,250	4,250	8,500	0	9,000
5 Dispatch/Clerk	30,000	31,250	16,125	16,125	32,250	0	35,000
1 Dispatch/Clerk (new position)	—	—	—	—	—	—	7,000
2 Deputy/Cadets	—	—	2,500	7,500	10,000	2,500	10,400

¹The Roman numerals indicate the classification of a job in terms of skills, responsibilities, and pay. The I is at the low end of the scale.

makers can know exactly what they are buying (see Figure 17).

The performance budget avoids the indiscriminate cutting that is often prevalent with line item budgets. When the decision-maker makes a cut, he can see exactly what is being removed in terms of work units. If the department's request to investigate 300 burglaries is slashed by 20, then its capability will be only 280 burglary investigations. Instead of the chief or sheriff having to guess at the impact of the reduced expenditures, the exact curtailment can be foreseen. The criteria used to determine whether a follow-up investigation will occur can be stiffened so that the projected rate of burglaries and the cases to be investigated will fall within the 280 cases authorized by the budget. The decision-makers can choose between services by actually budgeting for the workload for the next fiscal period.

While an improvement over the line item budget, the performance budget still leaves much to be desired, since it does not speak to the goals and objectives of the agency and its units. There is no overall direction or planning as to how the agency will meet and measure goals and objectives. For this, another type of budgeting system is needed.

The Program Planning Budget System (PPBS)

The Program Planning Budget System (PPBS) is extremely difficult to implement but offers many advantages to the police agency that outweigh the difficulties.[8] The chief advantage of the PPBS is that it allows the department to compare and evaluate its various programs and activities in terms of meeting the goals and objectives of the department. It allows for projecting into the future so that decisions can be anticipated and planned for, and it allows for greater control so that any changes deemed necessary can be made if the activity is not supportive of the goals and objectives.

When using the PPBS, the agency must develop a strong planning capability within both the organization and the jurisdiction. Objectives must be established, plans drawn, and controls established to measure progress. Present and projected revenues must

Figure 17
Sample of Performance Budget

CRIME AGAINST PERSONS

Crime Category	Average Hours per Case	Cost per Hour (Dollars)	Number of Projected Cases 1972-73	Cost per Case Investigated (Dollars)	1972-73 Request
Robbery	7	21	20	147	2.940
Assault	8	21	36	168	6.048
Homicide	24	23	3	552	1.656
Sex-Related	12	22	15	264	3.960
All Others	5	18	12	90	1.080
—	—	—	—	—	15.684

be understood and estimated, as must human and material expenditures. All the interrelationships among these factors need to be understood. If it is to be of use to the jurisdiction, PPBS will require managerial and personnel support.

The Program Planning Budget, when examined closely, resembles the budgets previously described. The difference is in the format used prior to the actual budgetary requests. The budgetary decision-maker, whether the manager of the agency or jurisdiction or an elected official, is first given descriptions of the program and subprograms. Next he is told the objectives and given an analysis of how the objectives will be accomplished and the various alternatives that are available. From that point, the PPBS takes on the more familiar and traditional format. What follows is a rather extensive PPB System that was developed for one unit of a police agency. To provide a shorter example would result in the loss of the essence of the system. Such unit programs, taken together, could comprise a PPB System for the entire agency. PPBS example (selected parts of actual PPBS):

Bureau of Investigation
Budget Request, Burglary Unit, 1973–1974

An Overview

During the previous budget year we have found that through a change in our approach to the rising burglary rate, we are able to detect a small, and as yet unproven, trend in the burglary pattern. This trend is not necessarily a descending number of reported cases; it appears as a decrease of a projected anticipated increase occurring during the latter months of 1972. It indicates that if our enforcement thrust remains directed toward the present intermediate goals, we may be able to control or at least influence the burglary pattern. If this is possible, further application of improved approaches could well lead us to our long-range goal—the reduction in number of incidents reported.

By reallocating the existing manpower through reorganization, we were able to direct our activities toward special problem areas—residential burglaries and receivers of stolen property. Residential burglaries occur almost three times as often as do commercial burglaries. Receivers of stolen property had received little or no attention in the past. Because of the close relationship between the thief and those who buy stolen goods, enforcement was applied to close this conversion outlet.

The program and subprograms described in the Burglary budget are an attempt to expand enforcement effort to those areas where optimistic results are indicated. Included are improvements necessary to refine and make more effective our enforcement process. Built into the program is the necessary flexibility that will allow us to change the direction of enforcement thrust when necessary to meet any changes in the criminal pattern.

Program	Burglary Investigation	Activity A
Subprogram	Burglary Intelligence (new)	Activity B
	Safe Burglary	
Subprogram	Pawnshops, Second-Hand Dealers and Flea Markets	Activity C
Subprogram	Receiving Stolen Property	Activity D

Additional Personnel

No.	Classification	Full-time/ Part-time	Duties	Sworn or Civilian
10	Sergeants	Full	3 Burglary Investigation 3 Burglary Intelligence/ Safe Burglary 2 Pawnshops, Second-Hand Dealers, and Flea Markets 2 Receiving Stolen Property	S
1	Steno II	Full	Clerical, Burglary Investigation	C
1	Typist II	Full	Clerical, half time Pawnshops, half time Receiving Stolen Property	C

See individual programs for additional information.

I. Program: Burglary Investigation

II. Summary of Program
Focus the resources of the Burglary Unit toward identification, apprehension, and successful prosecution of burglary suspects through the coordination of the separate activities of unit subunits.

III. Objectives

A. Reduce the incidence of burglary through increased apprehension and successful prosecution of offenders. The proposed program will reduce this anticipated increase to 9 percent (anticipated population growth: 5 percent).

B. Increase the effectiveness of the Burglary Unit, measured in increased adult burglary arrests.

C. Establish within the unit a subunit to maintain constant intelligence as to burglaries occurring and burglary suspects active.
This model will be incorporated into the Police Department Electronic Data Processing Program when operational.

1. *Modus operandi*

2. Vehicles used

3. Property stolen (identify fences by type of property received)

4. Description of suspects

D. Coordinate efforts of the unit through enforcement. Thrust toward arrest-prosecution of suspects and limiting outlets for stolen property.

E. Develop a mechanism in which each member ("component") understands his contributions.

IV. Alternative Approaches

A. Establish a strike force to provide saturation enforcement in high-incidence areas. A flexible, integral body assigned to a problem area with information as to suspects, vehicles, and *modus operandi.* In the absence of a favorable assignment area, this force works surveillance on known or suspected burglary suspects and known or suspected fences.

B. Continue with our time-worn methods and face a continual, ever-escalating burglary problem—a problem unsatisfactory to police and community. This approach requires a decision by department administration— acceptance of the level we now maintain or experimentation in possible improvements of operation.

C. Establish a case-weighing system that allows investigation of only those cases that appear to show promise of solution. Present reporting quality would not permit such a system and would undesirably place the decision at too low an organizational level. This alternative has at least two undesirable aspects:
   1. Lack of attention to a majority of reported cases quite possibly would allow valuable physical evidence to be lost, causing a decline in the number of prosecutions.
   2. It is felt that the citizen-public should receive police attention when he is victimized.

V. Line Item Breakdown
   A. Personnel

	No.	Classification	Full-time/ Part-time	Duties	Sworn or Civilian
Present	16	Sergeant	Full	Investigation	S
	1	Steno III	Full	Secretary	C
Add	3	Sergeant	Full	Investigation	S
	1	Steno II	Full	Records-filing	C

Justification:
16 Detectives, 1972: 9,600 reported cases, 3.8 man-hours each case.
19 Detectives, 1973: 10,500 reported cases, 4.1 man-hours each case.
In 1972 a clearance rate of 17.6 percent was achieved. Even though this compares favorably with the national average, we cannot accept it as a satisfactory level. It does little to stop the rising incident rate, the primary objective of our effort. The clearance rate will have to be raised appreciably before realization of a lowering incident rate. By increasing the man-hours per case and incorporating the necessary coordination between unit subgroups, the clearance rate will be increased and incident rate lowered.
At present, 1 Steno III handles work generated by 19 detectives, 9,600 cases reported. This is totally unrealistic. Shortage of adequate clerical support jeopardizes the

Item	Cost	No. Existing	Justification
3 Desks	$ 300	16	Additional detectives
3 Chairs	$ 75	16	Additional detectives
2 Handi-Talki Radios	$1,600	0	Surveillance channel
4 Manual Typewriters	$ 400	4	Two of the existing typewriters are worn out and unserviceable.
1 8½x11 5-drawer files	$ 75	4	Additional report filing
C. Vehicles			

Number	Kind	Special Equipment
10	Police-Equipped Sedan	Emergency equipment and radios to meet H-Car specifications

      effectiveness of the unit and results in highly paid detectives doing clerical work.

  B. Permanent Equipment

  C. Vehicles

  D. Nonpersonnel Needs

    1. Supplies, $3,000

    2. Dues and subscriptions: burglary investigators, $200

    3. Printing and advertising

    4. Contractual and professional services

  E. Travel

    1. Investigations

    2. Extraditions: two @ $500 = $1,000

    3. Associations and conferences: safe burglary investigators, September 11–13, 1973, cost $200

    4. Training anticipated

  F. Miscellaneous

    1. Public works

    2. Capital improvements: space for 3 detectives

    3. Anticipated overtime needs: 1,200 hours

    4. Other

VI. Evaluation

  A. Was the incident of reported burglaries decreased from the anticipated projected level? Was this attributed to the program? Monitored monthly, the production level of the unit—cases cleared and adult burglary arrests—can be compared to current conditions. As well, the current burglary patterns can be developed and compared to those of previous years.

B. Continuous evaluation of unit production and burglary patterns will allow attention to critical areas provided by the flexibility of the program. The degree with which this flexibility can be exploited is a measure of the success of the program.

VII. Additional Information

A. Current statistical data necessary from Bureau of Technical Services.

B. Comparative adult burglary arrests:
   1970—624
   1971—674
   1972—615

The appearance of these figures would indicate that if burglaries are increasing, adult burglary arrests should also increase, producing a higher percentage of case clearance and lower incident rate.

I. Subprogram: Pawnshops, Second-Hand Dealers, and Flea Markets

II. Summary of Subprogram

A. Provide increased control of city-licensed second-hand dealers, Municipal Code 6707 and 21626 Business and Professions Code (200 licensed dealers in city).

B. Raise the level of police control of all second-hand dealers in the city to the present control maintained on pawnshop activities.

The city has within its boundaries two flea markets, one of which is the largest of this type in the state. One flea market has 1,500 to 2,000 dealers selling, exchanging, and buying an immense amount of property. This property, for the most part, is used or second-hand property, the source of which we have yet to determine. At this point we are familiar enough with the operation to know that stolen property moves through this outlet. In 1972, under the authority of Sections

21626 and 21628 Business and Professions Code, a reporting system was established for the flea markets. Briefly, this reporting system requires that each dealer who sells second-hand merchandise under the license issued to the flea market owner must report all identifiable property he intends to sell on a standardized Police Department form. The volume of paperwork and necessary police supervision that this reporting system generated is enormous, overwhelming our present staff. Police supervision is necessary in this area to monitor the trade conducted at the flea markets and recover all the stolen property moving through these dealers. For many years, the Police Department has policed the 5 licensed pawn shops, gun dealers, and a few jewelry stores who trade for second-hand merchandise. This supervision requires the attention of a full-time detective and a part-time records clerk. There are 200 licensed second-hand dealers in the city. To monitor their level of trade and recover the stolen property they might deal in requires additional police staff. It appears inequitable that the city requires reporting from all and yet supervises only a small percentage of the dealers they have licensed. Until we provide this supervision, we can be certain that stolen property will continue to escape our efforts.

In recent years, private garage sales have become extremely popular. There is no local ordinance that controls this activity. The same applies for those who advertise second-hand property for sale in newspapers and periodicals. Enforcement in these areas should not infringe on individual rights; however, some cities have restricted the garage sale activity through ordinance, and provision should be made to at least allow the police to monitor the exchange of second-hand property in these areas.

To understand the burglary problem requires that first understanding must be gained as to what the burglar steals. Primarily the burglar steals personal property that he can easily convert to cash, drugs, or other items of value. The burglar must find a market for his stolen goods. If the police have closed these markets to him or if he faces apprehension by dealing with those markets that the police monitor, he will soon learn that it is unprofitable for him to steal. Likewise, those persons who deal in stolen property while operating what is normally a legitimate business will cease this activity, knowing that they also face prosecution because of police supervision of their transactions.

III. Objectives
   A. Intercept and recover stolen property moving through these outlets.
   B. Suspend all receiving-stolen-property activity of second-hand merchants.
   C. Establish close supervision of second-hand dealers, flea markets, garage sales, and sales reporting.
   D. Determine volume of unlawful trade performed by dealers.
   E. Provide equitable enforcement of similar merchants.

IV. Alternative Approaches
   Proper control of second-hand dealers is authorized under Section 6706.7 of the Municipal Code and 21626 Business and Professions Code. Due to lack of sufficient staffing in the past, this area has been neglected. This program will provide the personnel to supervise and establish adequate enforcement in this necessary area.
   D. Nonpersonnel Needs
      1. Supplies: reporting forms, $200
      2. Dues and subscriptions
      3. Printing and advertising: law familiarization brochure-pamphlet, $100
   E. Travel: None anticipated
   F. Miscellaneous
      1. Public works needs: None
      2. Capital improvements needed: space allocation for three detectives

V. Evaluation
   A. How many arrests and convictions for receiving-stolen-property violations?
   B. What volume of stolen property recovered? (Compare A and B to recent history.)
   C. Were outlets for stolen property closed?
   D. What level of equitable enforcement reached?

7. LINE ITEM BREAKDOWN
A. Personnel

	No.	Classification	Full-time Part-time	Duties	Sworn or Civilian
Present	1	Sergeant	Full	Supervise Pawn-shops and Second-Hand Dealers	S
	2	Sergeant	Full	Supervise Pawn-shops and Second-Hand Dealers	S
Add					
	1	Typist II	Part	Filing and paper-work generated by unit	C

B. Permanent Equipment

Item	Cost	No. Existing	Justification
2 5-drawer, 8½ x 11 files	$150	1	Maintain records
1 5-drawer 3 x 5 file	$5	0	Maintain records
1 Electric Typewriter	$100	0	Additional Typist II
1 Desk	$100	0	Additional Typist II
1 Chair	$25	0	Additional Typist II

C. Vehicles

No.	Kind	Special Equipment Needed
2	Sedan	Police emergency equipment, H-Car specifications

VI. Additional Information and Comments

The effect of this program is felt by Burglary, Fraud, and Auto Theft Units. Coordination is maintained between units through exchange of information.

Summary

Such a vast amount of literature on budgeting is available that even to attempt a description and analysis in one chapter is frustrating. The reader is strongly encouraged to read further.

This chapter has attempted an overview of kinds of budgets with an emphasis on the budgeting process. Without an adequate understanding of budgets and budgeting, the police manager will have difficulty in attempting to translate financial resources into workable programs and operations. A thorough knowledge of the community and of the relationships between police activities and goals will assist the manager in effectively planning his budget.

Substantial attention in this chapter has been given to a PPB System example. Within that example, the line item approach was employed as well. Taken together, these approaches provide the most effective kind of community police budget, because the manager must establish goals, programs, and alternatives and relate them all to costs. Normally, more effective decisions result from such efforts.

Suggested Reading

Argyris, Chris. *The Impact of Budgets on People.* New York: Controllership Foundation, 1954.

Bierman, Harold, Jr., and Smidt, Seymour. *The Capital Budgeting Decision.* New York: Macmillan, 1960.

Buchanan, James N. *The Public Finances.* Homewood, Ill.: Richard D. Irwin, 1970.

Burkhead, Jesse, and Miner, Jerry. *Public Expenditure.* Chicago: Aldine-Atherton, 1971.

Crecine, J. P. *Governmental Problem-Solving: Computer Simulation of Municipal Budgeting.* Chicago: Rand McNally, 1969.

Hinrichs, H. H., and Taylor, G. N., eds. *Program Budgeting and Benefit Cost Analysis.* Pacific Palisades, Calif.: Goodyear, 1969.

Leahy, Frank J., Jr. *Planning-Programming-Budgeting for Police.* Hartford, Conn.: Travelers Research Corporation, 1968.

Lee, Robert D., Jr., and Johnson, Ronald W. *Public Budgeting Systems.* Baltimore: University Park Press, 1973.

Mushkin, Selma, et al. *Implementing PPB in State, City and County.* Washington, D.C.: George Washington University, 1969.

Sharkansky, Ira. *The Politics of Taxing and Spending.* Indianapolis: Bobbs-Merrill, 1969.

Shoup, Donald C., and Mehay, Stephen L. *Program Budgeting for Urban Police Services.* Los Angeles: University of California at Los Angeles, 1971.

Smithies, Arthur. *Budgetary Process in the United States.* New York: McGraw-Hill, 1955.

Wildavsky, Aaron. *The Politics of the Budgetary Process.* Boston: Little, Brown, 1964.

CHAPTER 8

Organizing: Traditional and Systems Approaches

In Chapter 1, the process approach to management (that is, planning, organizing, leading and motivating, and controlling) was introduced as the basic framework of this book. This chapter discusses the functional activity of organizing. The purpose of the chapter is to analyze general organizational structuring concepts as applied to community police agencies.

The specific areas to be covered include the following: (1) a discussion of concepts derived from three organizational schools of thought—classical, neoclassical, and systems (2) brief descriptions of some existing organizational models used by community police, and (3) a suggested integrated traditional-systems model of organization as applied to community police agencies.

Traditional Organizational Concepts

As used in this chapter, the word *organizing* has a specific meaning. *Organizing* applies to the concepts and processes used to structure the activities and relationships of persons engaged in a joint effort. Organizing should not be confused with the broader term *organization*, which can, and often does, apply to all managerial and employee activities in a police agency. When the police manager draws an organizational chart (usually lines and boxes or circles) depicting the functional activities of a police agency and their reporting relationships, he is establishing a formal organization. The process of organizing involves the arranging of activities in such a way as to coordinate the resources in moving toward a desired goal.

Historically, the bodies of knowledge concerning organizing activities and relationships can be divided into three schools of thought—classical, neoclassical, and systems. The classical and neoclassical schools of thought consist of the same concepts, but the neoclassical is less rigid in defining and applying them. Both of these schools of thought can be considered as a traditional approach to organizing. The neoclassical approach is, essentially, a behavioral science critique of the classical approach and was prompted by the human relations approach to management described in Chapter 1. It was also an attempt to compensate for the shortcomings discovered in the classical approach. The systems approach, to be described later in the chapter, emphasizes different concepts in organizing.[1]

Certain key concepts in the traditional approach to organizing have been applied in structuring community police agencies: division of labor, span of control or management, unity of command, the organizational hierarchy, formal and informal organizations, and centralization/decentralization.

Division of Labor

The most basic concept in the traditional approach to organizing is division of labor.[2] This concept is also known as specialization, functionalization, and, at times, departmentation. The two terms to be used in this discussion are *specialization* and *depart-*

mentation. Specialization is the dividing up of the labor, or work, to be performed into tasks and/or processes. A process is two or more tasks occurring in sequence. The following discussion will illustrate how specialization takes place in a community police agency.

Figure 18 outlines a very general eight-task process involved in responding to a reported crime. The tasks can be broken down even further. For example, steps in task 1, answer the phone, could be: (1) pick up the receiver, (2) ask pertinent questions, (3) make appropriate notations, and so on. The tasks listed in Figure 18 are used for illustration only and are not meant to represent all the tasks possible.

Figure 18
Task Process in Responding to Crime

Tasks	Activity
1	Answer the phone (to receive call)
2	Transmit, via radio, to patrol unit location and nature of call
3	Receive call; respond to scene
4	Investigate case: Initial
5	Prepare report
6	Investigate case: Follow-up
7	Prepare case
8	Appear in court (if necessary)

In considering the eight-task process in Figure 18, five community police agencies of different sizes will be used. The size groupings are somewhat arbitrary but are useful in illustrating the manner in which specialization occurs. The groupings are as follows:

Group	Size (in number of total personnel)
A	0–20
B	21–50
C	51–100
D	101–250
E	over 250

In a very small police department (Group A), it is conceivable that one person could successfully perform all eight tasks. In a one-man department, this may be unavoidable. In such cases a police officer may wait at a stationary location such as the police station, the jail, or his home until he receives a call, and then respond to it. Or he may rely on a general city operator or perhaps have a telephone in his vehicle. As a department increases in size, however, a typical specialization takes place when tasks 1 and 2 are separated from tasks 3 through 8. This division, typical of Group A departments, has resulted from the desire to have some police units mobile (patrolling), the technology available (car telephones have not always been available, and they may be too expensive), the need to have someone available at the office or station to handle "drop-in" requests for service, and, as the number of police increases, the need to have communications coordination among all units. The police officer, who handles all activities associated with a case (tasks 3–8), remains a generalist in that he is involved in all aspects of the case's development.

As police agencies grow from Group A to Group B, or in existing Group B organizations, specialization normally occurs in two ways. First, tasks 3 through 5 are separated from tasks 6 through 8, and second, tasks 5 and 7 are broken into subtasks, or more specific tasks. The first division is that between patrol and investigations. This is an important decision for the police manager, because it is here that the first division between *operational activities* (also called *field activities*) occurs. Operational activities are those *directly related* to achieving the organizational goals. The Group A specialization was essentially between *operational activities* and *support activites*. The second specialization in Group B agencies is essentially an operational-support division in that report-writing and case development are divided into preparation by the officer and typing by a clerk. While there is some question as to the economy of this arrangement, it occurs in many agencies.

The differences between the classical and neoclassical schools of thought are important in this decision. The arguments for specializing the operational functions are that specialization will improve the technical competence of the personnel involved in the activity, and they will thus be able to do more and do it faster. Permitting patrolmen to do their own follow-up as the workload increases also takes them out of the field, and they lose valuable patrol time. In addition, it may be difficult to follow up on some cases immediately after the event; the patrolman may not have the experience to do the follow-up or to decide when a follow-up investigation is not necessary, and he may then work too much overtime. Theorists of the classical school of organizational thought would definitely support this kind of specialization on the grounds that a worker with great technical competence in performing only a few tasks will perform them most efficiently.

Theorists of the neoclassical school of thought would advise proceeding with caution in specializing at this point, or at any time, without considering the following arguments.

1. The greater the specialization, the greater the interdependence in the organization, and therefore, the greater the coordination problems, and the greater the organizational stress. When and if the police manager decides to divide general police work into patrol and investigations specialties, he creates two units that are dependent on each other. These two units must communicate effectively and get along with each other. If patrol does not pass along information to investigations, and vice versa, then both will be less effective. If investigators criticize the initial reports of patrol, stress will result, emphasizing in part the need for improved coordination. In smaller police agencies, such as those in Groups A and B, the inevitable face-to-face contact can offset many of these problems, but in larger agencies, extensive specialization produces many managerial problems of communication and coordination. If the manager is aware of these problems he can attempt to alleviate them. However, the stress produced in the intradepartmental conflict of specialists is not all counterproductive. Conflict can, and often does, lead to desirable changes in the organization. For example, the stress created by investigators criticizing patrol reports should lead to improved training in report-writing and in quality control of written reports.

2. When a new specialty is created, it has the potential of becoming an "empire." When individuals specialize they take on a role identity. This means that the individuals in the specialty begin to see their performance, and often their primary loyalty, as being associated with the specialization and not the agency. Perhaps the most obvious example in community police agencies

is the separate identities that often develop for patrol and traffic specialties. Individuals identified as traffic officers see their role, or job, as primarily writing traffic tickets, investigating accidents, and perhaps conducting follow-up investigations in traffic-related criminal incidents. They may resent any other assignment, including patrolling, other types of cases, and even backing up a patrol unit in serious cases. The traffic officer's argument is that these other duties are "not his job." He does not have a patrol role identity because of his specialization. As the number of individuals in a specialized unit grows, as in investigations, for example, the role identity may create a primary loyalty to the investigative unit and not the entire police agency. In other words, the investigative unit's leadership may "build an empire" to the detriment of the whole department. In order to build an empire, a unit must look good and protect itself; this often leads to withholding information from other units, manipulating statistics used in evaluating the unit, demanding a disproportionate share of the organization's resources, and resisting organizational change. All of these activities, if they occur, are detrimental to organizational success.

3. Specialization can also create problems in motivation of employees and development of personnel. Motivation has been discussed in Chapter 2 and will not be expanded here. Generally speaking, the more specialized the job in police work, the greater the possibility that the individual will become increasingly unmotivated and less productive. Proper placement of personnel would offset this somewhat but not entirely. One task of the manager is the development of personnel competency with the ability to accept increasing responsibility for organizational success. This is sometimes difficult to do in highly specialized organizations because some individuals may work only in one or two jobs and therefore are limited in their ability to function effectively, especially in supervisory and managerial positions. A more generalist approach, or time in each specialty, usually provides for a better foundation of experience on which to build effectiveness as a supervisor and manager.

These arguments emphasize the importance of the decision to establish patrol and investigations specializations. While some police agencies resist this specialization, most agencies do create an investigative specialty.

Another reason for establishing specialties, other than a desire to improve technical competence and the other reasons already mentioned, is that assignment to the specialty is often considered to be a promotion. Promotional opportunities are significant in police departments because they are a means of motivating employees by providing recognition and status. Some positions are considered to be more prestigious, or to have more status, than others because of what goes with the position. In the case of the investigator, the status may be promotion, more money, wearing plain clothes rather than a uniform, working days rather than shifts, and having more freedom. All these attributes associated with the position of investigator give it status. Often specialized positions, such as traffic or a tactical patrol unit, provide status as well. The official status in an organization comes through the rank structure, or organizational hierarchy. The process by which that hierarchy is created will be discussed later in the chapter. The manager should remember that when considering the establishment of a specialized position, he is doing far more than just improving the technical competence of his personnel. There are many other factors—positive and negative—to be considered.

Returning now to the eight-task process, the specializations that have taken place in Group B departments are: (1) separating operational and support activities, (2) separating patrol and investigations, and (3) separating report development (operations) by an officer from report-writing or typing (support) by a clerk.

As organizations increase in size from Groups A and B into Groups C, D, and E, three functional divisions occur in addition to task-process specializations:

1. The operational function continues to be divided by purpose or type of case and client.

2. The support function continues to be divided by operational specialty unless offset by coordination and efficiency considerations.

3. A third major function, administration, emerges at some point in organizational growth and begins to be specialized according to purpose.

The operational function is directly related to the achievement of the agency's goals. After the initial separation of duties between patrol, or general policing, and investigations, specialization occurs by purpose or type of case and client. For example, in Group C agencies (and perhaps even in Group B), a traffic specialty may develop. This is specialization based on a type of case, or a purpose. It is also possible that in Group B and C agencies, a juvenile specialty will develop. While this is related to the type of case, it is more directly concerned with the client, or the juvenile. Initially, many community relations units were created to respond to one type of client; however, the community relations concept was, and is, intended to be much broader in scope.

As police agencies grow in size, operations become even more specialized. In investigations, some detectives work on crimes against persons and others on crimes against property, and perhaps others on vice. As agencies grow still larger, investigative specialists emerge based on homicide, rape, and other specific crimes. Traffic, too, becomes more specialized. Patrol tends to be slower to specialize than other operational activities because of the reactive nature of the unit. In other words, patrol is designed to handle problems as they occur. What problems will occur, and when, is not always known or even predictable. In some urban communities, however, patrol is specialized in that some patrol units handle only felony calls while others engage in aggressive patrol. In some communities, patrol is becoming increasingly specialized because of limited resources. Lack of manpower has forced some police agencies to create a priority in responding to demands for service. This is a form of specialization in that it results in patrol officers' responding only to the most serious cases (often violent) or those that have a reasonable probability of being solved.

The specialization of the support function is based on three major factors: specialization of the operational function, efficiency, and coordination. Supporting activities in a police agency are those that provide basic support for the operational activities. Examples are communications (tasks 1 and 2), records (an extension of the communications process), secretary-clerical work, maintenance, crime lab, property and evidence control, and so on. For reasons of efficiency and coordination, many support activities normally remain centralized and are not divided according to the specialization of operations. Each operational specialty does not need its own communications and records system (unless perhaps specialties are dispersed over a wide geographical area) because of the resulting inefficiency and the fact that communications and records are a coordinating center for all operational activities, as are a crime lab and a property and evidence control unit. Clerks and secretaries can, and often do, follow the lines of both operational and support specialization. However, their growth should be based on the workload to be performed, because several individuals can often share the time of secretaries and clerks.

Administrative activities constitute the third major function in police organizations. Administration involves managing the operational and support functions and specialties that develop. Normally, these activities are performed by those people designated as supervisors and managers, but as the organization grows in size, there is a tendency for more managerial activities to become specialized—research and planning, finance or budgets, personnel, training, and so on. Generally, the specialization of administrative units does not take place until after operational and support specializations are reasonably well developed. At some point, the police manager begins to realize that the function of administration in itself is vital, and his response is to develop administrative specialties in certain areas. The initial step may be to designate one individual to assist the chief of police as an administrative assistant, but if the organization continues to grow, more administrative specialties are likely to be established.

The three major functions that have been described—operations, support, and administration—are related to departmentation. While specialization involves task and process divisions, departmentation is the grouping of like specialties together. The suggested basis for departmentation in community police agencies is the similarity or likeness of tasks or processes as they relate to (1) doing the job (operations); (2) supporting the job (support); or (3) managing the job (administration). The difference between specialization and departmentation is often confusing because at times no difference exists. When a secretary is initially employed to provide support, her job represents a specialization, because tasks formerly performed by police officers are given to her. Her job represents departmentation, too, because it is a support job, fulfilling a different major function from that of operations. When the division between patrol and investigations takes place, it is specialization but not departmentation, because it is a separation by process *within* a major function—operations. The reader may well ask why this is important. It is important in terms of traditional organizational theory, because as police organizations grow in size, the number of specialties continues to increase beyond that which can be effectively coordinated. It becomes necessary to group these specialties, based on some criterion of likeness. This grouping, or departmentation, has been by these three major functions.

To this point, several bases for specialization and departmentation have been described. For specialization, these are:

1. Purpose (function)
2. Task
3. Process (two or more tasks)
4. Case (which may also be considered purpose or process since both are involved in case specialization)
5. Client (for example, juvenile; this may also be a case specialization)

For departmentation, the basis is by major function only. Frequently, two other criteria are cited as a basis for both specialization and departmentation decisions. These are time and area. The authors consider these factors to be related more to manpower allocation decisions than to specialization or departmentation decisions. Time and area decisions usually are made *after* the decisions concerning specialization and departmentation. Time and area decisions involve whether certain specialties should work all shifts or should be assigned to a district station, but the latter is more a question of centralization or decentralization than it is a matter of specialization or departmentation. One exception to this, and there may be others, is if a police manager decides to have investigators work by geographical area rather than by case or client. In such a situation an investigator would work all cases in one area, instead of all cases of a certain type or types. Where investigations is still general in nature, the investigator does work all cases, but as the number of investigators grows, each usually specializes by case and client. If the community is large enough, however, the manager must consider whether the investigators will be decentralized to areas.

The manager should keep in mind the importance of the decision to specialize. The systems approach to organizing, discussed later in the chapter, is in part a response to the problems inherent in specialization.

Span of Control or Management

Division of labor provides for horizontal growth of the organization. Vertical growth, or scalar growth, is suggested in the previous section by the mention of managers and supervisors. Vertical growth—the establishment of levels, or layers, in the organizational hierarchy—is created by two factors: (1) building down through delegation of authority and responsibility and (2) applying the concept of span of control, or, as it will be called here, span of management.[3] Span of management means the number of people that one person—the manager or supervisor (who is a manager in a broad sense)—can effectively supervise or manage. The word *management* is used instead of *control* because of the limited connotations of the latter word.

The concept of span of management and its importance to organizational development are most appropriately illustrated through an analysis of the growth of one police agency. In the following rather extensive example, both span of management and specialization are discussed as an organization grows vertically and horizontally.

Some Organizational Considerations
in the Growth of a Community Police Agency: A Case Example

In a one-man police department, the police manager (chief of police in this example) decides that his workload requires a second person. With the approval of community officials, he appoints a second man. Initially, the organizational chart looked like the one in Figure 19.

Figure 19
Organizational Chart
for One-Man Police Department

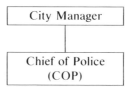

After employment of the second man, the police organization chart looked like the one in Figure 20.

Figure 20
Organizational Chart
for Two-Man Police Department

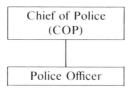

The title of the new employee does not matter; he could be called assistant chief of police, for example. The point is that the new employee creates a second level in the police organization, and the organization has grown both horizontally and vertically. Although there is one manager and one worker, on two levels, the work performed is similar for both individuals. The tasks associated with policing the community are now divided; in employing the second man the chief of police delegated some of his authority and the responsibility to perform certain activities. The division of the work at this stage is basically by time, for each individual probably performs the same tasks at different times. The chief also has some additional administrative responsibilities.

As the workload increases, the police manager—the chief—believes that more police officers are needed to provide around-the-clock service. He decides that he needs to employ three new officers in addition to himself and his assistant. The chief himself will still engage in some operational activities along with administrative duties. The organizational structure now looks like the one in Figure 21.

The chief of police now has a span of management of four patrol officers.

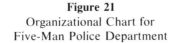

Figure 21
Organizational Chart for
Five-Man Police Department

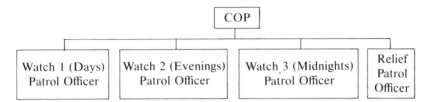

However, they are not working at the same time, nor are they working in one location. Either at this point, or after a slight increase in the number of patrol officers, the manager becomes concerned with supervising these officers. In addition, the administrative work continues to increase. This concern results in a new position, and level, in the organization (Figure 22).

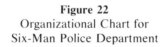

Figure 22
Organizational Chart for
Six-Man Police Department

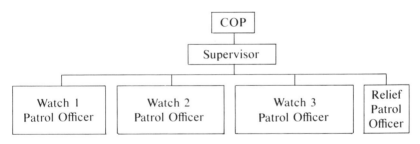

The supervisor may be called a sergeant, a lieutenant, or a captain. The supervisor's span of management is four, and the chief's is now one. Again, however, the chief and the supervisor probably work at different times to insure supervision around the clock. Now the organization has three levels; how quickly it moves to a fourth will be determined by its growth rate, the available resources, and the manager's perception of effective spans of management.

As the organization continues to grow in size, several important questions will have to be answered by the manager:

1. How many more employees are needed?
2. Is specialization desirable, either between operations and support or

within operations (patrol-investigations, patrol-traffic, patrol-investigations-traffic)?

3. How much work does the manager have to delegate in order to accomplish administrative responsibilities effectively?

4. What is an effective span of management?

The organization continues to increase in size until it has four or more patrolmen on each watch, a supervisor for each watch, a relief supervisor, one investigator, one traffic officer, one secretary, and one clerk-typist. Now the organizational chart looks like the one in Figure 23.

Figure 23
Organizational Chart for Police Department
with Threefold Operations Specialization

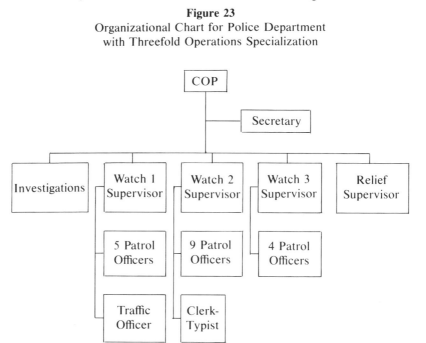

The organizational chart in Figure 23 reflects several important decisions by the police manager:

1. Operations and support are now separate specialties; there are now a secretary and a clerk-typist for support.

2. Operations has a threefold specialization: patrol, investigations, and traffic.

3. The investigative specialty (a unit, division, or bureau) has been given an official status equivalent to that of patrol supervisor.

4. The traffic officer has been given the status of a patrol officer.

5. The clerk-typist is on Watch 2 because of the workload and is supervised by the individual in charge of that watch.

6. The secretary is supervised by the chief, working the same hours as he does and providing administrative and clerical support for the chief and Watch 1 and 3 activities.

The police manager, the chief of police, now has a span of management of six employees; the Watch 2 supervisor has a span of management of 10; the Watch 1 supervisor has 6; and the Watch 3 supervisor has 4. Is this too many or too few?

In the traditional schools of management thought, the classical concept of span of *control* suggested that from 5 to 8 individuals could be effectively supervised by one person. The neoclassical critique suggests that span of *management* should be based on the type of work performed, where it is performed in relation to the supervisory source, the competence of the supervisor, the competence of the personnel supervised, and the managerial philosophy. In general, the neoclassical school holds that spans of management broader than 5 to 8 persons are possible and desirable in organizations.

According to the classical school of thought, the span of management of the Watch 2 supervisor should be changed. According to the neoclassical school of thought, all or none could be changed. The police manager in this case decides that both his span of management and that of the Watch 2 supervisor are too great. The former decision is based on the chief's lack of mobility to effectively supervise around the clock; the latter is based on his belief that the Watch supervisor has too many individuals to supervise. On two evenings each week, all nine patrolmen and the clerk-typist are present. The new organizational chart looks like the one in Figure 24.

In this new organization, the top manager or executive has a span of management of two—the middle manager and the secretary. The middle manager can be titled lieutenant, captain, director, and so on. This new position has a span of management of six, and each supervisor on Watch 2 has a span of management of from four to seven employees, depending on whether both supervisors are working and on the number of employees working.

The decision by the chief that his span of management was too broad resulted in creating a new organizational level. Now there are essentially four levels where before there were only three:

Level I employees, along with the investigator, have direct responsibility for performing the basic tasks of the organization even though they have different statuses. Operational employees at level I usually are paid more than support workers even though both are at the same basic organizational level. The investigator has probably been given the same salary and official status as the supervisors, although he may perform no supervisory

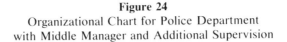

Figure 24
Organizational Chart for Police Department
with Middle Manager and Additional Supervision

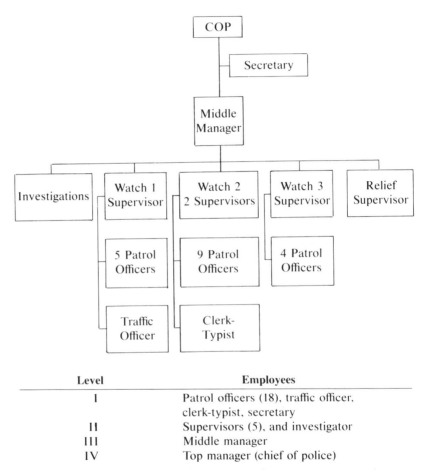

Level	Employees
I	Patrol officers (18), traffic officer, clerk-typist, secretary
II	Supervisors (5), and investigator
III	Middle manager
IV	Top manager (chief of police)

tasks. The new middle manager has been provided more money and status by virtue of his prestige ranking in the organizational structure.

In this discussion, the important point is that the decision of the chief to narrow his own span of management created another organizational level. This is positive in that it created a promotional opportunity, yet it has possible negative consequences in terms of communication. The more levels in the organization, the greater the likelihood that communication will be hindered. Complete and accurate communication is crucial to effective organizational performance; the more organizational levels, the more complex is the communication process.

The span of management strongly influences the "flatness" or "tallness" of organizational structures. The narrower the spans of management, the taller the hierarchy, or the more levels it will have. The broader the spans of management, the flatter the hierarchy, or the fewer the levels in the organization. For example, assume that the management of an organization with 1,000 workers believed in a span of management of no more than five employees. The organization levels in terms of number of employees would look like this:

Level	Number of Employees
VI	1
V	2
IV	8
III	40
II	200
I	1,000

With a span of management of five employees, 1,000 workers would require 200 supervisors (1,000 ÷ 5). These 200 would be the second level in the organization. The 200 supervisors would require 40 supervisors to manage them. This would create a third organizational level. The base of 1,000 employees ultimately means six organizational levels. If the span of management were broadened to ten employees, the organization would have four levels:

Level	Number of Employees
IV	1
III	10
II	100
I	1,000

There is a difference of two levels, which could result in an improvement in vertical communication. However, other theories of the neoclassical school of thought should be considered in determining spans of management.

Unity of Command

In the foregoing example, the traditional organizational concept of unity of command was evident in the organization charts.[4] Unity of command, in essence, means "one man, one boss." Expressed another way, it means that any one employee should have only one person to whom he is directly accountable and to whom he reports. A patrolman should report to only one supervisor, and that supervisor is held responsible for that patrolman.

Division of labor "builds" the organization horizontally; applying the concepts of span of management and unity of command builds the organization in a hierarchical structure to facilitate coordination and control. In the classical school of organizational thought, the "one man, one boss" idea is meant to insure designated areas of responsibility, to insure accountability, to enhance the feeling of security of the employee, and to control the organization.

The neoclassical school is less rigid and suggests such possible deviations as the *functional supervisor*. To explain the concept of functional supervision, let us return to the example in Figure 24. There, unity of command is apparent. The watch supervisors are directly responsible for patrol officers, and those patrol officers are directly accountable to the watch supervisors. Further, the channel of communication is the chain of command— through the supervisor, to the middle manager, to the chief of police. Observance of chain of command is designed to improve coordination and upward communication, place responsibility for actions, and encourage decision-making at the appropriate level of authority.

It is possible, however, that a watch supervisor would not be the most effective boss in some situations. For example, at the scene of serious crimes, the investigator could assume functional supervision in on-the-spot searches. This functional relationship would be depicted on the organizational chart by a dotted line from the investigator's box to the patrol officers' boxes, accompanied by an explanation as to when functional supervision was appropriate. Such an explanation is normally available in position descriptions of investigator, patrol officer, and supervisor.

Many functional supervisory relationships are possible in large, complex organizations, but the number of such organizational relationships can create conflict for those supervised. Whereas a few functional relationships may be desirable in increasing effectiveness in certain tasks, an employee with a supervisor for each separate task may become confused. Only the most mature, competent, and highly motivated employee could work successfully in such a situation. The traditional approach to organization adheres to unity of command with some functional supervisory exceptions.

The Organizational Hierarchy

A *hierarchy* can be defined as an "arrangement into a graded series." Division of labor, span of management, and unity of command create an organizational hierarchy with different specializations and levels. Each specialization and level has a role definition and a status based on both formal and informal considerations.

The hierarchy assumes the shape of a pyramid, with formal authority flowing from the apex. The hierarchy, or formal organization, is often considered to be structured in two basic parts, line and staff. This is somewhat confusing in police organizations because of staff's relationship to both support and administrative activities. In the original distinction, the *line* are those who do the job; the *staff* are those who advise as to how the job should be done. However, police organizations have defined staff in several other ways:

1. Staff is *all* the employees of the organization.

2. Staff is all, or part, of the supervisors and managers, regardless of work performed.

3. Staff is service and/or administrative activities.

Given the different usages of the term *staff*, and the three basic police functions, the distinction between line and staff is not a particularly important concept except as it applies to unity of command. Operations is line; service is also line in most cases; administration, when specialized, is generally staff. The relationship between advisory roles (planning, personnel) and operational roles (patrol, traffic) should be well defined, and if functional staff supervision is provided, the relationships of all concerned should be well defined.

Much has been written about staff and line conflict, because staff persons often are considered the "experts" who want to tell line workers how to do their jobs. Line and staff often have misconceptions about each other. On a formal level, their relationship can be spelled out by definition of roles and responsibilities. On an informal level, their relationship is somewhat more complicated.

Formal and Informal Organizations

The formal organization is the one represented by the hierarchy as depicted by the organizational chart. It is consciously designed to represent the pattern of relationships, activities, and communication that are defined through job descriptions and policy and procedure manuals, shown by charts, and displayed as the rational plan to be used in achieving organizational goals. The informal organization develops as a result of the interaction among people who work in the organization. Rarely, if ever, does the formal organizational chart depict what really happens in terms of relationships and communication. This occurs for many reasons, some of which were discussed in Chapter 2.

One useful approach in analyzing the informal organization is that of John M. Pfiffner and Frank P. Sherwood.[5] They use a series of "overlays" to show the several informal organizations that exist within a formal structure.

1. The *sociometric* overlay represents the social relationships of people based on the perceived desirability or undesirability of association.

2. The *functional* overlay represents the intellectual, knowledge, or expertise relationships.

3. The *decision* overlay represents the true decision centers in the organization.

4. The *power* overlay represents the pattern of influence in the organization.

5. The *communication* overlay represents the channels through which information actually flows.

The formal organizational structure plus the five overlays create an intricate network of relationships, because the five overlay organizations do not usually follow formal organizational lines. All the overlays interact to create the informal organization. A useful way of illustrating the impact of the overlays on the formal structure is through a series of questions:

1. Who in the organization is your immediate supervisor?
2. Who in the organization do you like the most? Who do you like the least?
3. Who do you think knows most about your job?
4. If you wanted a decision made concerning your job and you could not make it, who would you go to see?
5. Who has the most influence affecting you and your job?
6. If you obtain an important piece of information concerning the success of the organization, to whom would you tell it first? Is there anyone with whom you would not share it?

These questions, in order, are designed to indicate first the formal organization and then the five overlays: sociometric, functional, decision, power, and communication. The authors have asked these questions of numerous police managers. Rarely has one person's name been given in answer to all six questions, and rarely have six separate names been provided. Most police managers respond with three or four names. If the formal and informal organizations were highly integrated, few separate names would appear in the six questions; probably no more than one or perhaps two. In the ideal formal model of an organization, the immediate supervisor is liked—perhaps not the most liked, but certainly not disliked. He has expertise or knows his job and those of the employees he supervises, has the authority to make decisions, has the power to carry them out, and is open to communication and has created a desire in the employee to be aware of, and communicate, important information. Unfortunately, most organizations and supervisors do not fit the ideal model. The informal model, in all aspects suggested by the overlays, can function to negate the formal plan. Happily, in some cases, the informal structure makes the formal structure more effective. In either case, the manager should be aware that there are relationships and patterns of activity and behavior apart from those designed to occur in the rational plan. Undesirable formal-informal conflict will be reduced if the managerial concepts discussed in this book are considered in administering a police agency. However, some conflict undoubtedly will always be present and will provide an impetus for change. People are not boxes on a piece of paper; they are not that predictable.

Being aware of the informal organization, however, does not

mean that police managers should not be concerned about organizing in a formal way. They should, and general guidelines for traditional organizing are provided below:

1. Establish and be aware of objectives. Organization is a tool by which objectives are realized. It is not an objective in itself.

2. Divide work, by workload, into component activities but not into single, repetitive tasks. This precludes overspecialization and demotivation.

3. Group similar organizational activities, or specializations, together based on the operational, support, and administrative criteria.

4. For each activity, outline the duties to be performed and the relationships to be maintained.

5. Recruit, train, and assign qualified personnel (see Chapter 9).

6. Delegate the necessary authority and responsibility.

7. Restructure based on progress toward objectives.

Centralization/Decentralization

A recurring issue that faces community police agencies as they grow in size is centralization *versus* decentralization. This issue has two dimensions—philosophical and geographical. In the former, the managerial philosophy is in question. To what degree is decision-making authority and responsibility delegated to lower levels in the organizational hierarchy? A manager who gives a wide latitude in decision-making to subordinates is operating under a philosophy of decentralization. On the other hand, a manager who prefers to make as many decisions as possible himself and does not delegate readily is operating under a philosophy of centralization. Managerial philosophy, in terms of centralization and decentralization, relates to the Theory X and Theory Y managerial outlooks and the 9/1 and 9/9 leadership styles. (The Theory X manager views employees negatively; the Theory Y manager, positively. The 9/1 style manager has a low concern for people; the 9/9 style manager, a high concern, while both have high concern for production.)

The geographical dimension of the issue is important to police because of community concerns about control and participation.

Creating substations, district stations, and so on is geographical decentralization. Closing them down is usually an attempt to centralize. The arguments for centralization focus on economy; it is cheaper to centralize. The arguments for decentralization focus on responsiveness, ability to meet the unique needs of any given neighborhood. In large cities, a return to walking beat patrol officers and basic car plans are forms of decentralization that move policemen closer to the public. Placing policemen in cars and keeping them there except for calls allows more mobility and coverage within a larger area. However, this often provides for less interaction and responsiveness to local needs.

The police have long been faced with this issue and will continue to be. Centralization was a trend in police agencies until the mid-1960s. As noted, arguments for centralization focus on cost but also reflect an increasing desire to control the police officer by having him work out of one location. The responsiveness issue was raised in the 1960s, a period of rising crime rates and civil disorders, and decentralization in response to citizen demands for participation and local control was, and is, prevalent in many communities. Of course, some areas are so large that geographical decentralization is unavoidable. Where possible, however, support and administrative services should be centralized and responsiveness assured through various operational alternatives that will place the police officer in more positive relationships with the citizen.

Traditional Police Organizational Models

The previous subsections concerned the traditional approach to organizing as described through analysis of some major concepts and issues. The discussion could not be inclusive, of course, and the manager should read the suggested books at the end of the chapter for additional material.

Before discussing the systems approach and its criticisms of traditional theories of organizing, let us look at several examples, or models, of community police organizational charts (Figures 25, 26, and 27). These models were taken from research material prepared by the Police Science Department of Los Angeles State College for the President's Commission on Law Enforcement and Administration of Justice. The terminology is not always the same as that used in the examples in this chapter, nor does the process of increasing growth follow the process described. These differences emphasize an important point—*there is no one right way to organize.* The models in the figures suggest a useful guide; the previous examples suggest another. Each manager should be aware of the underlying concepts and develop a model to meet his own agency's unique needs.

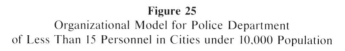

Figure 25
Organizational Model for Police Department
of Less Than 15 Personnel in Cities under 10,000 Population

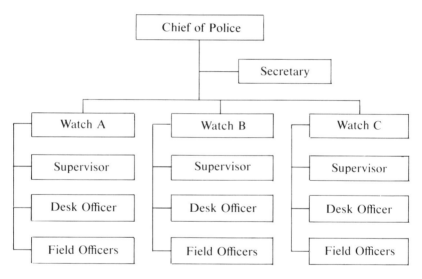

The Systems Approach

General systems theory has emerged in the last two decades, contributing a body of knowledge important to managers of any type of organization.[6] The systems approach is concerned with an analysis of wholes rather than individual parts of the whole, with how those parts are interrelated and interdependent, with how the complex interaction of interrelated and interdependent parts influences and changes each part *and* the whole. Viewing an organization from a systems perspective results in a more comprehensive understanding of the whole. In this chapter, the "whole" is the community police organization.

Figure 26
Organizational Model for Police Department
of 15–75 Personnel in Cities of 10,000–50,000 Population

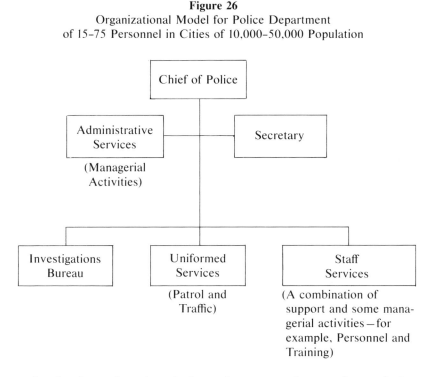

In the foregoing description of systems, the words *analysis, influences,* and *changes* are used. To understand the meanings of these words, one needs a frame of reference. For the organization as a whole, this frame of reference is provided by its goals and objectives. In order to view the organization as a whole, the manager must be aware of goals and objectives so he can evaluate the organization's effectiveness and efficiency. The goals and objectives of the organization are major links with the environment of that organization. As the organization engages in certain activities in pursuit of goals and objectives the environment reacts and often influences future organizational activities. This reaction, as in the communication process described in Chapter 2, is called *feedback.*

To summarize, in taking a systems view of an organization, the police manager should remember certain key ideas:

1. Organizational environment and feedback

Figure 27
Organizational Model for Police Department
of 75–400 Personnel in Cities of 50,000–250,000 Population

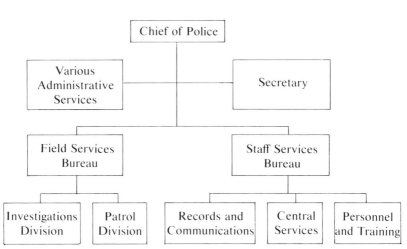

Note: Beyond this point in growth, Administrative Services becomes equal to Field Services (operations) and Staff Services (support and some managerial activities). In much larger cities—over one million or so, operational geographical decentralization is suggested with some limited administrative and supporting services. Specialization in each major function continues to take place.

2. Organizational goals and objectives
3. Organizational parts that make up the organizational whole
4. Organizational interdependency and interaction of parts
5. The dynamics of relationships of organizational parts as they influence realization of goals and objectives

Traditional and Systems Perspectives: A Comparison

The following example and analysis illustrate the differences in perspective between a systems view of organizing and a nonsystems or traditional view.

In 1972, the Academy City Police Department received numerous complaints from citizens about the behavior of some police officers. Concerned by this problem, the chief of police decided to establish a police–community relations unit to contact citizens and improve communications and community-police relationships. He established the unit and assigned several officers. All but one of these were police officers from a minority group. The members of the unit started going to community meetings, explaining the police job in the community, responding to citizen grievances, and, in general, giving the impression that the police department was sincerely interested in improving relationships with the minority citizens who were the most concerned with, and complaining about, police activity.

For the first three months after the specialized unit was established, complaints to the department declined, but in the fourth month they began to increase, and at the end of the sixth month, there were twice as many complaints as before the community relations unit was established. The chief was dumbfounded. What had happened?

The police manager was not successful in alleviating the community-police relationship problem for several reasons. In considering the problem, the manager made an incorrect assumption; he assumed that the citizen complaints were groundless, while in fact there were several cases in which they were not. This assumption is reflected in the activities of the specialized unit, such as "explaining the police job." In other words, the chief believed that if the citizens understood why the police did what they did, then they would be less likely to complain. The failure to adequately research and analyze the problem and plan a more effective response was one of the reasons why the problem was not satisfactorily resolved. Proper research, analysis, and planning, however, are not the primary concerns of this chapter except as planning reflects alternatives in organizing. In this particular example, a traditional view of organizing resources is apparent.

The police manager decided to establish a specialized unit to deal with the community problem. Division of labor, or specialization, is the basis for traditional organizational structures. In establishing such a unit, the police manager, in effect, was saying that the "community relations problem" was the responsibility of one unit and that other units in the department (such as patrol, traffic, and investigations) should not be concerned with citizen complaints or with citizen relationships. The community relations unit was identified with a certain *role*—to pacify the community. This unit became known as the "song-and-dance team." Their *status* was low because, although they were assigned in the *formal organization* to work directly under the chief of police, they were seen as "social workers" and not "police officers." (This basic distinction in *role identity* is similar to the counselor *versus* enforcer role discussed in Chapter 1.)

An antagonistic relationship between the community relations unit and operational units soon developed, leading to personal bitterness between certain individuals and a nearly complete breakdown in communication. There was constant bickering between operational units and community relations about what each was doing. Support unit personnel (records, communications, and so on) were forced to "choose sides" in the dispute. The chief of police became aware of the extreme differences when he asked the managers in charge of the patrol unit and the community relations unit to submit a list of ten outstanding patrol officers to send to a specialized training program. The program was to prepare these officers to become field trainers to break in new policemen. The two lists submitted did not have one identical name; obviously, the perceptions of each of the two managers as to who were the best police officers and therefore the most effective were completely different. It was apparent that the managers did not agree on the organization's goals and objectives.

The community (which represents part of the environment of the police agency) initially responded favorably to the establishment of the community relations unit, for they believed that something was being done to alleviate perceived police abuses. Unfortunately, this only added to the problem, because nothing really changed. The operational unit personnel believed that the complaints were the problems of the police–community relations (PCR) unit and saw no need to change their activities or behavior. The citizens, whose expectations were higher because of the community relations unit, began to see that nothing had changed, and they now were told by some patrolmen when they complained to 'take it to PCR." This angered many of the citizens even more. As their complaints increased, the operational units became more defensive and aggressive. Faced with more complaints, community relations officers began to identify more with the citizens and became more critical of operational personnel. Citizens became militant, and the cycle continued; somehow it had to be stopped or erupt into a major confrontation.

It is, of course, an oversimplification to suggest that establishment of a specialized community relations unit was about to cause a riot. On the contrary, many other factors would have to be present before such an event could occur. However, the police manager's traditional view of organizing in response to a perceived problem certainly contributed to the turn of events. Taking a systems view of the organization and organizing could have precluded some of the difficulties that developed in the organization.

The Systems Approach in Organizing

Had the police manager taken a systems view of the community relationship problem and the police organization, he would have considered the following:

1. No organization can be effective unless it can adapt to and accommodate its environment. In the case of the community police agencies, the environment includes the social, economic, and political attitudes and behavior of citizens and groups in the community.

2. The relationship of the organization to its environment is defined by the changing goals and objectives of the organization as a result of its adapting to the environment. Effectiveness is measured by the degree to which goals and objectives are realized.

3. The organization as a *whole* is made up of numerous parts that are interrelated and interdependent. Changes in one part influence other parts, and those changes in turn influence the original part. The *parts* of an organization for consideration in the systems view include:
   a. Individuals
   b. The formal organizational structure comprised of specialized unit parts

    c. The informal organization comprised of the various overlays previously discussed

    d. The interaction of the formal and informal organization as they create role and status "parts" of the organization.

4. The parts of the organizational whole are linked together through communication processes, and communication, or the transfer of accurate and complete information, is absolutely essential to organizational effectiveness. Effectiveness in organizations is the result of decisions made concerning all organizational and managerial activities. Effective decision-making results from the analysis of organization problems relative to goals and objectives. And analysis, of whatever type, requires accurate and complete information. The transmission of information is not possible if communication processes in the organization are impeded. The individuals, the formal organization, the informal organization, and role and status concepts can all impede communication.

5. The systems view of organizing emphasizes the importance of communication, in addition to coordination and control, in structuring organizations. While division of labor, or specialization, is not discounted as an important organizing concept, communication is considered more important, and specialization is considered a possible barrier to effective communication. Consequently, the systems approach seeks to develop organizing models that will improve communication without the loss of the benefits of specialization.

6 Specialization and communication have both horizontal and vertical dimensions. Not only are organizations specialized horizontally into such areas as patrol, traffic, and investigations; they are also specialized vertically into workers, supervisors, and middle managers. Both types of specialization are potential barriers to effective communication.

If the police chief who established the police–community relations unit had taken a systems view of the police–community relations problem, he probably would have arrived at a different solution to the problem. For purposes of illustration, the following example shows how the police chief could have considered the problem from a systems perspective. This is a conversation between the chief, Bob, and another police manager, Bill, who has more of a traditional approach to both organizing and the police role.

Bob: The number of citizen complaints against the men has really increased the last few months.

Bill: I know. There is always that 10 percent who will complain, and they're usually the criminals anyway.

Bob: Perhaps you're right, but I can't help thinking there's more to it than that. Our job is not only to catch individuals suspected of crimes but to keep the citizens thinking positively about the department. Sometimes I think our men are concerned too much about doing the catching and not enough about what citizens think.

Bill: We're not in any popularity contest; our job is to get the creeps off the streets and to keep them off. If we have to step on a few toes to do it, that's tough.

Bob: I certainly agree that we should do everything within the law to arrest offenders, but if we become too aggressive or abrasive we'll turn a lot of the citizens off. This is especially true in the minority community, where much of our activity is. If they don't respect us, they won't cooperate—not only in investigations and with information, but at budget time. If we're to be effective, we have to have the cooperation of the community, especially from those groups with whom we have frequent contacts.

Bill: Well, maybe you're right, but you can go too far. We're cops and not social workers. Maybe we should try to pacify them. If they understood our problems, I think they'd stop complaining. Let's set up a community relations unit, put some of those liberal college kids and minority officers in it, and send them out to tell our story.

Bob: I think we should do something to improve community relations, but I'm not sure if we should create a specialized unit. What would the reaction of the patrol officers be?

Bill: I think they'd welcome it; then they could go out and do their job and stop trying to pacify the gripers.

Bob: But isn't part of their job to be responsive to the citizens?

Bill: Well, yes, I guess so.

Bob: If we create this specialized unit then we'd be telling the men that community relations isn't their job. This might make them even more abrasive and make the citizens more resentful of us. Do you think that could happen?

Bill: It might, and if it did, it could even create conflict between patrol and the community relations unit.

Bob: How is that?

Bill: Well, if patrol goes out and makes the citizens mad and community relations has to come along and try to make up, it probably wouldn't be too long before patrol and community relations wouldn't even talk to each other.

Bob: I think you're right; maybe we should think about this problem some more. There's more to this than we first thought.

Bill: You're certainly right about that.

This discussion goes through several important stages. First Bob identifies the problem, and Bill responds with a rather narrow analysis of its causes. Then the men discuss agency goals, Bill emphasizing the enforcer aspects and Bob underscoring both the enforcer and responsiveness dimensions of the police role. Bill finally agrees that Bob may be correct, and as Bob begins to point out some of the implications of Bill's suggestion that a specialized community relations unit be established, Bill begins to see that the problem, and the possible solutions, are more complex than he had originally thought.

The systems perspective is evident throughout Bob's comments. He displays a concern for the importance of the organization's relationship with the community (environment) and the importance of agreement on organizational goals. Bill's response to establish a specialized unit is addressed by Bob in terms of role and status concerns. Bill quickly picks up on this point, and as he begins to take more of a systems perspective, he comments on the possible communication problems that could develop. The conversation ends with a decision to continue to think about, and analyze, the problem.

At this point, Bob and Bill do not have the necessary information to make the most effective decision. As analysis of the problem continues, alternate concepts of organizing will undoubtedly be considered. The systems approach to the solution of the problem would first require the identification of the objectives to be realized in respect to the community relations problem. In this case, that objective might be to improve the attitudes of citizens toward police officers and consequently increase their willingness to support and communicate with officers.

The next step would be to determine the extent of the problem and its causes. The identification of causes is extremely complex, and the manager is likely to discover that some, if not most, causes that can be identified cannot be influenced or controlled by him; poverty, poor housing, poor education, unemployment, lack of transportation, lack of recreational activities, and so on are all potential contributors to citizen hostility toward police, and police managers may have little if any influence over them.

Some causes, however, such as inappropriate officer behavior, enforcement policies, and police programs, can be influenced by the manager. Once the causes are identified, the police manager needs to develop systematic programs to alter or modify them, but in a manner that reflects consideration of a systems approach in the organization. Training programs designed to alter the behavior of patrol officers should probably include the entire organization. Changes in policies and programs can affect the entire organization and the citizens who have positive attitudes toward the police. A transfer of resources to a program designed to improve protection in one area will probably result in moving those resources from another area or organizational activity. What kinds of problems will result? Can balance be achieved? These are questions of the systems thinker and the manager who employs the systems approach in problem-solving.

The Team Organization and the Matrix Organization

The *matrix organization* is an attempt to integrate the traditional and systems approaches to organizing.[7] The *team organization*—another systems model—is also an alternative for the police manager. However, the team organization model, in discussions of team policing and team management, has received substantial attention in police journals and books.[8] Consequently, only a brief discussion will be provided in this chapter, and the major emphasis will be on the matrix organization.

Team organizational concepts have been applied to police in the form of team policing and/or team management. Team policing is an attempt to integrate horizontal specialties (patrol, investigations, traffic) into general teams. Team management is an attempt to integrate the vertical specialties created by the organizational hierarchy (supervisors, middle managers, executives). The purpose of both team approaches is to improve communication and decision-making and to be more responsive in addressing organizational problems. Advocates of the team organization would undoubtedly suggest that traditional organizational structures, with specialization, narrow spans of management, and unity of command, are often characterized by inadequate communication, ineffective decision-making, and slow and inflexible responses to changing organizational problems.

The matrix organization attempts to overcome such problems through use of projects, which require a type of team effort, without the loss of some necessary and desirable features of the traditional structure. Figure 28 depicts a matrix organizational structure. This figure indicates an integration of the major functions of the police organization through development of a project capability. A *project*, for purposes of a police agency, is defined as an integrated functional team effort designed to respond to an unusual, or serious, police problem. Projects normally have specific goals and are limited in terms of time. An integrated functional team effort means that representatives from several police functions or specialties form a team to accomplish a specific goal within a given time period. The team working on a problem to accomplish a goal is called a *project*. For purposes of illustration, Projects A, B, and C in Figure 28 will be considered projects in community relations, auto theft prevention, and annexation, respectively.

Project A: Community Relations

The community relations problem described earlier in this chapter could have been handled with a project approach. If, analyzing the problem, the chief had decided that community relations should be every employee's concern, an integrated project effort would have been most desirable and perhaps most effective. Bringing together individuals from all functions, especially the operational units, to address the problem is necessary to alter the apparent negative community relations attitude. Giving this team the goal of reducing citizen complaints through educating citizens concerning the police task *and* educating the police concerning citizen needs, would be an appropriate utilization of the project concept.

Project B: Auto Theft Prevention

It is not uncommon for communities, from time to time, to

Figure 28
Matrix Organization for a Community Police Agency

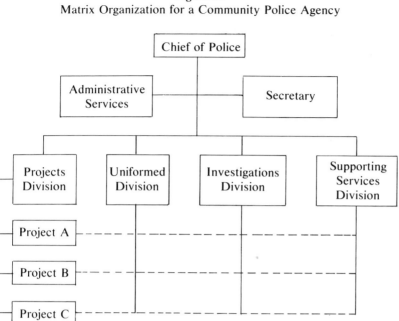

experience a sharp increase in certain types of crime. When this happens, the necessary response to the problem may be difficult through existing functions. Such a problem could be an increase in automobile thefts. The project format is useful here in that individuals from several functions can be brought together to analyze the causes of the increase and respond with specific goals oriented toward reducing this crime.

Patrol officers, investigators, and evidence technicians can work in a project framework to deal with an auto theft problem. Or on a broader scale, these specialized officers from several police agencies could work on a project designed to respond to auto theft problems over a wide area. While auto theft is an ongoing police problem, it can become unusually serious and require an unusual response. Again, a project capability is useful in this regard.

Project C: Annexation

Annexation is the incorporation of a geographical area, often with inhabitants, into a community or county. This often results in an immediate and significant increase in needed manpower to respond to the police service demands of the incorporated area. Annexation can result in rather drastic changes for an organization and requires careful planning by all units involved. Since all functions in the organization are affected by annexation, an integrated functional response in planning and implementation is desirable. A project is ideal for this type of response.

An important consideration for the police manager is at what point, or in what circumstances, a project should be developed.[9] It is difficult to give a specific guide in this regard; when unusual problems develop, such as a sudden and major community relations problem that has never occurred before, or an annexation possibility, the use of a project is a logical choice. However, at what point does an ongoing problem of a police agency, such as particular types of crime, training problems, or communication and record-keeping problems, become *serious* enough to warrant utilization of a project approach?

There are no easy answers to this question. To some degree extraordinary efforts, such as special projects, will be dictated by community concern about a particular police-related problem. This is especially true in crime problems, because increasing community concern is often backed up with additional resources. This has occurred in numerous police departments since the late 1960s with the availability of state and federal monies. However, project development does not have to await a crisis in the community. The manager can develop his own guidelines in the use of projects.

For the administrative and supporting services, projects should be used not only in major problems but on a regular basis. Projects can be used as an audit system to evaluate every phase of the organization as to its efficiency and effectiveness. A police manager should constantly assess his organization in order to make improvements, and a project team with personnel from several functions is a useful device for such an assessment.

In operational problems such as crime and community service activities, in the absence of community pressure, the police manager should attempt to establish criteria that would automatically activate a project team. One method of doing this is to decide, for example, that an increase in any type of crime of more than a certain percentage would require the development of an interfunctional project team to analyze the increase, isolate the causes, develop a plan to reduce the number of crimes, and implement and coordinate that plan. Unfortunately, if several crimes increased by more than the given percentage, then so many projects would be required that it would be difficult to respond to ongoing problems. Therefore, a more effective target for a project team would be the crime or crimes with the largest increases for a given period (six months or a year, for example). The manager should then develop as many projects as resources will permit. The project participants may discover methods of responding to crime problems that can be integrated into ongoing functional unit activities.

Projects can be utilized not only *within* a police organization but also between police organizations and between agencies within community government. If an auto theft problem is area-wide (covering an urban area or a county, for example), then several police agencies should be involved in project development. For a local problem in juvenile delinquency, the police department can work with health, education, probation, and perhaps other governmental units in the project format. Numerous police problems that arise can be effectively handled through use of the matrix model of organization.

When projects are used, the police manager should carefully consider the coordination problems that will arise between project manager and functional unit manager. The project manager will have a goal, certain financial and manpower resources, and a certain time period within which to work. The functional unit managers should be consulted as to which personnel are to be assigned to projects. The project and functional managers should work together to avoid conflict between their respective activities. This coordination, through regular discussion and outlining of procedures, should be initiated at the outset of any project.

Properly utilized, the matrix organization can improve the effectiveness of the police organization. The use of project teams in addition to functional activities will permit the needed multidimensional analysis of problems, improve communication, and generally make the organization more flexible and therefore more responsive to its changing environment.

Summary

This chapter has presented a general discussion of organizational theory from three major schools of thought—the classical and neoclassical, or traditional, and general systems theory. The emphasis in the chapter was to criticize each school of thought with concepts derived from the other schools. Neoclassical concepts were used to criticize the classical school, and systems theory concepts were used to criticize the classical and neoclassical schools. The chapter concluded with a description of a matrix organization model applied to a community police agency of moderate size.

As in all the other chapters in this book, the discussion of the particular subject matter is limited in scope. The literature on organizing concepts is vast, and the police manager is encouraged to consult sources in the footnotes and suggested readings for additional information.

Suggested Reading

Churchman, C. West. *The Systems Approach.* New York: Delta, 1968.

Dale, Ernest. *Organization.* New York: American Management Association, 1967.

Eastman, George D., and Eastman, Esther M., eds. *Municipal Police Administration.* 6th ed. Washington, D.C.: International City Management Association, 1969.

Etzioni, Amitai. *Modern Organizations.* Englewood Cliffs, N.J.: Prentice-Hall, 1964.

Lazzaro, Victor, ed. *Systems and Procedures.* 2nd ed. Englewood Cliffs, N.J.: Prentice-Hall, 1968.

Levinson, Harry. *Organizational Diagnosis.* Cambridge: Harvard University Press, 1972.

Milsum, John. *Positive Feedback.* New York: Pergamon Press, 1968.

Optner, Stanford L. *Systems Analysis for Business and Industrial Problem Solving.* Englewood Cliffs, N.J.: Prentice-Hall, 1965.

Price, James L. *Organization Effectiveness.* Homewood, Ill.: Richard D. Irwin, 1968.

Wilson, O. W., and McLaren, Roy C. *Police Administration.* 3rd ed. New York: McGraw-Hill, 1972.

CHAPTER 9

Recruitment, Selection, and Training of Personnel

The criminal justice system and its law enforcement component is primarily a system of *people*. The bulk of a police department's budget is devoted to the salaries and benefits of its personnel; the quality of service delivery depends on the type of personnel involved; and even the public's reception or rejection of that service reflects the degree of professionalization achieved by the agency. Literally, the entire success or failure of the law enforcement agency to serve its jurisdiction may very well depend on the care and emphasis it places on the recruitment, selection, and training of its personnel.

Recruitment and Selection

Before recruiting or selecting, the manager must know exactly what he wants a police officer to be. Once the manager knows what he wants in employees, he must determine what knowledge and skills can be developed by training. Once he knows what an individual can be trained to do, the manager can arrive at a rough estimate of just what qualities the person should already have when employed. When recruiting and selecting, the manager should seek these qualities and train "up" to the standards desired.

Only recently has anyone attempted to examine and state police qualities or requirements. In the past, the common tool for the manager has been the Department of Labor's "Generic Functions and Qualifications for Police" (see Table 8). Of particular interest is the Department of Labor's requirements. Key phrases such as "capacity to learn," "verbal ability," "tact," "ability to perform," "equanimity," "organizational ability," "assurance of manner," "physical stamina," "dexterity," "honesty," "dependability," "initiative," and "ability to adjust" indicate characteristics sought by law enforcement agencies. Some of these qualities can be increased by training or education, while others must be present when the person is employed. In addition, most of them can be summed up in one phrase—common sense—a phrase most peace officers will use first when asked what a policeman or deputy needs most.

More recent than the Department of Labor's efforts has been Project STAR. Based on research in four states, the Project STAR has developed a description of the characteristics of police officers that may prove useful to the recruitment and selection of police officers as well as in their training (see Chapter 1 and Table 9).

A method that is expensive and often beyond the means of small agencies is thoroughly analyzing the tasks performed by persons in each position in the organization. While the Project STAR did just that, there are, of course, many unique jurisdictions that require special skills or traits of the police officer if he is to function effectively in the local environment. Only by thoroughly documenting each and every kind of task and knowing just what is required to complete it can one get some idea of the kind of person and the training needed. Again, this analysis is expensive and is often beyond the capabilities of small agencies except for a rather crude analysis of such items as an officer's activity sheet.

Table 8
Generic Functions and Qualifications for Police

SOURCE: U.S. Department of Labor, *Dictionary of Occupational Titles* (Washington, D.C.: U.S. Government Printing Office, 1965).

I. **Functions**
   Operational
      Guard, search, and detain prisoners
      Guard and search establishments or stores
      Control pedestrian and automotive traffic
      Collect evidence of violations of laws, etc.
      Report violations
      Report public hazards
      Investigate, analyze, and report accidents
      Prevent disturbances
      Investigate persons and establishments
      Conduct raids
      Arrest violators
      Provide first aid
      Inform and interpret laws, regulations, etc.
      Conduct routine patrol
   Administration and Support
      Instruct recruits
      Direct, supervise, etc. (at various levels)
      Maintain discipline, standards, etc.
      Command (at various levels)
      Report on operations, facilities, equipment, etc.
      Use tactical communications

II. **Requirements**
   Capacity to acquire knowledge of laws and regulations
   Capacity to learn investigative procedures and methods
   Verbal ability to converse with people at various levels
   Tact and diplomacy in order to establish rapport with
      people
   Ability to perform under stress
   Equanimity in the face of danger or resistance
   Organizational ability in order to gather and evaluate
      facts
   Assurance of manner that will gain confidence and
      respect
   Physical stamina
   Manual dexterity and motor coordination for use of
      firearms
   Honesty and dependability
   Ability to exercise initiative in relating to people
   Ability to adjust to fluctuating situations

Table 9
Project STAR Police Tasks

Note: For more complete information, see Chapter 1.
Advising
Booking and receiving prisoners
Collecting and preserving
  evidence
Communicating
Controlling crowds
Defending self and others
Deterring crime
Interacting with other agencies
Interviewing
Investigating
Making arrests
Managing interpersonal conflict
Moving prisoners
Participating in community rela-
  tions/educational programs
Participating in pretrial conferences
Patrolling/observing
Preparing reports
Providing public service
Regulating traffic
Searching
Testifying as a witness
Training
Using equipment

Recruitment

Once the agency has determined exactly what type of people it wants, it must recruit people of that type. In its simplest form, recruitment is the active seeking of persons with the characteristics deemed essential to function in the position to be filled. Once these individuals are identified, the manager must encourage them to apply for the position. In law enforcement today, this does not occur except on rare occasions. Probably the reason is the fact that law enforcement theorists have paid scant attention to the recruitment process. Recruitment has simply meant occasional "help wanted" advertisements placed in local newspapers, a few notices placed on the bulletin boards of college police science programs, development of reserve and cadet programs for manpower pool purposes, or the announcement of positions through all the available media.[1] What is needed is a strong and active program in which the administrator, once the agency knows the characteristics of the men and women it seeks, develops plans to bring the available jobs to their attention and then encourages them to come forward and seek out a career in law enforcement.

An active plan of recruitment should begin with an identification of just where these people are. Are they in high schools, evening trade schools, police science programs? Are there provisions for beat patrolmen to identify young candidates and bring them to the attention of recruiters? Are career counselors in the schools, labor departments, and community agencies briefed on departmental personnel needs, and do they have ways to identify individuals and bring them to the agency's attention? A good plan will include the answers to these questions. The plan should also include ideas for the different types of individuals identified.

Everett N. King, a reserve police buff, hit on an excellent idea when he proposed that administrators must "... first, create the interest; second, demonstrate the need and value to the individual; and third, stimulate potential members to action by offering some benefit."[2] What King is saying is simply that the agency must know what creates initial interest and eventually motivates the individual to become an applicant. For a field whose workers must daily use street psychology and gain information about criminal activities, law enforcement has ignored some valuable psychological and human observations of what makes police work attractive and how to get people who have the desirable characteristics motivated to enter the profession. The recruitment plan should develop the means to motivate people.

The potential applicant must see that it is in his or her interest to serve. The welfare of the applicant's family and the members of his or her community is increased. The tasks to be performed are challenging and well within his or her capability. The applicant should feel that by being involved in law enforcement, his or her life will be more meaningful and the bonds between the individual and the community will be far greater than would be the case in any other profession or occupation. Finally, there is the great challenge of law enforcement itself, working toward goals that have value and will make life in the community a little better.

If recruitment materials are possible within the financial resources of the agency, they should be developed. The material should provide the potential applicant with the information that is needed to make a career decision. It should spell out exactly the types of duties performed and the qualifications sought so that the individual will know exactly what to expect and what the agency will expect from him or her. All too often, applicants get images from the media of what law enforcement is all about, and they are quite shocked when they are informed, or discover, what being a policeman actually involves.

Someone in the agency should be assigned the task of recruiter. The recruiter should be thoroughly familiar with all the jobs available in the department and the personal characteristics needed for success in each position. He should also be familiar with preservice training—adult education, community colleges —and the training the department or state agency provides. He should contact prospects and know how to motivate those who have the desired characteristics, and he should provide some career counseling to those who might be interested. The agencies that rely solely on a central personnel office should not be totally dependent on that office unless it is completely familiar with the needs of the profession.

How often should recruiting be undertaken? Ideally, the manager should be searching for potentially qualified personnel all the time so that when openings occur he will have a known quantity of potential applicants. Notice of the opening should be sent to those individuals at the same time it is being broadcast through other recruitment channels. If recruitment is continual, the agency will be assured that the selection process will have sufficient quality candidates to fill the needs of the agency.

In summary, whatever the methods used, there should be a plan based on the following:

1. The needs of the agency in the immediate and far future
2. Specific responsibility in the agency for recruiting personnel to meet the identified needs
3. Means for bringing likely prospects and the recruiter together

4. Continual search for and motivation of quality people

As Joseph Kimble has pointed out:

It is time to divert the resources of the organization from certain of their traditional paths. Planning and research programs must be established that will continually seek to identify the techniques and methods that will best aid the department in procuring manpower within its own particular community. In addition, there must be developed throughout the department a growing awareness of the important role recruitment plays in the future hopes and goals of the agency.[3]

Selection

After the agency has had an opening, and a suitable number of qualified applicants for the position have become available, selection begins. Several steps are involved in the selection process, and their purpose is to ascertain whether in fact the individual applicant has the necessary qualifications and attributes sought by the department so that a decision of acceptance or rejection can be made. The steps in this process can be any combination of those listed in Table 10. The actual employment of any or all of these steps depends on a variety of factors ranging from budgetary considerations to community attitudes toward the law enforcement agency. For instance, a community that has a large number of questionable incidents among recently employed police officers may spend far more time and effort with each and every step than one that is homogeneous, has a high degree of community-police cooperation, and recruits the bulk of its police officers directly from the community. Each community law enforcement agency will have to choose the steps that reflect the degree of professionalism it desires, the resources available, and any other factors at work in the environment.

Lee J. Cronbach and Goldine C. Gleser have developed a model of the selection process that applies no matter what combination of steps is used.[4] The parts of the Cronbach and Gleser selection model that should be used by the police manager emphasize three areas:

(1) the individual candidate about whose characteristics the selection or rejection decisions are aimed, (2) the criteria or

Table 10
Steps in the Police Selection Process

1. A set of minimum qualifications
2. A comprehensive application
3. An audit of the application
4. An application interview
5. A test for aptitude, intelligence, and/or interest
6. A test of physical agility
7. A medical examination
8. An oral interview by a board
9. A community character inquiry
10. A psychiatric evaluation
11. A polygraph examination
12. A thorough background investigation

characteristics sought by the law enforcement agency that contribute to the acceptance or rejection, and (3) the decision to accept or reject the applicant on the basis of weighing the desired characteristics against those possessed by the applicant. These components or parts appear at each step employed in the process and in the final decision. The model then would appear to be a series of steps in which the information about the candidate is measured against departmental selection criteria so that a terminal decision can occur. Rejection (a terminal decision) can occur at any time, but acceptance (a terminal decision) can occur only on the completion of each step to the satisfaction of the personnel selection decision-makers (see Figure 29).

Set of Minimum Qualifications. A set of minimum qualifications is the first step to be considered in the screening process. The applicant is, in effect, asked to meet these standards before submitting an application. By establishing and making known these minimum standards, the administrator is spared the problem of rejecting the most obviously unqualified candidates. Often, these minimum standards are set by the states through peace officer commissions on standards and training.

The minimum qualifications are fairly standard.[5] They are United States citizenship, minimum age of 21 (18 in some areas), maximum age of 35–40, a high school education, good physical condition, residency when required, a specific height range (often 5'8" to about 6'3" but is always changing) and weight proportion-

Figure 29
Model of Selection Process

Information about Candidate:	▼Step Decision
	*Terminal Decision

→minimum qualifications ————————→ criteria —⌇--→reject*

⌐→comprehensive application————————→ criteria—⌇--→reject*

⌐→application audit————————————→ criteria—⌇--→reject*

⌐→application interview————————————→ criteria—⌇--→reject*

⌐→aptitude/intelligence/interest test————————→ criteria—⌇--→reject*

⌐→physical agility test————————————→ criteria—⌇--→reject*

⌐→medical examination————————————→ criteria—⌇--→reject*

⌐→oral interview————————————————→ criteria—⌇--→reject*

⌐→community character inquiry————————→ criteria—⌇--→reject*

⌐→psychiatric evaluation ————————————→ criteria—⌇--→reject*

⌐→polygraph examination————————————→ criteria—⌇--→reject*

⌐→thorough background investigation————→ criteria—⌇--→reject*

accept*

Adapted from Lee J. Cronback and Goldine C. Gleser, *Psychological Tests and Personnel Decisions,* 2nd ed. (Urbana: University of Illinois Press, 1965).

al to height. By simply measuring oneself against these standards, the individual can screen himself before approaching the management.

A Comprehensive Application. The primary purpose of a comprehensive application is to provide the administration with sufficient information to make a preliminary decision about the applicant and to make a more detailed background investigation later. Some applications are so extensive that they test the perseverance of the applicant! Application forms can be developed so that the personnel manager can predict with some accuracy the chances for successful selection. Data that can be used in evaluating success potential are items such as education,[6] employment records, interests, special skills, and so on. Once he has some experience, the decision-maker learns to weigh certain sections of the application to help evaluate the chances of a candidate.

The application is often submitted with such supporting documents as a birth certificate; a diploma or certificate verifying educational attainment; a driver's license; military papers such as draft classification card, discharge, and DD 214; and a letter authorizing the release to the agency of information concerning the applicant.

An Audit of the Application and an Interview. The recruiter, personnel administrator, or whoever receives the application should review it and see that the information is complete and clear. If any information learned so far predicts the failure of the candidate, the reviewer should either advise the applicant of the chances of satisfactorily passing the selection steps or at least report his evaluation of the candidate's suitability. In the interview, the manager should further explain the nature of police work and allow the applicant to ask questions about the department and the work. Some departments allow the reviewer to reject the applicant at this step if it is obvious that he is unsuitable.

Test for Aptitude, Intelligence, and/or Interest. George W. O'Connor reported in his 1962 survey of metropolitan police departments that only 7 of the 368 agencies responding did not require some written test to measure mental dexterity.[7] Law enforcement authorities constantly call for professionalization of agencies by assuring that police officers be chosen for their aptitude, interest, and intelligence. If agencies are to choose personnel with favorable characteristics, then they must administer suitable tests that can measure these characteristics. Tests are available to measure values (Allport-Vernon Scale of Values), interest (Kuder Preference Record, Strong Vocational Interest), attitudes (Rokeach Dogmatism Scale), judgment (Social Intelligence Test, Cordall Test), and intelligence (Wechsler, Miller Analogies Test, Otis' Army General Classification, Thurstone, revised Army Alpha). Other tests evaluate academic level of competence (California Achievement Tests, Iowa Test of Educational Development, Cooperative School and College Ability Tests, Hermon-Nelson Tests, Lorge-Thorndike Tests, SRA Primary Mental Abilities). If the manager has a characteristic in mind, there is probably some test somewhere to measure it. In a small district, he might ask a local high school counselor for advice and even "recruit" the counselor to help the agency choose appropriate personnel. With the increasing concern about affirmative action and other employment of minorities, many agencies are having to reconsider these tests and every other step in the selection process. Essentially, the concern is that employment criteria should predict successful job performance and not simply exclude groups or classes of individuals.

A Test of Physical Agility. Most recruitment material distributed by agencies mentions that the applicant should be physically fit. In addition to passing a medical examination, the physically fit applicant must be adept enough to perform the tasks that may be demanded of a police officer. Despite this announced requirement, a study by Robert D. Keppel in 1967 indicated that only 56 per cent of 79 city police departments require any kind of physical agility test.[8]

There is little literature or research concerning the physical agility required of police officers. Occasional articles argue that good physical condition increases the safety of the policeman's work or improves his attitude toward the tasks to be performed. Little is available concerning what should be measured at the entry level. The Public Personnel Association has suggested a test that is designed to measure the natural or unskilled physical characteristics or abilities that make possible easy and effective training in one or more physical job skills.[9] Some are muscular strength, muscular endurance, circulatory endurance, agility, speed and body balance. A thorough consideration of physical agility would include tests for some or all of these characteristics.

A Medical Examination. Most commonly the applicant must submit to an examination by an appointed medical doctor or, if the agency has one, by a doctor retained for the examination of all its personnel. The applicant is examined on the premise that he must be of sound health if he is to give long and fruitful service. Managers often fear that the unfit will perform below standards and become pensioners before completing their service time. Although there are no widely accepted standards, the lines suggested by the Professional Standards Division of the International Association of Chiefs of Police are reasonable.

An Oral Interview. A fairly common feature of every selection process is the oral interview. For police candidates, the interview is conducted by an interview board whose composition varies from agency to agency. Most boards have from three to six members chosen by a variety of means. The composition is generally determined by the manager charged with the selection process. Often peace officers are chosen because of their familiarity with policing needs, but community representation is increasing.

A skillful oral board with an interview plan can greatly assist in the selection process. The board sees the applicant in action— how he looks and speaks and his bearing and manner. They can see how he interacts with the board—how he responds to questioning, his trains of thought, and how he reacts to others. Developing an interview plan takes time, and the effectiveness of the plan often requires verification by careful study of the cases in which it failed to reveal certain of the candidate's characteristics. Because of the weight given to oral boards, care must be exercised in the selection of board members and an oral board plan developed. John Guidici provides the manager with some excellent guidelines for oral boards.[10] These concern knowing exactly what the board is to do; knowing exactly what traits, attitudes, and characteristics the board should consider and evaluate; knowing exactly what is meant by the traits, attitudes, and characteristics possessed by the applicant; and knowing the scoring system for evaluating the applicant. A good plan will allow the board to take accurate measures of the candidates and determine which ones are satisfactory for the job.

A Community Character Inquiry. The writings of police managers refer to only one inquiry—the background investigation. This single step is premised on the fact that the behavior of an applicant will be consistent over a long period of time, and therefore an estimate of future behavior can be ascertained. What is suggested here is that two investigations be conducted—one a short character inquiry to assure the jurisdiction that the selection process should be continued, and the other an extensive search into the individual's full background.

The community character inquiry is a short examination of the individual—a search of criminal records and motor vehicle license history, brief contact with employers, teachers, neighbors, and so on. A summary of this "suitability check" should be supplied to the manager so that he can decide whether the process should continue. It may even be worthwhile to institute this step earlier in the process. Sometime during the process, a thorough background check must be made. Because of the expense, any findings that may reflect on the candidate should be brought to the manager's attention as soon as possible.

A Psychiatric Evaluation. One of the greatest concerns of police managers is the emotional stability of prospective police officers. Administrators often call this "common sense" and regard it as the number one requirement. Yet few agencies conduct any psychological evaluation of their personnel.

Formal programs that do exist for psychiatric or psychological evaluation of applicants vary from jurisdiction to jurisdiction. Thomas W. Oglesby's survey showed a wide variety; George W. O'Connor's later survey confirmed the diversity.[11] Despite this diversity, the programs have been successful at discovering emotional disturbances, severe character defects, judgment defects, and questionable motives that might otherwise have gone unnoticed.

One study shows the validity of psychiatric evaluation and testing. Nick J. Colarelli and Saul M. Siegal, with the cooperation of the Kansas State Highway Patrol, were able to rate highway patrolmen as "good" or "poor" risks.[12] Their results were compared with monthly ratings by supervisors. They found that by evaluation testing, they could predict future performance. With one exception, every man predicted to be a "poor" risk was eventually terminated or viewed by his supervisors as a poor patrolman or marginal in job performance. Similarly, those judged "good" risks were rated excellent or above average by their supervisors.

Psychological evaluation and testing in the selection process can help identify the mentally disturbed, those lacking "common sense," and those who will be unable to perform effectively. Used correctly, the findings can contribute to the total profile of the applicant while providing some assurance that the best men are being chosen.

A Polygraph Examination. The primary reason for using the polygraph is to verify the information obtained. Applicants may have been deceptive or misleading in the data they provided. A character or background investigation can also be defective because of personnel limitations, the difficulty of checking on a person in a highly mobile population, or the reluctance of many individuals, when interviewed, to provide negative information. Another reason may be that many acts of deviant behavior go undetected. The polygraph examination substantiates the results of other screening devices and increases the assurance with which a decision can be made.

Despite the fact that polygraphs are often used in law enforcement, polygraph tests are rarely employed in selection. Polygraph testing is expensive; the operator requires considerable training, an extensive internship, and continued practice; special facilities are required; and some states have laws about use of the polygraph as a condition of employment. In 1964 Charles D. Gooch reported that only 23 agencies out of 118 used the polygraph.[13] The polygraph is an excellent step in the process if the agency uses it correctly.

A Thorough Background Investigation. The last segment of the selection process is a thorough background investigation. The character of the peace officer should be above reproach. No department should ever accept a candidate until his background is comprehensively explored and the investigator can assure the administration that the applicant's habits, prejudices, and emotional stability (among the many characteristics to be investigated) are such that he can perform his duties with credit to the profession. Anything less is unacceptable.

The mechanics of a background investigation have been explained elsewhere.[14] It is only recently that the Rand Institute and the New York Police Department have confirmed what police administrators have known intuitively all along. The Institute confirmed that characteristics discovered in the background had a tendency to reappear in work.[15] So the money invested in an extensive background investigation pays off later.

Training

A law enforcement training program has three major objectives: (1) to provide the newly hired peace officer with the basic skills necessary for him to successfully complete his task assignments within the agency, (2) to introduce the new officer into the work setting or environment, and (3) to assist him in the further development of skills to meet a changing world and insure professional growth. The objectives can usually be accomplished by a four-phase training program consisting of recruit training, induction (familiarization training), in-service training, and advanced training.

Training involves all the processes of law enforcement management and should be aimed at providing skilled and professional manpower capable of achieving the objectives of the agency and providing whatever additional services are demanded by the community.

The management functions of planning, directing, controlling, and budgeting are important when developing a training plan for the agency. The manager should view the training of personnel as it relates to the problems facing the agency and the strategy and tactics to be employed in meeting these problems. Undirected training is a waste of scarce public resources. Coordination of efforts necessitates uniform methods to assure that any unnecessary effort is prevented and the agency is moving toward the solutions of the community's problems. To keep the costs involved reasonable and to insure adequate corrective action if required, control and budgetary constraints must be so exercised that trained personnel are developed and that they are developed for working at capacity.

Determining Training Needs

The manager and his training officer must think of training each officer in the acquisition of specific skills, knowledge, and attitudes relative to correct job performance. In order to do this, it is first necessary to determine exactly what the agency wants its personnel to do and just how it wants it done. They must also consider the future utilization of their personnel.

A training program or plan is then devised in which the newly selected peace officer acquires the skills and knowledge necessary to do the tasks assigned and to become a true professional capable of meeting society's future demands. Last, the manager must be capable of determining the degree of success or failure and be able to devise and implement whatever corrective or remedial steps are necessary to achieve the objectives. The primary tool now used in law enforcement for designing training is the job description.

To assure adequate training, the manager should itemize the duties and functions performed by the police officer in order to let the training officer know just what should be covered in the training plan. This itemization is actually a job description, and it should detail the important features of the assignment and identify the subject areas in which training is required. The breakdown of the tasks performed then becomes the guide to the training that the officer will receive. In essence, the well-developed plan outlines what tasks will be achieved, how they will be achieved, and when and where they will be accomplished.

Thomas N. Frost provides the manager with several methods of determining what should be included in the job description content of the training plan as well as how it should be developed.[16] After these determinations the basic curriculum can be developed for training newly hired employees as well as employees in any other position in the agency. In addition to the job description, Frost suggests that subject matter can also be ascertained through an analysis of the community as to its needs for police services, present and future.

Although basic job information and knowledge of the community are key determinants of the agency's training plan, the manager should not rely on them alone. Other excellent methods of determining needs, as well as current weaknesses, is to tap the knowledge gained by supervisors, middle managers, and executives through inspections, conferences, surveys, and measurements of field performance and service delivery. No techniques of determining needs or effectiveness should be overlooked in any training plan.

Recruit or Induction Training

In 1965, the International Association of Chiefs of Police surveyed some four thousand police departments throughout the country and reported that about 85 per cent of all police officers were placed on the streets without receiving initial training.[17] This percentage has probably declined, but in a period of high crime rates, intensive disruption in cities, violence, and social unrest, an untrained peace officer is a disservice to society, and an agency composed of such individuals is a scandal. Despite the movement since the 1920s toward higher standards, "no person, regardless of individual qualifications, is prepared to perform police work on native ability alone."[18]

The objective of recruit or induction training is to develop the skills and knowledge necessary for the competent performance of initial duties. There has been little analysis of just what should be taught or what contribution the instruction makes to assuring that skills are developed and knowledge gained. In many cases, the states themselves set the minimum amount of training and determine the subjects to be taught. Harry Diamond argues that the training needs must be determined by the agency itself by use of routine inspections, examination or tests, surveys, staff conferences, and review and analysis of performance, as well as the traditional "job description."[19] What has often occurred is that some standard format, recommended and based on the job description of someone in another agency, has been adopted as a whole, with the result that many new police officers study procedures, policies, practices, and even laws that are of little value since they may rarely, if ever, apply. Much of what is taught is useless when specialized units exist within the agency to handle particular calls for service. The training given initially should only be that which is necessary to perform the functions assigned and the responsibilities given. If more knowledge and skills are required later, such training should occur later, when it will have the most meaning for the learner. Recruit or induction training is needed, but it must be realistic.

The Professional Standards Division of the International Association of Chiefs of Police (IACP) recommends a two-hundred-hour basic program (see Table 11). A slightly different approach is recommended by Charles B. Saunders, Jr. (see Table 12). Whatever the format chosen, it should reflect and meet local needs, since the traditional American agency is local and must be responsive to local needs.

The Induction/Familiarization/Probation Phase

After a recently "graduated" officer is introduced into an agency, he begins a familiarization and probationary period. For most, familiarization will begin with more training, either through assignment to a field training officer if the new officer will be serving with the uniformed patrol division, or perhaps through a formal familiarization program designed to acquaint the individual with all the divisions in the agency. During this period the new officer has probationary status.

The probationary period is the time during which the agency closely evaluates the individual, his use of acquired skills, his intelligence, and his ability to function in the environment. Regardless of the care taken in the selection process and the effectiveness of the initial training, a few unacceptable individuals will always be appointed. Obviously, they should be eliminated as soon as their inadequacies become apparent.

Because of the close supervision of a field training officer (FTO), this period often discloses shortcomings either in the individual or the training. The newly hired officer's initial experiences in the police environment will have a strong influence on his future usefulness. His early impressions and experiences will eventually shape his career, his acceptance by co-workers, and his service to the public. If he has adjustment difficulties or acquires poor habits, they will affect him later. This is why the period is extremely crucial to both the department and the individual and why the neophyte should be under the guidance of an experienced and knowledgeable FTO.

The FTOs and familiarization officers should be carefully chosen, trained to teach on a one-to-one basis, and well versed in the techniques of evaluation. The failure to choose these trainers carefully or to indoctrinate them properly in the objectives of the program can lead to poorly trained, poorly screened, and even disillusioned officers. Once the new officer is comfortable in the

Table 11
200-hour Basic Course Recommended by IACP

Subject Area	Hours
Introduction to Law Enforcement	3
Criminal Law	16
Criminal Evidence	8
Administration of Criminal Law	2
Criminal Investigation	54
Patrol Procedures	38
Traffic Control	20
Juvenile Procedures	6
Defensive Tactics	14
Firearms	26
First Aid	10
Examinations	3

SOURCE: Professional Standards Division, International Association of Chiefs of Police, *Model Police Standards Council Program* (Washington, D.C.: International Association of Chiefs of Police, 1968), pp. S/7-1-S/7-19.

organization and operating environment, he can be given full responsibility and be expected to function effectively.

Another advantage of closely supervised field training during the probationary period is that only in the field, operating in the environment, can the new man visualize and experience the connection between what he is doing and what others are doing. With the assistance and guidance of the FTO, or in the familiarization program, the intense study and theory of recruit school can be integrated with the real problems encountered on a daily basis, and expected standards of performance can be made more explicit. Training will then have real meaning. The new officer can begin by assisting and then gradually assume duties and responsibilities.

In-Service Training

Even after careful and thorough selection and familiarization, further training on a continuing basis is necessary if the officer is to continue performing efficiently. New needs or demands on the agency by the community, growth of technology, changes in law, weaknesses in existing services or practices, discrepancies in early training, and new policies and procedures all necessitate a program of continued training.

Table 12

Knowledge and Skills Which Should Be Conveyed to All New Officers

Administration of Justice: foundations of criminal justice, state and federal constitutions, state criminal statutes, local codes and ordinances, court systems and procedures, laws of arrest, search and seizure, testimony in court, rules of evidence, the functions and duties of criminal justice agencies, juvenile court procedures, civil rights, and civil law.

Patrol Procedures: patrol techniques, preliminary investigations, report writing, communications procedures, responding to calls for service, and handling criminal cases, non-criminal cases, and disaster cases.

Traffic Enforcement: state and local traffic codes, traffic direction, officer-violator contacts, summons issuance procedures, traffic court procedures, accident investigation, and drunk-driving cases.

Social Science: basic psychology, abnormal psychology, human relations, crime and delinquency causation, geography, and public relations.

Investigation: conduct of interviews, interrogation, case preparation, investigation of crimes against persons, investigation of crimes against property, organized crime and vice, crime scene procedures, collection of evidence, scientific crime detection, and personal identification.

Emergency Medical Services: basic first aid, emergency childbirth, recognition and handling of the mentally disturbed.

Physical Training and Skills: proper use of firearms, defensive tactics, mechanics of arrest, crowd and riot control, and prisoner transportation.

Agency Standards and Procedures: department rules and regulations, code of ethics, general and specific orders, jail procedures, records procedures, vehicle and equipment care and use, department organization, and personnel procedures.

SOURCE: Charles B. Saunders, Jr., *Upgrading the American Police: Education and Training for Better Law Enforcement* (Washington, D.C.: Brookings Institution, 1970), pp. 122–123.

Numerous authorities agree that an in-service training program is a necessity.

The form taken for in-service training varies from agency to agency. The most popular is the regularly scheduled program attended by personnel on a rotating basis during "quiet" periods. Some use roll-call instruction, first developed in Los Angeles, in which short training periods occur before the officers go on duty. In-service training also includes refresher training and special training designed for special needs. The variety is staggering.

State standards organizations, federal agencies, and even police science programs at junior colleges sponsor refresher and specialized courses. The only problem with these is that they often ignore local conditions or functions that may be unique to a few agencies.

The greatest problem with in-service training is that it rarely includes drill or field practice. Classroom sessions without practice can defeat the in-service efforts of the administrator. Often the new officer gets a sound basis in theory but does not really know how to carry out theories in the field.

Advanced Training

There are two general types of advanced training. The first is specialized training for assignment to a particular department or for performance of a certain task. The other is generalized training aimed at developing the individual for an executive or leadership position at a later date. Both forms of advanced training should be provided before or shortly after assignment to higher levels in the organization or assignment to the specialized functions.

The most common form of specialized training is investigator's courses. The variety of training available varies from state to state and region to region. For instance, basic investigator's courses are often available through both local colleges and state standards and training commissions. Sometimes the state reimburses jurisdictions for training conducted by the colleges.

Generalized training is usually for personnel who show promise for or who have recently been promoted to supervisory or management levels. Supervisory, middle management, and executive development training is often available from standards and training commissions of the states and from other sources.

Summary

This chapter has briefly described some of the major concerns, and possible managerial responses, in recruitment, selection, and training. Historically, these processes have been quite diverse in the United States because of a decentralized governmental structure, limited local resources, and the need to respond to unique community needs.

A most basic activity of police managers is identifying, securing, and developing individuals to become effective and professional police officers. The developing phase is beginning to include more than just training, however, as evidenced by a recent study in Los Angeles.[20] The limits of this chapter do not permit a description of the study, but the reader is encouraged to secure and read the document.

Suggested
Reading

Bauhr, M. E., et al. *Psychological Assessment of Patrolman Qualifications in Relation to Field Performance.* Washington, D.C.: OLEA, DOJ, 1968

Bloomington, Minnesota, Police Department. *Joint Recruitment by Hennepin County Suburban Police Departments.* Bloomington, Minn.: Personnel Department, 1963.

Cottle, William C. *Interest and Personality Inventories.* Boston: Houghton Mifflin, 1968.

Cronbach, L. J. *Essentials of Psychological Testing.* 2nd ed. New York: Harper & Row, 1960.

Donovan, J. J., ed. *Recruitment and Selection in Public Service.* Chicago: Public Personnel Association, 1968.

Dunnette, Marvin D. *Personnel Selection and Placement.* Belmont, Calif.: Wadsworth, 1966.

Flippo, Edwin B. *Principles of Personnel Management.* 3rd ed. New York: McGraw-Hill, 1971.

Gagné, R. M. *The Conditions of Learning.* New York: Holt, Rinehart & Winston, 1965.

Germann, A. C. *Police Executive Development.* Springfield, Ill.: Charles C. Thomas, 1962.

Guion, Robert M. *Personnel Testing.* New York: McGraw-Hill, 1965.

Lawske, Charles H., and Balma, Michael J. *Principles of Personnel Testing.* New York: McGraw-Hill, 1966.

McManus, G. P., et al. *Police Training and Performance Study.* Washington, D.C.: Law Enforcement Assistance Administration, Department of Justice, 1970.

Mandell, M. M. *Selection Process: Choosing the Right Man for the Right Job.* New York: American Management Association, 1964.

Miller, M. W., ed. *On Teaching Adults.* Chicago: Center for Study of Liberal Education for Adults, 1960.

Public Personnel Association. *Test Catalogue, 1968.* Chicago: Public Personnel Association, 1968.

Staton, Thomas F. *How to Instruct Successfully.* New York: Harper & Row, 1971.

CHAPTER 10

Evaluation and Controlling

This final chapter covers the last stage of the managerial process: controlling. Inherent in the controlling process is evaluation—of people, of programs, and of the organization. Without evaluation and control, the manager cannot learn about the organization and therefore cannot effectively run it.

This chapter is divided into four major sections. The first presents a general overview of the controlling process; the second discusses concepts of productivity, efficiency, and effectiveness; the third analyzes the personnel evaluation process; and the fourth examines the concept of professionalism as a method of control.

Some of the material in this chapter is taken from Jack L. Kuykendall, "Police Management Controlling," *Law and Order* 21 (May 1973): 22–34. Permission to reprint has been granted.

The Controlling Process

Definitions of controlling are numerous. Those provided below cover the rather broad range of concerns of police managerial controlling.

Control is the constraining of activities and resources to conform to a plan of action. [David I. Cleland and William R. King, *Management: A Systems Approach* (New York: McGraw-Hill, 1972), p. 359.]

A successful control process is one which effects corrections to the system involved before the deviations become serious. [Leonard J. Kazmier, *Principles of Management*, 2nd ed. (New York: McGraw-Hill, 1969).]

... a measuring of what we are actually accomplishing against what we planned to achieve. [Norman C. Kassoff, *The Police Management System* (Washington, D.C.: International Association of Chiefs of Police, 1967), p. 34.]

Controlling is assuring ourselves that what has been planned is actually happening. [Paul M. Stoker, *A Total Systems Approach to Management Control* (New York: American Management Association, 1968), p. 14.]

Controlling is concerned with comparing events with plans and making necessary corrections where events have deviated from plans. [Herbert G. Hicks, *The Management of Organizations* (New York: McGraw-Hill, 1967), p. 205.]

Control is the process of checking to determine whether or not plans are being adhered to, whether or not proper progress is being made toward the objectives and goals, and acting, if necessary, to correct any deviations. The essence of control is action which adjusts performance to predetermined standards if deviations occur. [Theo. Halmann, *Professional Management: Theory and Practice* (Boston: Houghton Mifflin, 1962), p. 485.]

Fundamentally, control is any process that guides activity toward some predetermined goal. The essence of the concept is in determining whether the activity is achieving the desired results. [W. Warren Haynes and Joseph L. Massie, *Management: Analysis, Concepts and Cases*, 2nd ed. (Englewood Cliffs, N.J.: Prentice-Hall, 1969), p. 319.]

When the central elements are extracted from these definitions, the concept of controlling as a managerial activity takes on substance:

1. Control requires comparison; therefore, there must be a plan, objective, or criterion for the manager to use as a yardstick in evaluating and controlling the activity of the organization.

2. The yardstick becomes the measuring device the manager employs to determine whether or not the organizational activity is "correct."

3. If it is not correct, then a deviation from the desired standard, or yardstick, has occurred. The manager needs both a yardstick and an awareness of all activity in the organization to determine whether a deviation has taken place.

4. When a deviation is recognized, the reasons must be discovered and action taken to correct the deviation.

5. The action can take many forms, but generally it involves changing the activity to conform with the plan or yardstick being used, or changing the plan to conform to the activity being performed. The former is by far the more common controlling approach in management.

To summarize, the essentials of a controlling system for a manager are standards, the ability and opportunity to observe deviations, a method to compare a standard with a deviation to determine the cause of the deviation, and the willingness, confidence, and knowledge to take corrective action.

Methods of Controlling for Police Managers

Some methods of control are common to most organizations, including community police organizations. The following are methods common to community police organizations:

1. The organizational hierarchy has built-in control. Supervisors control workers; managers control supervisors; and so on. Some organizations also have separate controls, such as inspection units. These are usually, but not always, found in large police organizations. An important concern in controlling both hierarchy and special units is motivation. Controlling and inspections should be made as positive as possible so as not to demotivate employees and cause them to try to "cover their trails" out of fear.

2. The budget can be an excellent controlling method because it makes explicit what resources will be expended for what purposes.

3. Many organizations, including the police, have regular written reports that can be evaluated. Among the most common for police are investigative reports, both initial and follow-up ones. Such reports provide an excellent source of information for checking the activity and performance of officers and units. Other regular reports also can be used or developed; these include general and statistical reports on the performance of individuals and units. When such reports are utilized, however, some standard for comparison is needed. The regular types of reports that can be developed by a police agency are numerous. As knowledge about effectiveness increases, reports on all phases of the police operation may become available.

4. Special reports on unusual problems, management audits and surveys, research grants, and so on are all forms of controlling for a manager.

5. A major controlling factor for consideration for a police organization, and therefore an important source of controlling information, is the environment. As noted in Chapter 1, the political, social, economic, and legal environment strongly influences the activities of police organizations. Police managers often get valuable insights and data about the activities and behavior of their police by being sensitive to the organizational environment. The problem for the police manager is deciding what source of information in the environment is the most complete and reliable.

6. One of the most effective controlling devices is simple observation. The manager can go to the scene and observe what is taking place. While often time-consuming, this method should be employed at times.

The number and type of controlling methods available to police managers is limited only by the creativity of the manager and the time he can give to this managerial activity. The concept of controlling, once understood, can take numerous forms in practice. One such practical system of controlling is suggested in the next subsection.

A General Police Management Controlling System

A general police management controlling system can be based on the following elements: (1) standards of performance, (2) key indicators of performance, (3) methods of checking key indicators, and (4) corrective action.[1]

Standards of Performance. Standards of performance can be defined by examples of some typical standards. These include policies, procedures, methods, rules and regulations, and objectives.

1. A *policy* is a guide to be used for deciding whether an activity or behavior is appropriate or inappropriate. An example of a policy is: "Noninjury traffic accidents will be investigated only if property damage to both vehicles totals more than $100. The estimate of damages is to be made by the investigating officer."

2. A *procedure* is a specified manner of acting once the decision to act has been made. For example, once the decision was made to investigate a noninjury accident, a procedure should exist to describe how the investigative process should proceed.

3. A *method* is one stage, or step, of a procedure. For example, a step within the investigative procedure is the method of completing the accident report.

4. A *rule or regulation* is a statement that specifies what will or will not be done. For example, a regulation might state that all officers will wear hats while outside their vehicles during accident investigations.

5. *Objectives* are statements expressing desired results and behavior. These statements may be qualitative and/or quantitative. For example, a qualitative objective could be courteous behavior by the officer while investigating the accident. A quantitative objective could be completion of the investigation of each noninjury accident within a specific time period (for example, forty-five minutes).

Each of these is a standard of performance in that it defines the activity and behavior expected by the organization. The establishment of standards of performance occurs during planning stages. Obviously, these standards should be based on the best available knowledge as to what is most effective in accomplishing the overall police mission. Policies, procedures, methods, and rules and regulations should be systematically developed in response to the recurring activities and problems confronting police departments. Objectives should first be established for the entire organizations in the form of broad qualitative statements, or goals. More specific and, if possible, quantifiable objectives should be set for each functional unit of the organization (patrol, investigations, records, and so on) and for each individual in the organization. Quantification of objectives can be in the form of numbers, percentages, and time. Both qualitative and quantitative objectives should be flexible enough to make allowances for possible exceptions.

Key Indicators of Performance and Methods of Checking. A key indicator is a piece of essential information that tells the police manager whether the standard of performance is being met. The method of checking the key indicator is the way in which the essential information is brought to the manager's attention. Key indicators should be as few as possible because of the importance of a manager's time, yet the indicator should be significant in determining whether standards of performance are met. As noted, methods of checking indicators include direct observation by supervisors or managers, inspections, verbal reports, ongoing written reports (case reports; weekly, monthly, or quarterly summaries of crime; time on calls; response times), special reports on unique problems, and input from community groups and other governmental agencies.

Police managers normally use most, if not all, of these methods of controlling. The frequency with which certain methods are employed by the manager and the information sought relate to the key indicators. For example, an objective described earlier was that noninjury accidents normally be investigated in forty-five minutes. A possible key indicator would be the monthly (or other time period) average time on calls for noninjury accidents.

If this average time was more than a few minutes different from the standard of forty-five minutes, corrective action might be required. Of course, the establishment of any such standard assumes that enough systematic research has been done to develop reasonable standards.

A summary of this example is: An objective is that no more

than forty-five minutes will be spent investigating noninjury accidents (standard of performance), and this standard will be
checked by the manager through a monthly written report (method of checking) of the average for that month of time per noninjury accident call (key indicator).

Corrective Action. Once the manager discovers a deviation in
a standard of performance, he must take action. First he must
determine the cause of the deviation. Is the standard itself appropriate and accepted by employees? If the standard is appropriate,
then the cause lies within the organization and/or with the employee. Possible examples within the organization include inac-
curate information, information incorrectly computed, an
unusual number of extensive noninjury accidents, and inadequate communication. There are many possible reasons why
organization and/or employees do not perform as desired. All
the knowledge in this and other books is needed to analyze the
cause of controlling problems and to decide what action to take.

Internal and External Controls

A distinction needs to be made between internal and external
controls. External controls are illustrated by the system described in this chapter. They are generally controls by management that are extended to the employees. An external control
system is necessary for effective police management; however,
there are limits to the effectiveness of the external control system
on the behavior of employees. All employees have their own
internal control systems. This means that they have a certain
degree of personal motivation and commitment. In numerous
situations, employees can engage in activity considered inappropriate by organization standards, and not be discovered. If, however, the employee is highly motivated and committed to the
performance standards that are part of the external system, then
he is more likely to comply by behaving appropriately. The successful police manager must give careful consideration to methods of selection, training, and motivation. As discussed in
Chapter 2, motivation and commitment are often increased
through employee participation in the establishment of performance standards. Another important internal control concern is

related to professionalism, which will be discussed in a later section.

Productivity, Efficiency, and Effectiveness

Generally speaking, the broad categories of standards for police organizations are productivity, efficiency, and effectiveness. Productivity has many possible definitions, but in general it is the relationship between the inputs and outputs of an organization. If a measure of output for an agency were the number of arrests made, then the agency might be considered more productive if the number of arrests increased while the number of employees to make the arrests remained constant or declined. As defined, productivity is essentially an efficiency measure, because efficiency is also concerned with the input-output relationship. However, if efficiency were considered in terms of cost and not in terms of productivity, then efficiency could decrease even when productivity increased. For example, if 10 investigators arrested 200 individuals in 1973, the ratio would be 1 investigator (input) for 20 arrests (output). If each investigator's salary was $10,000, then the direct cost per arrest was $500 ($10,000 divided by 20 arrests). If, in 1974, the same 10 investigators made 210 arrests, then the ratio would be 1 investigator for 21 arrests. However, if the salary increased to $11,000 per investigator, then the cost per arrest would be approximately $524. Assuming that the real value of the money remained constant, then while productivity (as defined) increased, efficiency (as defined relative to costs) decreased. This is only one of the confusing possible relationships among efficiency, effectiveness, and productivity.

Effectiveness is determined by the degree to which the organization realizes its goals or objectives. Continuing with the previous example, assume that the unit objective for investigations was an average of 25 arrests per year per investigator. In 1973, with an average of 20 arrests, the investigations unit was 80 percent effective (20 divided by 25); in 1974, it was 84 percent effective (21 divided by 25). Therefore, both productivity and effectiveness increased while efficiency declined; or if productivity had been judged on a monetary basis, then effectiveness would have increased and both productivity and efficiency would have declined. To make the example even more complicated, assume that the goal of the organization—the reduction of crime—is used to measure effectiveness. If the crime rate increased between 1973 and 1974, then even though arrests increased, effectiveness decreased in terms of achieving the organization's goal.

If this seems confusing, that is because it *is* confusing. What is important to remember is that while efficiency and effectiveness have been consistently defined in management, productivity has not. Police managers should remember the following when considering development of standards in planning to be used in controlling:

1. Efficiency is defined as the relationship between inputs and outputs, often, but not always, in terms of cost per output unit.

2. Effectiveness is defined as the degree to which organizational goals or objectives are realized. Cost-effectiveness is the relationship between cost and effectiveness. In the example, in 1973, 80 percent effectiveness in investigations cost $100,000 (10 investigators times $10,000 per investigator); in 1974, 84 percent effectiveness cost $110,000 (10 times $11,000). The 4 percent improvement in investigations cost $10,000. The manager must decide whether the increase in effectiveness was worth the increase in cost—in other words, whether the change was cost-effective.

3. Consideration of input-output raises the issue of what inputs and outputs are. Inputs will be discussed later. Outputs are either what police do (patrol, investigate, and so on) or outcomes, the result of what police do (crime changes, changes in behavior, and so on). A most difficult problem for police managers is determining the relationship between what police do and what happens as a result of police activity. This complicates considerations of efficiency, effectiveness, and productivity, because the relationship is influenced by many factors outside police control.

Each police manager must be careful in using the three broad standards described in this section. Productivity is a flexible concept, and the authors suggest that it be defined as the degree to which the police influence outcomes—that is, what happens as a result of what the police do—rather than as output—that is, what the police do. Such a definition will require constant attention, through evaluation methods, to the output-outcome relationship.

Input Processing

In considering productivity and changes in productivity in an organization, not only is the input-output-outcome relationship important, but so is the processing phase of inputs into outputs—in other words, the ways in which inputs are transformed into outputs. The productivity analysis process is depicted in Figure 30. Organizational inputs, such as human and physical resources, are processed as a result of the organizational structure and management practices to produce outputs, or police activities, such as patrolling, investigations, and so on. Outcomes are the things that happen as a result of outputs and include changes in crime rates, citizen attitudes, and citizen behavior toward the police. Productivity is improved by improving the quality and quantity of inputs, processing them to obtain greater motivation and effectiveness, and directing resources to the output activities that will achieve the most desirable outcomes.

Figure 30
Productivity Analysis Process

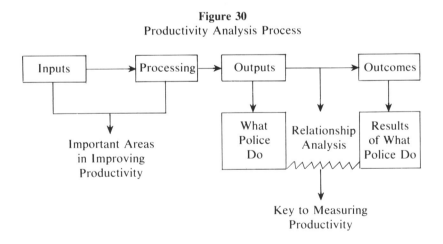

Inputs can be discussed in three broad categories: labor, tangible capital, and intangible capital. Labor is normally computed in time worked (usually man-hours). While this quantifies labor, it indicates nothing about the quality of the labor. Quality can change as a result of changes in employees' innate ability, education, training, and experience. A calculation of total labor input also does not consider the differences in levels of labor—that is, operational, support, and management. Another problem is deciding how to count "time worked" in determining the numbers of man-hours. For example, should total paid labor hours be used, or should coffee breaks, vacations, illnesses, and so on be subtracted? Often total hours are used because data on hours actually worked are not available. It would not be difficult to develop records concerning "time worked"; the relative contributions of the other factors, however, are more difficult to assess.

Tangible capital includes the structure, plant, equipment, and materials available for production. Tangible capital can also be measured in cost; however, if this is done, and if tangible capital is to be related to labor in determining total input, then labor must also be calculated in cost. If cost is used, a constant dollar or deflated dollar must be the basis for calculations. Changes in dollar value must be controlled through an index to some base period.

Intangible capital can include investment of funds to improve the quality of labor or investment in various research projects to improve the output or the processes generating outputs. Intangible capital is probably most effectively measured by cost, but its relationship to changes in output is difficult to identify.

The separate use of labor, tangible capital, and intangible capital as inputs in determining productivity results in only partial productivity. More complete is *aggregate productivity* or *total factor productivity*. This would include a measurement of all three categories of inputs added together by use of a common measuring system. Ideally, the relative weight of each category would also be known so that a change in one would result in a known change in productivity.

Just as changing inputs can alter productivity, so can the processing or transforming of the inputs into outputs. Numerous factors bear on this processing. These will be discussed in three categories: technology, organization, and management. *Technology* should not be confused with tangible capital in the form of machinery. Technology is used in this context to apply to means of doing the work, which would include man-machine combinations in processing activities. As defined *organization* concerns the patterns and structuring of activities among people and tasks. Moreover, the organizing of an endeavor determines what the productive processes will be and how they will work together. *Management* includes organizing, but it also involves such related activities as planning, goal-setting, motivation, leading, controlling, and overall organizational growth and renewal.

Technology, organization, and management are difficult to quantify in terms of their relative contributions to productivity. Technology may be evaluated most effectively on a program-to-program basis. For example, a computer terminal in a police car may permit faster and more accurate decisions in arrests than does a two-way radio. If so, the man-machine combination of police officer–computer terminal has potential for improved productivity.

Organization and management may be evaluated in terms of recent research as to what is most predictive of optimizing output. The material in previous chapters and suggested reading provides sources of information in this regard.[2]

An area not previously discussed but worth mentioning is organizational development, a rapidly growing organizational and management field. If separate frameworks are not desired for measuring organizational and managerial effectiveness, guidelines of organizational development can be used. While still somewhat new, organizational development emphasizes the establishment of trusting and open relationships among organization members to facilitate goal-oriented problem-solving. In many cases this requires both changes in organizational structure (for example, the use of teams) and management styles (for example, changing methods of leadership, motivation, and control).

Figure 31 shows a general model of productivity determination in police organizations. Only inputs and processing are outlined, because outputs and outcomes have already been generally discussed. The model is an attempt to identify input and processing factors that can assist the manager in improving productivity. Theoretically, if any of the input or processing factors increased or were made more effective, productivity would be improved.

Certainly this model is not all-inclusive, and more factors can be added if more detail is desired, or the factors can be stated in

Figure 31
General Model of Factors of Productivity
Determination in Organizational
Inputs and Processing

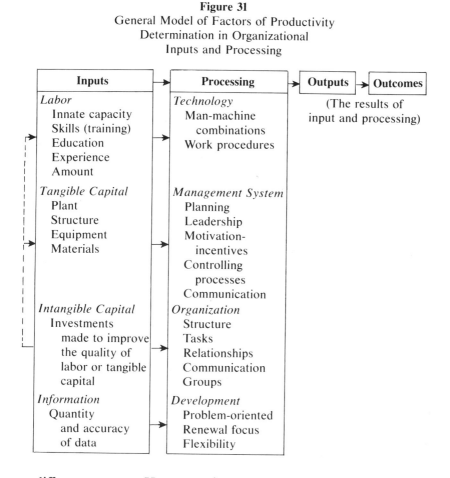

Inputs	Processing	Outputs	Outcomes
Labor	*Technology*	(The results of	
Innate capacity	Man-machine	input and processing)	
Skills (training)	combinations		
Education	Work procedures		
Experience			
Amount			
Tangible Capital	*Management System*		
Plant	Planning		
Structure	Leadership		
Equipment	Motivation-		
Materials	incentives		
	Controlling		
	processes		
	Communication		
Intangible Capital	*Organization*		
Investments	Structure		
made to improve	Tasks		
the quality of	Relationships		
labor or tangible	Communication		
capital	Groups		
Information	*Development*		
Quantity	Problem-oriented		
and accuracy	Renewal focus		
of data	Flexibility		

a different manner. However, the model is useful in determining factors of importance in improving productivity.

The model has several features that previous explanations have not covered. Input factors include "Information" because of the importance of this input to police agencies. Without information, in both quantity and quality, a police agency cannot function effectively. In processing factors, "Communication" is listed under both "Management System" and "Organization" because of the impact that both can have on the communication process. A "Development" heading reflects the need to be constantly aware of the importance of a flexible problem orientation and the importance of renewal of the organization toward intended organizational goals.

One obvious factor of importance that is not included in the model is environment. The political, social, and economic environments of any organization are constantly interacting to influence inputs and processing. People and groups in the environment react to the quality and quantity of outputs, and their reaction is important to the manager who is concerned about how the outputs are produced. Feedback provided from the environment is an important consideration in altering inputs and processing.

While the model is useful in identifying factors that can influence productivity, possible combinations of input factors with processing systems are not discussed. Each element of the model might be viewed on a positive-negative continuum—positive-negative in terms of the impact of the element on a change in productivity. With all the elements that exist in the model, numerous positive-negative combinations exist. Research is needed to increase managers' knowledge of the interactive dynamics of positive-negative factors in sequence and in combination.

Personnel Evaluation Process

The appraisal of employee performance is an important concern of many supervisors and managers. Richard S. Barrett says that "management has no choice as to whether it will have a program of performance evaluation. It has a program . . . formal or informal, and the results are continuously used."[3]

Not only is performance appraisal inevitable, it is also important. According to Felix M. Lopez, "Unless an organization pursues a policy of viewing continuously the past performance, present progress, and future prospects of its human resources, it must manage by intuition and tradition. Sound management in the modern organization setting seems to make a formal employee performance evaluation program essential."[4]

Many police organizations engage in some form of personnel

Most of the material in the section "Personnel Evaluation Process" is taken from Jack L. Kuykendall and Orville Butts, "Performance Appraisals in Police Organizations," *Journal of California Law Enforcement* 7 (1973). Permission to reprint has been granted.

appraisal. The purpose of this section is to analyze some of the existing methods, and suggest a system to improve police personnel appraisal.

Performance Appraisal: An Analysis

Performance appraisal can generally be defined as action taken by an organization to evaluate the performance of its employees. Dale S. Beach says employee appraisal is "the systematic evaluation of the individual with respect to his performance on the job and his potential for development."[5] Leonard D. White states that the purposes of performance appraisals are to furnish a basis of judgment in handling personnel; to protect employees against snap judgments, prejudice, and the ill will of some supervisors; and, in well-managed organizations, to point out to employees their strong and weak characteristics.[6] George N. Beck found that most police departments use performance appraisals for personnel transactions, for evaluation of training techniques, and for improving employee performance.[7] *Municipal Police Administration* lists two basic purposes for employee appraisal: one is to assist in employee counseling, and the second is to assist in making administrative decisions.[8] A. C. Germann says that police performance appraisals should improve employee and supervisory effectiveness and personnel processes.[9] Robert C. Myrtle has noted the following "categories of use" for performance appraisals:

A. Administrative
1. As a basis for salary considerations for exceptional performance
2. As a guide to status changes for employees, such as promotions
3. As a control device to uncover organizational weaknesses
4. As a planning tool in identifying changing skills and future personnel needs

B. Motivation
1. To determine where the employee stands and what is needed in terms of performance
2. To integrate individual and organizational goals

3. To permit input of employees to improve efficiency and effectiveness

C. Employee Development

1. To enlarge and enrich jobs via a consultative process
2. To stimulate career development via job rotation, training, and so on
3. To facilitate change and innovation[10]

Lopez has identified sixteen basic methods, or techniques, of performance appraisal. These methods can be classified as either person-oriented or results-oriented.[11] Table 13 provides a breakdown of these sixteen methods by orientation. Each of these sixteen methods is briefly defined in Tables 14 and 15.[12]

Table 13
Categories and Methods of Performance Appraisal

Person-Oriented Methods	Results-Oriented Methods
Discrete Category Scales	Output Data
Graphic Scales	Efficiency Indexes
Adjective Scales	Financial Indexes
Simple Ranking	Field Review
Paired Comparison	Critical Incident
Forced Distribution	Performance Standards
Free Response Reports	Management by Objectives
Performance Checklists	
Forced Choice	

SOURCE: Felix M. Lopez, Jr., *Evaluating Employee Performance* (Chicago: Public Personnel Association, 1968).

Person-oriented appraisal methods are those evaluation procedures that rate personal traits, compare one employee with another, or describe how the employee performs his duties. Results-oriented approaches are based on evaluating the employee's performance rather than the employee himself. They are concerned primarily with qualitative and/or quantitative, narrative, and consultative procedures used in evaluating results obtained by employees.

Person-oriented appraisal methods suffer from numerous shortcomings. Some of these are the following:

1. *The error of leniency* occurs when the rater marks most of

Table 14

Person-Oriented Methods of Performance Appraisal

Method	Definition
1. Discrete Category Scales	Identification of personal or job traits which are evaluated in terms of a series of categories such as: Needs Improvement | Standard Performance | Outstanding Performance The number of categories usually ranges from 2 to 5, but there can be more.
2. Graphic Scales	Identification of traits, but evaluated on the following type of scale: Unsatisfactory Poor Good Superior Excellent This is a more flexible version of the discrete category scale. Responses can be placed anywhere on the continuum.
3. Adjective Scales	Identification of traits that are more complete in evaluative response. An example is: Handles situations clumsily; ignores policy, etc. | Judgment often illogical; tends to overlook policy, etc. | Acts judiciously under most circumstances, etc. | Judgments impartial and logical, etc. | Thinks soundly and logically, etc. This is a more descriptive version of the graphic scale.
4. Simple Ranking: *a.* Simple Order	Ranking of "best" to "worst" employee.

Table 14 — Continued

Method	Definition
b. Alternative Ranking	Employees halved into "highest" and "lowest" performing groups. Highest half ranked from top down; lowest half from bottom up.
c. Group Ranking	Criterion groups established to represent specific levels of performance. Employees being evaluated are placed in groups appropriate to their levels of performance.
5. Paired Comparison	Every employee compared with all others being evaluated. Employee receiving highest number of favorable comparisons is ranked highest; conversely, fewest favorable comparisons results in lowest ranking.
6. Forced Distribution	The "bell-shaped curve" or normal frequency distribution is employed; an example would be allocating 10% for highest and lowest rankings, 20% for next highest and lowest groups, and 40% for the middle group.
7. Free Response Reports	Evaluation of employee in "rater's own words."
8. Performance Checklists	Checklist of desirable traits, behavior, etc. provided. Rater checks those that apply to employee. Items checked can be given different weights to determine total rating.
9. Forced Choice	Sets of descriptive statements concerning performance are used and the rater selects those which "best describe" the employee's performance.

SOURCE: Felix M. Lopez, Jr., *Evaluating Employee Performance* (Chicago: Public Personnel Association, 1968).

Table 15

Results-Oriented Methods of Performance Appraisal

Method	Definition
1. Output Data	Measurement of such output as cases cleared, people interviewed. complaints received. etc.
2. Efficiency Indexes	Establish indexes concerning tardiness. absences. accidents, complaints. etc. Indexes should be correlated and selected for a particular situation.
3. Financial Indexes	Measurement of costs, budget performance, etc.. compared with some performance yardstick.
4. Field Review	Personnel specialist interviews supervisor of employee to determine performance. problems, developmental plans, etc.
5. Critical Incident	Critical incidents related to successful job performance are identified. Rater observes employee behavior during incidents and records observations for review with employee.
6. Performance Standards	Specific job requirements established for each employee.
7. Management by Objectives	Joint establishment of individual objectives – preferably quantifiable – between superior and subordinate. Individual objectives should be integrated with employee's organizational unit objectives and overall organizational goals. Periodic review of objectives is established.

SOURCE: Felix M. Lopez. Jr.. *Evaluating Employee Performance* (Chicago: Public Personnel Association. 1968).

the reports in the highest categories, thereby overrating the employee.

2. *The error of personal bias* occurs when the rater allows personal feelings about an employee to affect ratings. Likes or dislikes tend to limit the objectivity of the appraisal.

3. *The error of central tendency* occurs when the rater places all employees somewhere near the center of the rating scale. This occurs because the rater may not be aware of how the rating is to be used because he does not know his subordinates well, or because he is required to justify all extreme ratings.

4. *The error of related traits* occurs when the rater gives the same rating to traits that are considered related in some way. The value of rating each trait separately is lost, and the overall rating is less valid.[12]

5. *The halo effect* occurs when the rater lets one or two traits dominate the appraisal of an employee. The rater evaluates all remaining traits based on the dominant trait or traits.[13]

6. The rater's desire to avoid "playing God" in evaluating people negatively can result in overevaluating employees.

7. Many raters are not qualified to analyze the personality of employees.

8. Employees often react defensively to "personal" evaluations, resulting in a breakdown in communication with the rater.[14]

9. Use of personal traits does not provide needed guidance for performance improvement.[15]

10. There is a questionable relationship between traits used for evaluation and those required for successful performance.

Results-oriented approaches tend to be more objective, center on job performance rather than on individual traits, and generally result in more effective motivation. Moreover, the rater does not have to be a personality expert, and he can identify effectiveness of performance more readily. Albert W. Schrader says that men want their performance and not their character discussed during a performance review.[16]

However, results-oriented approaches also suffer from possible shortcomings. Some of these are:

1. The results identified (objectives, goals, standards) may not

be attainable. This can create frustration with a resulting decline in employee motivation.

2. The results may be established without employee participation. This can lead to misunderstanding and resentment by the employee and consequently have a negative impact on motivation.

3. In the police field, results that are oriented to crime-related objectives may act as incentives to subvert the procedural rights of citizens in order to be successful as determined by established objectives.

A Results-Oriented Appraisal System

The general appraisal system suggested in this section incorporates features of several results-oriented methods. These methods avoid many of the problems inherent in the evaluation of personal traits of the employee, and, if the system is based on participative management, it will increase the probability of achieving the desired results. Participative management emphasizes two-way communication between employee and rater, advocates that the employee become an active participant in determining the results to be used for evaluation, and places the rater in a supportive role with the employee in facilitating successful performance. The relationship between rater and employee should be based on mutual trust and confidence. In this setting, both rater and employee should be active participants in the appraisal process.

An initial step in establishing a results-oriented system is to develop employee objectives to be accomplished in a given time period. As discussed in Chapter 3, this is a difficult step in police agencies because of the qualitative nature of many of the services performed. Qualitative, as opposed to quantitative, objectives provide subjective criteria for evaluation, and evaluations may suffer from many of the shortcomings of person-oriented evaluations. In addition, when quantifiable objectives are selected, there may be a danger of establishing a quasi-official "quota system," or the objectives may function as an incentive to deviate from due process of law. These problems are not impossible to overcome if the proper intent of the objectives is established and systematic consideration is given to selecting objectives that are related to effective performance.

The appraisal process requires continuous observation and monitoring of the police officer's progress toward realizing established objectives. When problem areas are detected, or during periodic consultations, the rater's supportive role becomes important in seeking out causes and assisting the employee in finding productive solutions. At designated times, an appraisal session should be held between rater and employee to discuss job performance, objectives, strengths, weaknesses, and plans for improvement. The rater's role should be supportive and positive. If such a relationship cannot be established, a third party—preferably a behavioral scientist who is an internal or external consultant—should assist in developing relations between rater and employee. During the appraisal session, three primary activities should take place:

1. The police officer's past job performance should be appraised in relation to the accomplishment of previously developed objectives. Problems, if any, should be identified and discussed and solutions sought.

2. A plan for the further growth and development of the police officer should be designed, with special emphasis on eliminating weaknesses and shortcomings. The plan can include recommendations for more training and education, a job transfer, or any other reasonable action that the police officer can take to improve job performance.

3. New objectives should be developed for the next appraisal period.

On completion of this phase of the appraisal process, the rater should provide a detailed narrative report to his immediate supervisor in the three areas described. If the plan for improvement requires the approval of another individual, the report should be forwarded to the appropriate person. If the improvement plan is approved as written, the police officer is informed, and he proceeds to implement the recommended actions. If the plan is disapproved or modified, another discussion should be held between the rater and the police officer to develop a new plan or to discuss the acceptability of a modified plan. If a new plan is developed, the cycle is repeated until the plan is acceptable to all concerned. This process will facilitate integration of individual and organizational objectives.

Possible benefits of using a results-oriented appraisal system are as follows:

1. Changing evaluation from a controlling to a planning tool that will enhance employee development[17]

2. Changing from essentially subjective to objective criteria in appraisal

3. Changing from negatively-based to positively-based motivational techniques

4. Changing from a "personality analysis" that often angers employees to an open climate of free communication and willingness to discuss results and the problems in realizing those results[18]

5. Changing from an organization-directed "acceptable day's work" to employee-directed creative efforts

6. Reducing turnover and absenteeism as a result of higher job commitment

7. Improving individual performance and organizational productivity

Professionalism in Community Police Organizations

Professionalism is reserved for this final chapter for four reasons: (1) it is an appropriate way in which to conclude the book; (2) a commitment to some concept of professionalism is the most effective mechanism for controlling police, because such a commitment is closely related to internal control; (3) on both an organizational and an individual level, the historical concern for controlling police in the community has been a recurring issue; and (4) without some concept of police professionalism as related to democratic society, the effective control of police organizations by the community, and of behavior and activity of individual officers by the police manager, will be difficult if not impossible.

Professionalism can be considered from several perspectives—as recognized by others, as an attitude, and as a form of flexible, responsive behavior to changing community needs.

Some of the fields that have traditionally been considered

professions include law, medicine, and religion. These fields are recognized as such by society because they meet the criteria of professionalism:

1. A protracted period of formal education to acquire specialized knowledge
2. A strong commitment to service related to the professional area
3. Some form of licensing or certification
4. A high degree of mobility from job to job and community to community
5. Self-regulation or policing by peers

Other vocational pursuits are increasingly being considered as professions—teaching, engineering, nursing, and public administration, to mention a few. Persons in other vocations or occupations also often have the attitudes associated with professionalism. A professional attitude is normally a commitment to the objective and effective performance of the work involved in the occupation. Individuals in many occupations have a strong desire to do the best possible job. This reflects a professional attitude about their work and often carries over into work behavior.

Professional behavior is the consistent acting out of the commitment to be objective and effective and, in the case of police, to be equitable in law enforcement. For police, professional behavior is not rigid, or fixed and narrow, but is represented by responsiveness to changing needs in the community. The failure of some police in the 1960s to maintain a posture of behavioral professionalism often led to increasing demands for community control of police.

This community control movement has taken, and is taking, many forms. Suggestions include improvement of internal police investigations, citizen review boards, an ombudsman, and reorganization of police departments to insure that each identifiable community (blacks and youth, for example) politically shares "control" of the police agency.

If police can identify and maintain a strong commitment to behavioral professionalism, demands for community control of police are likely to occur less often and be less extreme. The concept of behavioral professionalism for police organizations is closely related to the discussion of policing styles. Each style, however, reflects varying degrees of professionalism. The most responsive, and effective, is the integrated approach to policing. Such a style will increase the professional orientation that police should seek. The status associated with being recognized as a profession, which the police are not as yet, may appear quite desirable, but the personal attitude of being a professional is an even more desirable goal.

In addition to considering the style of the community police agency in terms of its concept of professional behavior, each agency and officer must decide on a guiding philosophy of policing. Figure 32 depicts four possible philosophical orientations, or models, that are useful in characterizing available alternatives.

Figure 32
Professional Model of Policing Behavior

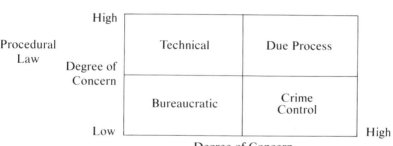

These orientations are based on the degree of concern for substantive law (that is, laws that define the elements of crimes) and procedural law (that is, the legal process associated with enforcing substantive law). The four possible combinations are as follows:

1. Low concern for substantive and procedural law (bureaucratic model)

2. High concern for procedural, low concern for substantive law (technical model)

3. High concern for substantive, low concern for procedural law (crime control model)

4. High concern for both substantive and procedural law (due process model)

Each of these models characterizes a philosophy of policing—a set of beliefs held by the police organization and/or officers concerning the role of the police in the community. It is often reflected in goals, policies, and individual officer behavior. A policing style includes not only the policing philosophy but also community expectations of the police role. A policing style is the adjustment of the philosophy to community expectations.

The bureaucratic philosophy is slow, rigid, sluggish, and indifferent. It reflects behavior that is concerned only with "getting by." The technical philosophy is overly concerned with the technicalities of procedural law and reflects relative inaction—only the "legalities" of contemplated action are considered. The due process and crime control models are concepts borrowed from Herbert C. Packard. The crime control philosophy reflects more of a concern for getting the job done and catching criminals than it does for the manner in which both are accomplished. The attitude of the crime control model is that the police are waging a war on crime and that any techniques are acceptable to win that war. The due process model reflects an equal concern for substantive and procedural criminal law. The police are concerned with individual rights and constitutional safeguards but are not fearful of being aggressive or taking action within the spirit of the law when the precise meaning of what is permitted is unclear.

The ideal model in moving toward behavioral professionalism is a combination of the integrated policing style with a due process philosophy of policing. Perhaps the most counterproductive, least professional, and most resented is the punitive style coupled with the crime control policing philosophy. These two together, unless checked by responsible action of police themselves, will inevitably lead to widespread complaints of brutality and repression.

The Outlook for Police Professionalism

Will police ever be recognized as professionals? This is a most difficult question to answer, but there are strong indications that the accepted criteria of professionalism are beginning to be realized, however gradually, in police agencies. Currently, over five hundred institutions of higher learning offer police or police-related degree programs. More and more police agencies are encouraging, and in some cases requiring, their officers to have some college training for employment and/or promotion. In addition, many states now have standardized training requirements for officers and provide some form of certification.

The knowledge to be transferred in the formal education process also appears to be increasing. More and more books, journal articles, government documents, and related materials are beginning to identify significant information useful to effective police performance.

The mobility criterion of a profession is not yet being realized in police organizations. While top police officials, such as the chief, and those at the bottom, the patrol officers, are often mobile, there is minimal mobility of ranks in between. Some efforts are being made to overcome problems of mobility, or lateral transfer, but there will probably be a long waiting period before lateral transfer is widespread.

The service commitment needed for recognized professionalism is often apparent among police, but the service ideal must have both form and substance. The form and substance are provided by consideration of a policing style and a guiding philosophy, or model, of policing behavior.

A recognition of professionalism can have an important meaning in the continued growth and development of American community police. However, the concept of behavioral professionalism is even more important, because it is through behavior—organizational and individual—that effectiveness and equity in the police-community relationship will be determined. Controlling the police will come primarily through an ideal of what policing is, and not through the controlling system that is created by the police organization. Police managers must come to grips with the policing ideal and inculcate that ideal in each and every police officer in the United States.

Summary

This final chapter has been concerned with the last, and first, stage of the managerial process. Controlling completes the planning-organizing-leading-controlling cycle, but the knowledge derived from the controlling stage provides the basis for starting to plan again. The managerial process is a cycle that is never over.

Controlling is the process by which standards are compared with activity and behavior, deviations are detected and analyzed, and corrective action is taken. Important concerns in evaluation and controlling include the general standard categories of efficiency, effectiveness, and productivity. All are important concepts in managerial controlling.

One of the most important areas of controlling is related to personnel evaluation. Human resources are the key to the success of any organized endeavor, and the way they are evaluated is important to insure high levels of motivation and learning.

Controlling discussions for managers tend to concentrate on externally described systems emphasizing standards, supervisors, and reports. More important is the concept of internal control, or a personal commitment to effective performance. The core of internal control for police is professionalism, both in the recognition of policing as a profession and in the activity and behavior of individual officers and community police organizations.

Suggested
Reading

Barrett, Richard S. *Performance Rating.* Chicago: Science Research Associates, 1966.

Beach, Dale S. *Personnel: The Management of People at Work.* New York: Macmillan, 1965.

Beck, George M. "Municipal Police Performance Rating." *Journal of Criminal Law, Criminology and Police Science* 51 (January–February 1961): 568–575.

Bristow, Allen P. "A Comparative Examination of Performance Rating Forms by Police Agencies." *Police* 5 (January–February 1961): 18–24.

Cleland, David I., and King, William R. *Management: A Systems Approach.* New York: McGraw-Hill, 1972.

Davis, Keith. *Human Behavior at Work.* 4th ed. New York: McGraw-Hill, 1972.

Eastman, George D., and Eastman, Esther M., eds. *Municipal Police Administration.* 6th ed. Washington, D.C.: International City Management Association, 1969.

Epstein, Sidney, and Jayman, Richard S. *Guidelines for Police Performance*

Appraisal, Promotion and Placement Procedures. Washington, D.C.: National Institute of Law Enforcement and Criminal Justice, 1973.

Flippo, Edwin B. *Principles of Personnel Management.* 3rd ed. New York: McGraw-Hill, 1971.

Germann, A. C. *Police Personnel Management.* Springfield, Ill.: Charles C. Thomas, 1958.

Halmann, Theo. *Professional Management: Theory and Practice.* Boston: Houghton Mifflin, 1962.

Iannone, N. F. *Supervision of Police Personnel.* Englewood Cliffs, N.J.: Prentice-Hall, 1970.

Kassoff, Norman C. *The Police Management System.* Washington, D.C.: International Association of Chiefs of Police, 1967.

Kepner, Charles H., and Tregoe, Benjamin B. *The Rational Manager.* New York: McGraw-Hill, 1965.

Kindall, Alva F., and Gatza, James. "Positive Program for Performance Appraisal." *Personnel Management Series,* reprints from the *Harvard Business Review,* pp. 97–104.

Lopez, Felix M., Jr. *Evaluating Employee Performance.* Chicago: Public Personnel Association, 1968.

Myrtle, Robert C. "Employee Evaluation Systems." In Gilbert B. Siegel, ed., *Human Resource Management in Public Organizations; A Systems Approach.* Los Angeles: University Publishers, 1973, pp. 510–558.

Schrader, Albert W. "Let's Abolish the Annual Performance Review." *Management of Personnel.* 8 (Fall 1969): 22–28.

Sloan, Stanley, and Johnson, Alton C. "New Context for Personnel Appraisal." *Harvard Business Review* 46 (November–December 1968): 4–10.

Stahl, O. Glenn. *Public Personnel Administration.* 6th ed. New York: Harper & Row, 1971.

Stokes, Paul M. *A Total Systems Approach to Management Control.* New York: American Management Association, 1968.

Notes

CHAPTER 1   MANAGEMENT OF COMMUNITY POLICE AGENCIES

1. Edwin Powers, *Crime and Punishment in Early Massachusetts, 1620–1692* (Boston: Beacon Press, 1966), pp. 424–426.

2. Eugene F. Rider, "The Denver Police Department: An Administrative, Organizational and Operational History, 1858–1905" (Ph.D. diss., University of Denver, 1971); and George A. Ketcham, "Municipal Police Reform: A Comparative Study of Law Enforcement in Cincinnati, Chicago, New Orleans, New York and St. Louis, 1844–1877" (Ph.D. diss., University of Missouri, 1967).

3. For some histories of American policing prior to the twentieth century, see the following: Roger Lane, *Policing the City: Boston, 1822–1885* (Cambridge: Harvard University Press, 1967); James F. Richardson, *The New York Police: Colonial Times to 1901* (New York: Oxford University Press, 1970); Patrick B. Nolan, "Vigilantes on the Middle Border: Study of Self-Appointed Law Enforcement in the States of the Upper Mississippi from 1840–1880" (Ph.D.

diss., University of Minnesota, 1971); Selden D. Bacon, "Early Development of American Municipal Police: Study of the Evolution of Formal Controls in a Changing Society" (Ph.D. diss., Yale University, 1939, 2 vols.); Hardean L. Bonkrude, "Crime and Its Treatment in Minneapolis and St. Anthony in 1880" (Ph.D. diss., University of Minnesota, 1970); and Phillip N. Spiller, "Short History of the San Antonio Police Department" (Master's thesis Trinity University, 1954).

4. Kevin E. Jordan, "Ideology and the Coming of Professionalism: American Urban Police in the 1920's and 1930's" (Ph.D. diss., Rutgers University, 1972).

5. Roland L. Warren, *Studying Your Community* (New York: Free Press, 1965).

6. Peter C. Unsinger and Harry H. Caldwell, "There's a Tavern on the Edge of Town: Impact of Tavern Locations on Police Patrol" (paper presented to the Northwest Science Association Meeting, April 1971).

7. Albert J. Shafter, "Numerical Strength of Small Police Departments," *Journal of Criminal Law, Criminology and Police Science* 52 (September–October 1961): 344–351.

8. John A. Gardiner, *Traffic and the Police: Variations in Law Enforcement Policy* (Cambridge,: Harvard University Press, 1969).

9. Harold D. Lasswell, *Politics: Who Gets What, When, How* (Cleveland: World, 1958).

10. Knowlton W. Johnson, "Police Interaction and Referral Activity with Personnel of Other Social Regulatory Agencies" (Ph.D. diss., Michigan State University, 1971).

11. William A. Westley, "The Police: A Sociological Study of Law, Custom and Morality" (Ph.D. diss., University of Chicago, 1951); Michael Banton, *The Policeman in the Community* (New York: Basic Books, 1964); and Jerome Skolnick, *Justice Without Trial* (New York: John Wiley, 1966).

12. James Q. Wilson, *Varieties of Police Behavior* (Cambridge: Harvard University Press, 1968).

CHAPTER 2   THE HUMAN ORGANIZATION

1. Keith Davis, *Human Behavior at Work*, 4th ed. (New York: McGraw-Hill, 1972), p. 390.

2. Adapted from Elizabeth Marting, Robert E. Finley, and Anna Word, *Effective Communication on the Job*, 5th ptg., rev. ed. (New York: American Management Association, 1963), pp. 293–295.

3. Adapted from Keith Davis, *Human Behavior at Work*, p. 396.

4. A. H. Maslow, *Motivation and Personality* (New York: Harper & Row, 1954).

5. J. W. Atkinson, *An Introduction to Motivation* (Princeton: D. Van Nostrand, 1958); David C. McClelland, *Assessing Human Motivation* (Morristown, N.J.: General Learning Press, 1971; and George H. Litnin and Robert A. Stringer, Jr., *Motivation and Organization Climate* (Boston: Graduate School of Business Administration, Harvard University, 1968).

6. Frederick Herzberg, *Work and the Nature of Man* (Cleveland: World, 1966).

7. William J. Reddin, *Managerial Effectiveness* (New York: McGraw-Hill, 1970), pp. 20–22.

8. Fred E. Fiedler, *A Theory of Leadership Effectiveness* (New York: McGraw-Hill, 1967); and Fred Luthans, *Organizational Behavior* (New York: McGraw-Hill, 1973), pp. 500–502.

9. Rensis Likert, *The Human Organization* (New York: McGraw-Hill, 1967).

10. Robert Blake and Jane Mouton, *The Managerial Grid* (Houston: Gulf, 1964). (Normally the grid system is illustrated, but that is not necessary for this discussion.)

11. Jay Hall, Jerry B. Harvey, and Martha Williams, *Styles of Management Inventory and Interpretive Score Sheet* (Conroe, Texas: Teleometrics International, n.d.).

12. Paul Hersey and Kenneth H. Blanchard, *Management of Organizational Behavior*, 2nd ed. (Englewood Cliffs, N.J.: Prentice-Hall, 1972), pp. 133–147.

13. Fiedler, *A Theory of Leadership Effectiveness*, p. 219.

14. Ideas taken from Rensis Likert, *The Human Organization*, and Robert Blake and Jane Mouton, *The Managerial Grid*.

15. Douglas McGregor, *The Human Side of Enterprise* (New York: McGraw-Hill, 1960).

16. Emette S. Redford, *Democracy in the Administrative State* (New York: Oxford Press, 1969), p. 56.

CHAPTER 3   MANAGEMENT BY OBJECTIVES/RESULTS

1. This MBO/R system was developed by the Systems Development Corporation for a California police agency.

CHAPTER 4   PLANNING CONCEPTS AND METHODS

1. Harold E. Pepinsky, "Police Decisions to Report Offenses" (Ph.D. diss., University of Pennsylvania, 1972), p. 93. The researcher found that when a dispatcher named the offense involved in the dispatch, the responding officer involved himself to a greater extent than when the dispatch excluded mention of an actual offense.

2. Department of Police, City and County of Denver, Colorado, *Research and Development Evaluation Survey*, July, 1972.

3. Michael E. Milakovich, "Politics of Block-Grant Law Enforcement Assistance: Impact of the Omnibus Crime Control Act on Local Government Agencies in Indiana" (Ph.D. diss., Indiana University, 1972); Committee on Government Operations, House of Representatives, 92nd Congress, 2nd Session, *Block Grant Programs of the Law Enforcement Assistance Administration* (Washington, D.C.: U.S. Government Printing Office, 1972); and Committee on the Judiciary, House of Representatives, 93rd Congress, 1st Session, *Hearings on Law Enforcement Assistance Administration* (Washington, D.C.: U.S. Government Printing Office, 1973).

4. For an excellent explanation of these OR techniques, see Robert J. Thierauf, and Richard A. Grosse, *Decision Making Through Operations Research* (New York: John Wiley, 1970).

CHAPTER 5   DECISION-MAKING AND POLICY FORMULATION

1. Sol N. Davidson, *The Cultivation of Imperfection: The Power of Negative Thinking* (New York: Frederick Fell, 1965), p. 38.

2. Robert R. Blake and Jane S. Mouton, *The Managerial Grid* (Houston: Gulf, 1964).

3. The continuum of leadership behavior developed by Robert Tannenbaum and Warren H. Schmidt is employed and liberties are taken with their theory. See "How to Choose a Leadership Pattern," *Harvard Business Review* 36, no. 2 (March–April 1958): 95–101.

4. David Braybrooke and Charles Lindblom, *A Strategy of Decision* (New York: Free Press, 1963); Charles E. Lindblom, *The Intelligence of Democracy: Decision-Making Through Mutual Adjustment* (New York: Free Press, 1965); and Charles E. Lindblom, *The Policy-Making Process* (Englewood Cliffs, N.J.: Prentice-Hall, 1968).

5. Robert E. Agger, Daniel Goldrich, and Bert E. Swanson, *The Rulers and the*

Ruled (New York: John Wiley, 1964). Although this book is drawn from the political realm of decision-making, many of the same processes are at work in law enforcement agencies.

6. Some authorities contend that each group musters support and often amends its position or solution until the decision desired appeals to the decision-maker(s). For a discussion of this phenomenon in mass movements and radical groups, see John W. Bowens and Donovan J. Ochs, *The Rhetoric of Agitation and Control* (Reading, Mass.: Addison-Wesley, 1971). For a discussion of how groups form and disappear over policy issues see William S. Riker, *The Theory of Political Coalitions* (New Haven, Conn.: Yale University Press, 1962). For a discussion of shared and unshared goals in the formation of groups and subcoalitions, see Richard N. Cyert and James March, *Behavorial Theory of the Firm* (Englewood Cliffs, N.J.: Prentice-Hall, 1963).

7. See Paul N. Whisenand and R. Fred Ferguson, *Managing of Police Organizations* (Englewood Cliffs, N.J.: Prentice-Hall, 1973, pp. 21–25 for an excellent analysis of the value systems at work in law enforcement.

8. See E. G. Bublitz, "An Analysis of Cynicism Within Law Enforcement" (Ph.D. diss., University of Utah, 1973) for examples of clarity and confusion of roles and the absence or presence of cynicism in the different agencies (Utah State Highway Patrol and Salt Lake City Police Department) and between divisions (patrol, investigation, and so on).

9. See Anthony Downs, *Inside Bureaucracy* (Boston: Little, Brown, 1967), and Preston P. LeBreton, *Administrative Intelligence—Knowledge and Policy in Government and Industry* (New York: Basic Books, 1967) for the problems involved in gathering and comprehending information.

10. First articulated in 1938, the concept remains valid. See Chester I. Barnard, *The Functions of the Executive* (Cambridge: Harvard University Press, 1966).

11. See footnote 6 as well as Victor Thompson, *Modern Organization: A General Theory* (New York: Alfred A. Knopf, 1961).

12. For examples of internal resistance to departmental policy decisions, see L. W. Sherman, C. H. Milton, and T. V. Kelly, *Team Policing: Seven Case Studies* (Washington, D.C.: Police Foundation, 1973), p. 32; and Robert R. LaBerge, "The Employment of Reserve Police Officers in Follow-up Investigations" (master's thesis, San Jose State University, 1973), p. 27.

13. Norton E. Long, "The Local Community as an Ecology of Games," *American Journal of Sociology* 63 (November 1958): 251–261.

CHAPTER 6   MANPOWER DETERMINATION AND ALLOCATION

1. This is perhaps the most common use of the workload-functional model. See John P. Kenney, *Police Administration* (Springfield, Ill.: Charles C. Thomas, 1972), pp. 156–180; and O. W. Wilson and Roy McLaren, *Police Administration*, 3rd ed. (New York: McGraw-Hill, 1972), pp. 692–704. The discussion by Wilson amd MacLaren emphasizes methods of allocation and distribution more than their determination, but several of the factors are related. See also Orville E. Butts, "Determining Police Manpower Needs" (master's thesis, California State University, San Jose, 1972).

2. George D. Eastman and Esther M. Eastman, eds., *Municipal Police Administration*, 6th ed. (Washington, D.C.: International City Management Association, 1969), pp. 130–131. This widely used primer in police management suggests that the investigative unit should be no more than 10 per cent of the total sworn personnel. The book also discusses general workload considerations. See Kenney, *Police Administration*, pp. 160–180, for a discussion of investigations.

3. See Kenney, *Police Administration*, p. 158, as an example. See Butts, "Determining Police Manpower Needs," pp. 91–112.

4. See Kenney, *Police Administration*, p. 156; Wilson and MacLaren, *Police Administration*, pp. 696–697; and Butts, "Determining Police Manpower Needs," p. 110.

5. See individual and coauthored articles of J. F. Elliott in the following issues of *Police:* November–December 1968, pp. 65–71; November–December 1968, pp. 51–55; May–June 1969, pp. 34–41; and May–June 1970, pp. 44–53. See also Richard C. Larson, *Urban Police Patrol Analysis* (Cambridge: Massachusetts Institute of Technology Press, 1972).

6. *Ibid.*

CHAPTER 7   BUDGETS AND BUDGETING

1. James A. Maxwell, *Financing State and Local Governments*, rev. ed. (Washington, D.C.: Brookings Institution, 1969), p. 127.

2. For some views on the politics involved in the budgetary process, see Arnold J. Meltser, *The Politics of City Revenue* (Berkeley: University of California Press, 1971) for the pressures exerted on how the jurisdiction will get the funds; and Aaron Wildavsky, *The Politics of the Budgetary Process* (Boston: Little,

Brown, 1964) for a discussion of the decisions of who will get what and how to spend it.

3. Marcel J. Jojola, "Rio Dell Community Mobilization" (paper developed for Middle Management Program, San Jose State University, September 1973).

4. Herbert Sydney Duncombe, *County Government in America* (Washington, D.C.: National Association of Counties, 1966), table, "Percent Distribution of General Revenues," p. 112.

5. For an excellent analysis of federal revenue sharing, see William Willner and John P. Nichols, *Revenue Sharing* (Washington, D.C.: Pro Plan International Ltd., Inc., 1973).

6. The descriptions of these phases of the budgeting process or cycle are based on information supplied by Capt. George C. Stephenson and Lt. James Scales of the Belmont, California, Police Department; Lt. Peter Quevada, Hayward, California, Police Department; Capt. Art Thomas, Compton, California, Police Department; and Chief Ray Shipley, Eureka, California, Police Department.

7. John F. Dolan, "The P.P.B. Concept," *The Police Chief* 35 (July 1968): 28–31; and Frank J. Leahy, Jr., "Planning Program Budgeting System," *The Police Chief* 35 (July 168): 16–27.

8. Materials developed and utilized on the PPBS were provided by Sgt. Richard Gummow, Sgt. Larry Thannisch, and Lt. Stanley Horton of the San Jose, California, Police Department.

CHAPTER **8** ORGANIZING: TRADITIONAL AND SYSTEMS APPROACHES

1. For an interesting discussion on these three schools of thought see William G. Scott, *Organizational Theory: A Behavioral Analysis for Management* (Homewood, Ill.: Richard D. Irwin, 1967), pp. 100–150.

2. *Ibid.*

3. For an analysis of this organizing guideline see Leonard J. Kazmier, *Principles of Management*, 2nd ed. (New York: McGraw-Hill, 1969), pp. 115–118.

4. Scott, *Organizational Theory*, pp. 100–150.

5. John M. Pfiffner and Frank P. Sherwood, *Administrative Organization* (Englewood Cliffs, N.J.: Prentice-Hall, 1960), pp. 16–32.

6. Scott, *Organizational Theory*, pp. 100–150; and David I. Cleland and William R. King, *Management: A Systems Approach* (New York: McGraw-Hill, 1972), pp. 29–114.

7. Cleland and King, *Management*, pp. 337–362.

8. Perhaps the most extensive analysis is provided in John P. Kenney, *Police Administration* (Springfield, Ill.: Charles C. Thomas, 1972), pp. 55–102.

9. David I. Cleland and William R. King, *Systems Analysis and Project Management* (New York: McGraw-Hill, 1968), pp. 135–284.

CHAPTER 9   RECRUITMENT, SELECTION, AND TRAINING OF
PERSONNEL

1. Joseph Kimble, "Recruitment," in Richard Blum, ed., *Police Selection* (Springfield, Ill.: Charles C. Thomas, 1964), pp. 71–84; and O. W. Wilson, *Police Planning*, 2nd ed. (Springfield, Ill: Charles C. Thomas, 1958), pp. 233–234.

2. Everett N. King, *The Auxiliary Police Unit* (Springfield, Ill.: Charles C. Thomas, 1960), p. 70.

3. Kimble, "Recruitment," p. 84.

4. For a more complete description of a selection strategy model, see Lee J. Cronbach and Goldine C. Gleser, *Psychological Tests and Personnel Decisions*, 2nd ed. (Urbana: University of Illinois Press, 1965).

5. Professional Standards Division, International Association of Chiefs of Police, *Model Police Standards Council Program* (Washington, D.C.: International Association of Chiefs of Police, 1968).

6. For an interesting challenge to the big push for "educated" law enforcement officers, see Ivar Berg, *Education and Jobs: The Great Training Robbery* (New York: Frederick Praeger, 1972).

7. George W. O'Connor, "Survey of Selection Methods," *The Police Chief* 29, nos. 10, 11, and 12 (October–December 1962).

8. Robert D. Keppel, "Survey of Physical Agility Requirements and Current Application at the Entry Level of Law Enforcement" (master's thesis, Washington State University, 1967).

9. Forbes E. McCann et al., *Physical Condition Tests in the Selection of Public Employees* (Chicago: Public Personnel Association, 1963); and H. Harrison Clarke, *Application of Measurement to Health and Physical Education* (Englewood Cliffs, N.J.: Prentice-Hall, 1960).

10. John Guidici, "The Oral Board," in Blum, *Police Selection*, pp. 178–198.

11. Thomas W. Oglesby, "Survey of Psychiatric or Psychological Testing of Police Applicants" (master's thesis, University of Southern California, 1957); and O'Connor, "Survey of Selection Methods."

12. The four tests administered were the California Test of Mental Maturity,

The Allport-Vernon Scale of Values, The Edwards Personality Preference Schedule, and the Minnesota Multiphasic Personality Inventory. Nick J. Colarelli and Saul M. Siegal, "Method of Police Personnel Selection," *Journal of Criminal Law, Criminology, and Police Science* 55, no. 2 (June 1964).

13. Charles D. Gooch, "Inquiry into the Use of the Polygraph in Application Evaluation and Personnel Screening" (master's thesis, Michigan State University, 1964).

14. O. W. Wilson, *Police Administration*, 2nd ed. (New York: McGraw-Hill, 1963); and John N. Nickerson, "Appraisal of Selected Personnel and Training Characteristics Practices and Requirements in Municipal Law Enforcement Agencies and Their Impact upon the Functioning of Governmental Administration" (Ph.D. diss., University of Idaho, 1970).

15. Rand Institute, *Police Background Characteristics and Performance* (New York: Rand Institute, 1972).

16. Thomas N. Frost, *Forward Look in Police Education* (Springfield, Ill.: Charles C. Thomas, 1959), pp. 39–54. Although it is not specifically directed toward law enforcement, see also the Manpower Administration's *Handbook for Analyzing Jobs* (Washington, D.C.: Department of Labor, 1972).

17. International Association of Chiefs of Police, *Police Training: Report to the President's Commission on Law Enforcement and Administration of Justice* (Washington, D.C.: International Association of Chiefs of Police, 1966).

18. President's Commission on Law Enforcement and Administration of Justice, *Task Force Report: The Police* (Washington, D.C.: U.S. Government Printing Office, 1967).

19. Harry Diamond, "Factors in Planning and Evaluating In-Service Training Programs," *Journal of Criminal Law, Criminology and Police Science* 53, no. 4 (December 1962).

20. Los Angeles County Sheriff's Department, *Career Development for Law Enforcement* (Washington, D.C.: Law Enforcement Assistance Administration, 1973).

CHAPTER **10** EVALUATION AND CONTROLLING

1. The approach used to develop the controlling system is adopted from Paul M. Stokes, *A Total Systems Approach to Management Control* (New York: American Management Association, 1968), p. 14.

2. Rensis Likert, *The Human Organization* (New York: McGraw-Hill, 1967).

3. Richard S. Barrett, *Performance Rating* (Chicago: Science Research Associates, 1966), p. 1.

4. Felix M. Lopez, Jr., *Evaluating Employee Performance* (Chicago: Public Personnel Association, 1968), p. 25.

5. Dale S. Beach, *Personnel: The Management of People at Work* (New York: Macmillan, 1965), pp. 257–258.

6. Leonard D. White, *Introduction to the Study of Public Administration*, 4th ed. (New York: Macmillan, 1955), p. 393.

7. George M. Beck, "Municipal Police Performance Rating," *Journal of Criminal Law, Criminology and Police Science* 51 (January–February 1961): 568–575.

8. George D. Eastman and Esther M. Eastman, eds., *Municipal Police Administration*, 6th ed. (Washington, D.C.: International City Management Association, 1969), p. 186.

9. A. C. Germann, *Police Personnel Management* (Springfield, Ill.: Charles C. Thomas, 1958), p. 156.

10. Robert C. Myrtle, "Employee Evaluation Systems," in Gilbert B. Siegel, ed., *Human Resource Management in Public Organizations: A Systems Approach* (Los Angeles: University Publishers, 1973), pp. 510–558.

11. Lopez, *Evaluating Employee Performance*, p. 134.

12. N. F. Iannone, *Supervision of Police Personnel* (Englewood Cliffs, N.J.: Prentice-Hall, 1970), p. 189.

13. White, *Introduction to the Study of Public Administration*, p. 272.

14. Alva F. Kindall and James Gatza, "Positive Program for Performance Appraisal," *Personnel Management Series*, reprints from the *Harvard Business Review*, pp. 97–104.

15. Stanley Sloan and Alton C. Johnson, "New Context for Personnel Appraisal," *Harvard Business Review* 46 (November–December 1968): 4–10.

16. Albert W. Schrader, "Let's Abolish the Annual Performance Review," *Management of Personnel* 8 (Fall 1969): 22–28.

17. Sloan and Johnson, "New Context for Personnel Appraisal," pp. 4–10.

18. Kindall and Gatza, "Positive Program for Performance Appraisal," pp. 97–104.

Additional Reading

The education and growth of the law enforcement manager does not rely on a single book. The following bibliography was compiled to supply to the manager a list of books worthy of his further study. The bibliography does not include works already cited in the footnotes and suggested readings in each chapter of this book. Nor does the list include books published before 1960, since they are often unavailable for purchase. Should a book or books be of interest, the manager should consult the latest edition of *Books in Print* at his local library or bookstore to see whether the book is available.

Abt, Clark C. *Serious Games.* New York: Viking Press, 1970.

Ackoff, Russell L. *Concept of Corporate Planning.* New York: John Wiley, 1970.

Ackoff, Russell L., and Rivett, Patrick. *Manager's Guide to Operations Research.* New York: John Wiley, 1963.

Albright, Lewis A.; Glennon, J. R.; and Smith, Wallace J. *The Use of Psychological Tests in Industry.* Cleveland: Howard Allen, 1963.

Altshuler, Alan A. *The City Planning Process: A Political Analysis.* Ithaca, N.Y.: Cornell University Press, 1965.

American Management Association. *Computer-Based Management for Information and Control.* Management Bulletin 30. New York: American Management Association, 1963.

————. *Control Through Information.* Management Bulletin 24. New York: American Management Association, 1963.

————. *Motivation and Productivity.* New York: American Management Association, 1963.

Anderson, Richard C. *Management Strategies.* New York: McGraw-Hill, 1965.

Andrews, Kenneth R. *Concept of Corporate Strategy.* Homewood, Ill.: Dow Jones–Irwin, 1971.

Anthony, Robert N. *Management Accounting: Text and Cases.* Homewood, Ill.: Richard D. Irwin, 1965.

————. *Planning and Control Systems: A Framework for Analysis.* Boston: Division of Research, Graduate School of Business Administration, Harvard University Press, 1965.

Anthony, Robert N.; Dearden, John; and Vaneil, R. N. *Management Control Systems.* Homewood, Ill.: Richard D. Irwin, 1965.

Applewhite, Philip B. *Organizational Behavior.* Englewood Cliffs, N.J.: Prentice-Hall, 1965.

Archibald, R. D., and Villoria, R. L. *Network Based Management Systems.* New York: John Wiley, 1967.

Argyris, Chris. *Integrating the Individual in the Organization.* New York: John Wiley, 1964.

————. *Interpersonal Competence and Organizational Effectiveness.* Homewood, Ill.: Richard D. Irwin, 1962.

————. *Management and Organizational Development: The Path From XA to YB.* New York: McGraw-Hill, 1971.

————. *Understanding Organizational Behavior.* Homewood, Ill.: Dorsey Press, 1960.

Association of Pennsylvania Municipal Managers, 1962 Research Committee. *Inter-Governmental Purchasing Agreements.* Pittsburgh: University of Pittsburgh, Institute of Local Government, 1962.

————. *The Establishment of a Centralized Specification Agency.* Pittsburgh: University of Pittsburgh, Institute of Local Government, 1962.

Atkinson, John W., and Feather, Norman T. *Theory of Achievement Motivation.* New York: John Wiley, 1966.

Aurner, Robert R., and Wolf, Morris P. *Effective Communication in Business.* 5th ed. Cincinnati: South-Western, 1967.

Aussieker, M. W., Jr. *Police Collective Bargaining.* Public Employees Relations Library, n. 18. Chicago: Public Personnel Association, 1969.

Banathy, Bela H. *Instructional Systems.* Palo Alto, Calif.: Fearon, 1968.

Bartley, Ernest R., and Bair, F. H., Jr. *Mobile Home Parks and Comprehensive Community Planning.* Gainesville: Public Administration Clearing House, University of Florida, 1960.

Barton, Richard. *Primer on Simulation and Gaming.* Englewood Cliffs, N.J.: Prentice-Hall, 1970.

Bass, Bernard M. *Leadership, Psychology and Organizational Behavior.* New York: Harper & Row, 1960.

Bassett, Glen A., and Weatherbee, H. Y. *Personnel Systems and Data Management.* New York: American Management Association, 1971.

Batten, T. R. *Human Factor in Community Work.* New York: Oxford University Press, 1965.

Beer, Michael. *Leadership, Employee Needs and Motivation.* Columbus: Bureau of Business Research, Ohio State University Press, 1966.

Behavioral Research Service. *Performance Appraisal Based on Self Review.* Crotonville, N.Y.: General Electric Company, 1965.

Bell, G. D. *Organizations and Human Behavior.* Englewood Cliffs, N.J.: Prentice-Hall, 1967.

Bell, Wendell; Hill, Richard J.; and Wright, Charles R. *Public Leadership.* San Francisco: Chandler, 1961.

Bellman, Richard E., and Dreyfus, Stuart E. *Applied Dynamic Programming.* Santa Monica, Calif.: Rand Corporation, 1962.

Bellows, R.; Gilson, T.; and Odiorne, G. S. *Executive Skills: Their Dynamics and Development.* Englewood Cliffs, N.J.: Prentice-Hall, 1962.

Bennett, Thomas R. *The Leader and the Process of Planned Change.* New York: Association Press, 1962.

Bennis, Warren G. *Changing Organizations.* New York: McGraw-Hill, 1966.

———. *Organization Development: Its Nature, Origins and Prospects.* Reading, Mass.: Addison-Wesley, 1969.

Bennis, Warren G., et al., eds. *Interpersonal Dynamics: Essays and Readings on Human Interaction.* 2nd ed. Homewood, Ill.: Dorsey Press, 1968.

Bennis, Warren G., and McGregor, Caroline, eds. *The Professional Manager.* New York: McGraw-Hill, 1967.

Bennis, Warren G.; Benne, Kenneth; and Chin, Robert. *The Planning of Change.* 2nd ed. Toronto: Holt, Rinehart & Winston, 1969.

Berelson, Bernard, and Steiner, Gary A. *Human Behavior: Inventory of Scientific Findings.* New York: Harcourt, Brace & World, 1964.

Bergen, Garret L., and Haney, William V. *Organizational Relations and Management Action.* New York: McGraw-Hill, 1966.

Berkley, George E. *The Administrative Revolution: Notes on the Passing of Organization Man.* Englewood Cliffs, N.J.: Prentice-Hall, 1971.

Berne, Eric. *Structure and Dynamics of Organizations and Groups.* New York: Grove Press, 1966.

Berry, Dean F. *The Politics of Personnel Research.* Ann Arbor: Bureau of Industrial Relations, University of Michigan Press, 1967.

Black, Guy. *The Application of Systems Analysis to Government Operations.* New York: Frederick Praeger, 1968.

Black, James M. *Positive Discipline.* New York: American Management Association, 1970.

Blake, Robert R., and Mouton, Jane S. *Corporate Excellence Through*

Grid Organization Development: A Systems Approach. Houston: Gulf, 1968.

―――. *Group Dynamics: Key to Decision Making.* Houston: Gulf, 1961.

Blanchard, Robert E., et al. *Development of a Technique for Establishing Personnel Performance Standards.* Springfield, Va.: Defense Documentation Center, 1966.

Blau, Peter. *Exchange and Power in Social Life.* New York: John Wiley, 1964.

―――. *The Dynamics of Bureaucracy.* Chicago: University of Chicago Press, 1963.

Blau, Peter, and Scott, Richard. *Formal Organizations.* San Francisco: Chandler, 1962.

Bloomington, Minnesota, Personnel Office. *Joint Recruitment of Policemen by Bloomington and Burnsville, Minnesota: A Case Study.* Bloomington, Minn.: Personnel Office, 1965.

Blumenthal, Sherman C. *Management Information Systems.* Englewood Cliffs, N.J.: Prentice-Hall, 1968.

Blyth, John W., and Johnson, Robert G. *How to Conduct the Appraisal Interview.* New York: Argyle, 1967.

Boulding, Kenneth E. *Social Dynamics.* New York: Free Press, 1970.

Bradford, L. P., ed. *Group Development.* Washington, D.C.: National Training Labs, National Education Association, 1961.

Bradford, Leland P.; Gibb, Jack R.; and Benne, Kenneth D. *T-Group Theory and Laboratory Method.* New York: John Wiley, 1964.

Branch, Melville C. *City Planning and Aerial Information.* Cambridge: Harvard University Press, 1971.

Breth, Robert D. *Dynamic Management Communications.* Reading, Mass.: Addison-Wesley, 1969.

Brickner, W. H. *Decision-Making Process.* San Jose, Calif.: Lansford, 1973.

―――. *Future Planning and Strategy Development.* San Jose, Calif.: Lansford, 1972.

Bristow, Allen P. *Effective Police Manpower Utilization.* Springfield, Ill.: Charles C. Thomas, 1969.

Bristow, Allen P., and Gabard, E. Caroline. *Decision Making in Police Administration.* Springfield, Ill.: Charles C. Thomas, 1961.

Brush, E. C., and Chapman, J. F. *New Decision Making Tools for Managers.* New York: Mentor, 1963.

Buckley, Walter. *Sociology and Modern Systems Theory.* Englewood Cliffs, N.J.: Prentice-Hall, 1967.

Burnham, James. *The Managerial Revolution.* Bloomington: Indiana University Press, 1960.

Burns, Tom, and Stalker, G. M. *Management of Innovation.* London: Pergamon Press, 1961.

Burns, T. J. *The Use of Accounting Data in Decision Making.* Columbus: Ohio State University Press, 1967.

Bursk, Edward C., and Chapmans, John F., eds. *New Decision-Making Tools for Managers.* Cambridge: Harvard University Press, 1963.

Byham, William C. *The Uses of Personnel Research.* New York: American Management Association, 1968.

Caiden, Gerald. *Administrative Reform.* Chicago: Aldine, 1969.

————. *Dynamics of Public Administration: Guidelines to Current Transformations in Theory and Practice.* New York: Holt, Rinehart & Winston, 1971.

Callender, J. C., ed. *Time-Saver Standards: Handbook of Architectural Design.* New York: McGraw-Hill, 1966.

Caplan, Edwin H. *Management Accounting and Behavioral Science.* Menlo Park, Calif.: Addison-Wesley, 1971.

Carlson, P. G. *Quantitative Methods for Managers.* New York: Harper & Row, 1967.

Cartwright, Dorwin, and Zander, Alvin F., eds. *Group Dynamics: Research Theory.* 2nd ed. Evanston, Ill.: Row Peterson, 1960.

Carzo, Rocco, Jr., and Yanouzas, John. *Formal Organization.* Homewood, Ill.: Richard D. Irwin, 1967.

Chaiken, Jan J., and Larson, Richard C. *Methods for Allocating Urban Emergency Units.* R-680-HUD/NSF. New York: Rand Institute, May 1971.

Chapin, F. Stuart, Jr. *Urban Land Use Planning.* 2nd ed. Urbana: University of Illinois Press, 1965.

Chapman, Samuel G. *Police Manpower and Population Changes in Michigan Communities of 10,000 or More Population, 1950–60.* East Lansing: Institute for Community Development and Services, Michigan State University Press, 1961.

Chicago Police Department, Operations Research Task Force. *Allocation of Resources in the Chicago Police Force.* November 1969.

Cohen, Arthur R. *Attitude Change and Social Influence.* New York: Basic Books, 1964.

Colbert, John, and Hohn, Marcia. *Guide to Manpower Training.* Morningside Heights, N.Y.: Behavioral Publishing, 1971.

Collins, Barry E., and Guetzkow, Harold. *Social Psychology of Group Processes for Decision-Making.* New York: John Wiley, 1964.

Cooper, Joseph D. *How to Get More Done in Less Time.* New York: Doubleday, 1962.

Cornog, G. Y., et al. *EDP Systems in Public Management.* Chicago: Rand McNally, 1968.

Costello, Timothy W., and Zalkind, Sheldon S. *Psychology in Administration.* Englewood Cliffs, N.J.: Prentice-Hall, 1963.

Crecine, John P., ed. *Financing the Metropolis.* Beverly Hills, Calif.: Sage, 1970.

Crouch, Winston W. *Employer-Employee Relations in Council-Manager Cities.* Washington, D.C.: International City Management Association, 1968.

Dailey, Charles A., and Dyer, Frederick C. *How to Make Decisions about People.* West Nyack, N.Y.: Parker, 1966.

Dale, Ernest. *Management: Theory and Practice.* New York: McGraw-Hill, 1965.

Dalton, Melville. *Men Who Manage.* New York: John Wiley, 1960.

Dalton, R. H. *Personality and Social Interaction.* Boston: D. C. Heath, 1961.

Davis, Kenneth. *Human Relations at Work: Dynamics of Organizational Behavior.* New York: McGraw-Hill, 1967.

Dearden, John, and McFarlan, I. W. *Management Information Systems.* Homewood, Ill.: Richard D. Irwin, 1966.

DeGreene, Kenyon B., ed. *Systems Psychology.* New York: McGraw-Hill, 1970.

Department of the Interior. *Guide for Training Supervisors in Merit Promotion.* Washington, D.C.: U.S. Government Printing Office, 1969.

Department of the Navy. *Application of Decision Theory and Scaling Methods to Selection Test Evaluation.* Alexandria, Va.: Defense Documentation Center, 1967.

Department of Personnel, State of Washington. *Promotional Evaluation Manual for Supervisors.* Olympia: Department of Personnel, State of Washington, 1968.

Dimock, Marshall, and Dimock, Gladys. *Public Administration.* New York: Holt, Rinehart & Winston, 1964.

Drabek, Thomas E. *Laboratory Simulation of a Police Communication System Under Stress.* Columbus: College of Administrative Science, Ohio State University Press, 1968.

Drucker, Peter. *The Effective Executive.* New York: Harper & Row, 1967.

Dubin, Robert. *Human Relations in Administration.* Englewood Cliffs, N.J.: Prentice-Hall, 1961.

Due, John F. *Government Finance: Economics of the Public Sector.* 4th ed. Homewood, Ill.: Richard D. Irwin, 1968.

Duncan, Hugh Dalziel. *Symbols in Society.* New York: Oxford University Press, 1968.

Dunn, Delmer D. *Public Officials and the Press.* Reading, Mass.: Addison-Wesley, 1969.

Dynes, Russell R. *The Functioning of Expanding Organization in Community Disasters.* Columbus, Ohio: Disaster Research Center, 1968.

Eckman, Donald P., ed. *Systems: Research and Design.* New York: John Wiley, 1961.

Eckstein, Otto. *Public Finance.* Englewood Cliffs, N.J.: Prentice-Hall, 1964.

Elliott, J. F., and Sardino, J. F. *Crime Control Team: Experiment in Municipal Police Department Management and Operations.* Springfield, Ill.: Charles C. Thomas, 1971.

Ellis, David O., and Ludwig, Fred J. *Systems Philosophy.* Englewood Cliffs, N.J.: Prentice-Hall, 1962.

Emery, F. F., ed. *Systems Thinking.* Baltimore: Penguin Books, 1969.

Etzioni, Amitai. *Comparative Analysis of Complex Organizations.* New York: Free Press, 1961.

———. *The Active Society: Theory of Societal and Political Processes.* New York: Free Press, 1971.

Ewing, David W. *The Managerial Mind.* New York: Free Press of Glencoe, 1964.

Fagin, Henry. *The Policies Plan: Instrumentality for a Community Dialogue.* Pittsburgh: Institute for Local Government, University of Pittsburgh, 1965.

Feinberg, Mortimer R. *Effective Psychology for Managers.* Englewood Cliffs, N.J.: Prentice-Hall, 1965.

Fendrock, John J. *Goals in Conflict: Personal vs. Business Success.* New York: American Management Association, 1969.

Fennessy, Edward F., et al. *The Technical Content of State and Community Police Traffic Services Programs.* Hartford, Conn.: Travelers Research Center, 1968.

Filley, Alan C., and House, Robert J. *Managerial Process and Organizational Behavior.* Glenview, Ill.: Scott, Foresman, 1969.

Finn, Thomas A. *Local Government and Politics: Analyzing Decision-Making Systems.* Palo Alto, Calif.: Scott, Foresman, 1970.

Fishburn, Peter C. *Decision and Value Theory.* New York: John Wiley, 1964.

Fisk, Donald M. *Indianapolis Police Fleet Plan: Example of Program Evaluation for Local Government.* Washington, D.C.: Urban Institute, 1970.

Flagle, Charles D.; Huggins, William H.; and Roy, Robert H., eds. *Operations Research and Systems Engineering.* Baltimore: Johns Hopkins University Press, 1960.

Folsom, Marion B. *Executive Decision-Making.* New York: McGraw-Hill, 1962.

Ford, R. W. *Motivation Through the Work Itself.* New York: American Management Association, 1969.

Frieden, Bernard J., and Morris, Robert, eds. *Urban Planning and Social Policy.* New York: Basic Books, 1968.

Friedman, Robert S. *Professionalism: Expertise and Policy Making.* Morristown, N.J.: General Learning Corporation, 1972.

Gagné, R. M. *Perspectives on Curriculum Evaluation.* Chicago: Rand McNally, 1967.

Gagné, Robert M., ed. *Psychological Principles in System Development.* New York: Holt, Rinehart & Winston, 1966.

Galvin, Raymond, and Radelet, Louis. *A National Survey of Police and Community Relations.* East Lansing: Michigan State University Press, 1967.

Gardner, Neely. *Effective Executive Practices.* New York: Doubleday, 1963.

Gaudet, Frederick J. *Solving the Problems of Employee Absence.* New York: American Management Association, 1963.

Gawthrop, Louis C. *Bureaucratic Behavior in the Executive Branch: Analysis of Organizational Change.* New York: Free Press, 1969.

Gellerman, Saul W. *Management by Motivation.* New York: American Management Association, 1968.

———. *Management of Human Relations.* New York: Holt, Rinehart & Winston, 1966.

———. *Motivation and Productivity.* New York: American Management Association, 1963.

Gellhorn, Walter. *When Americans Complain: Governmental Grievance Procedures.* Cambridge: Harvard University Press, 1966.

General Electric Computer Departments. *Critical Path Method Program.* GE-200 Series, CD225KL 104 rev. November 1964. Phoenix: Computer Department, General Electric Company, 1964.

Glans, Thomas B., et al. *Management Systems.* New York: Holt, Rinehart & Winston, 1968.

Goeller, B. F. *Modeling the Traffic Safety System.* Rand Study RM-5633-DOT. April 1968.

Goldman, T. A. *Cost Effectiveness Analysis.* New York: Frederick Pracger, 1967.

Golembiewski, Robert T. *Behavior Organization.* Chicago: Rand McNally, 1962.

————. *Men, Management and Morality.* New York: McGraw-Hill, 1965.

Golembiewski, Robert T., and Gibson, Frank, eds. *Managerial Behavior and Organization Demands: Management as a Linking of Levels of Interaction.* Chicago: Rand McNally, 1967.

Golembiewski, Robert T., and Cohen, Michael, eds. *People in Public Service.* Itasca, N.Y.: Peacock, 1970.

Goodman, William I., and Freund, Eric C., eds. *Principles and Practice of Urban Planning.* Washington, D.C.: International City Management Association, 1968.

Gore, William J., and Dyson, J. W., eds. *The Making of Decisions: Reader in Administrative Behavior.* New York: Free Press, 1964.

Goslin, David A. *The Search for Ability: Standardized Testing in Social Perspective.* New York: Russell Sage Foundation, 1963.

Gottesman, Jay. *Personality Patterns of Urban Police Applicants as Measured by the MMPI.* Hoboken, N.J.: Stevens Institute of Technology Press, 1969.

Greenwood, P. W. *Long-Range Planning in the Criminal Justice System: What State Planning Agencies Can Do.* Santa Monica, Calif.: Rand Corporation, June 1970.

Greenwood, William T., ed. *Management and Organizational Behavior Theories: Interdisciplinary Approach.* Cincinnati: South-Western, 1965.

Grosser, Charles F. *New Directions in Community Organization: From Enabling to Advocacy.* New York: Praeger, 1973.

Guest, Robert H. *Organizational Change: The Effect of Successful Leadership.* Homewood, Ill.: Dorsey Press, 1964.

Hackman, Ray C. *The Motivated Working Adult.* New York: American Management Association, 1969.

Hacon, R. J. *Conflict and Human Relations Training.* London: Pergamon Press, 1965.

Haire, Mason. *Psychology in Management.* 2nd ed. New York: McGraw-Hill, 1964.

Hampton, David R., ed. *Modern Management: Issues and Ideas.* Belmont, Calif.: Dickenson, 1969.

Haney, William V. *Communication and Organizational Behavior: Text and Cases.* Rev. ed. Homewood, Ill.: Richard D. Irwin, 1967.

Hardwick, C. T., and Landuyt, B. F. *Administrative Strategy.* New York: Simmons-Boardman, 1961.

Hare, A. Paul. *Handbook of Small Group Research.* New York: Free Press of Glencoe, 1962.

Hare, A. Paul; Borgatta, Edgar F.; and Bales, Robert F., eds. *Small Groups: Studies in Social Interaction.* Rev. ed. New York: Alfred A. Knopf, 1965.

Hauser, Norbert, et al. *Computer Simulation of a Police Emergency Response System.* LEA Grant No. 030. Brooklyn: Polytechnic Institute, 1969.

Haveman, Robert H., and Margolis, Julius, eds. *Public Expenditures and Policy Analysis.* Chicago: Markham, 1970.

Hawley, Willis D., and Wirt, Frederick M. *The Search for Community Power.* Englewood Cliffs, N.J.: Prentice-Hall, 1968.

Healy, Richard J. *Emergency and Disaster Planning.* New York: John Wiley, 1969.

Hearle, Edward F. R. *Can EDP Be Applied to All Police Agencies?* Santa Monica, Calif.: Rand Corporation, October 1961.

Herber, Bernard P. *Modern Public Finance: Study of Public Sector Economics.* Rev. ed. Homewood, Ill.: Richard D. Irwin, 1971.

Hersey, Paul. *Management Concepts and Behavior: Programmed Instruction for Managers.* Little Rock, Ark.: Marvern, 1967.

Heyel, Carl. *Organizing Your Job in Management.* New York: American Management Association, 1960.

————. *Sharper Skills for Administrators and Managers.* Stamford, Conn.: Motivation, 1969.

Hill, George E. *Management and Improvement of Guidance.* New York: Appleton-Century-Crofts, 1965.

Hillier, F. S., and Lieberman, G. J. *Introduction to the Techniques of Operations Research.* San Francisco: Holden-Day, 1967.

Hirsch, Werner Z., et al. *Fiscal Pressures on the Central City: The Impact of Commuters, Non-whites and Overlapping Governments.* New York: Praeger, 1971.

Hodge, Barton, and Hodgson, Robert. *Management and the Computer in Information and Control Systems.* New York: McGraw-Hill, 1969.

Hoeh, David C., ed. *Collective Bargaining in the Public Sector.* Hanover, N.H.: University Press of New England, 1968.

House, Robert J., et al. *Management Development: Design, Evaluation and Implementation.* Ann Arbor: Bureau of Industrial Relations, University of Michigan, 1967.

Hovey, Harold A. *Planning-Programming-Budgeting Approach to Government Decision-Making.* New York: Praeger, 1968.

Huckshorn, Robert J., et al. *Cooperative Centralization of Purchasing for Idaho Municipalities.* Moscow: University of Idaho, Bureau of Public Affairs Research, 1962.

Hughes, James W. *Urban Indicators, Metropolitan Evolution, and Public Policy.* New Brunswick: Transaction, 1973.

Human Factors Research, Inc. *Factors Influencing the Judgment of Human Performance.* Santa Barbara, Calif.: Human Factors Research, Inc., 1966.

Huneryager, S. G., and Heckman, I. L. *Human Relations in Management.* 2nd ed. Cincinnati: South-Western, 1967.

Hunt, I. C., Jr., and Cohen, Bernard. *Minority Recruiting in the New York City Police Department.* Part I, "Attraction of the Candidates"; Part II, "Retention of the Candidates." Rand Corporation Study R-702-NYC, May 1971.

Hutchinson, John. *Management Strategy and Tactics.* New York: Holt, Rinehart & Winston, 1971.

Inbar, Michael, and Stoll, Clarice. *Simulation and Gaming in Social Science.* New York: Free Press, 1971.

Isard, Walter, et al. *Methods of Regional Analysis: An Introduction to Regional Science.* Boston: Technology Press of Massachusetts Institute of Technology, 1960.

Jacobs, P. I.; Maier, M. H.; and Stolurow, L. W. *Guide to Evaluating Self-Instructional Programs.* New York: Holt, Rinehart & Winston, 1966.

Jeffery, C. Ray. *Crime Prevention Through Environmental Design.* Beverly Hills, Calif.: Sage, 1971.

Jennings, E. M. *An Anatomy of Leadership.* New York: Harper, 1960.

———. *The Executive: Autocrat, Bureaucrat, Democratic.* New York: Harper & Row, 1962.

Jerome, W. T., III. *Executive Control: The Catalyst.* New York: John Wiley, 1961.

Johnson, R. A.; Kast, F. E.; and Rosenzweig, J. E. *The Theory and Management of Systems.* New York: McGraw-Hill, 1967.

Kahn, Alfred J. *Planning Community Services for Children in Trouble.* New York: Columbia University Press, 1963.

Kakalik, James S., and Wildhorn, Sorrel. *Aids to Decision-Making in Police Patrol.* R-593/594HUD/RC, 2 vols. Santa Monica, Calif.: Rand Corporation, February 1971.

Kanter, J. *Management Guide to Computer System Selection and Use.* Englewood Cliffs, N.J.: Prentice-Hall, 1970.

Karrass, Chester L. *The Negotiating Game.* Cleveland: World, 1970.

Kassoff, Norman C. *Organization Concepts.* Washington, D.C.: International Association of Chiefs of Police, 1967.

Katz, David, and Kahn, Robert L. *The Social Psychology of Organizations.* New York: John Wiley, 1966.

Kelleher, Grace J., ed. *The Challenge to Systems Analysis: Public Policy and Social Change.* New York: John Wiley, 1970.

Kellogg, Marion. *Putting Management Theories to Work.* Houston: Gulf, 1968.

———. *What to Do About Performance Appraisal.* New York: American Management Association, 1965.

Kennedy, Will C.; Brooks, J. Michael; and Vargo, Stephen M. *The Police*

Department in Disaster Operations. Columbus, Ohio: Disaster Research Center, Ohio State University Press, September 1969.

Kenney, John P., and Williams, John B. *Police Operations.* 2nd ed. Springfield, Ill.: Charles C. Thomas, 1968.

Killian, Ray A. *Managing by Design—or Maximum Executive Effectiveness.* New York: American Management Association, 1968.

King, Bert T., and McGinnies, Elliott, eds. *Attitudes, Conflict and Change.* New York: Academic Press, 1972.

Koontz, Harold, ed. *A Unified Theory of Management.* New York: McGraw-Hill, 1964.

Koontz, Harold, and O'Donnell, Cyril. *Principles of Management: Analysis of Managerial Functions.* 4th ed. New York: McGraw-Hill, 1968.

Larson, Richard C. *Measuring the Response Patterns of New York City Police Patrol Cars.* Rand Study R-673-NYC/HUD. New York: Rand Corporation, July 1971.

———. *Models for the Allocation of Urban Police Patrol Forces.* Cambridge: Massachusetts Institute of Technology Operations Research Center, 1969.

———. *Operational Study of the Police Response System.* Tech. report no. 26. Cambridge: Massachusetts Institute of Technology, 1967.

Lawrence, Paul R., and Lorsch, Jay W. *Developing Organizations: Diagnosis and Action.* Reading, Mass.: Addison-Wesley, 1969.

———. *Organization and Environment: Managing Differentiation and Integration.* Boston: Graduate School of Business Administration, Harvard University, 1967.

Lawrence, Paul R., et al. *Organizational Behavior and Administration: Cases, Concepts and Research Findings.* Homewood, Ill.: Dorsey Press, 1961.

Learned, Edmund P., and Sproat, Audrey T. *Organization Theory and Policy: Notes for Analysis.* Homewood, Ill.: Richard D. Irwin, 1966.

LeBreton, Preston P. *General Administration: Planning and Implementation.* New York: Holt, Rinehart & Winston, 1965.

Lee, Alec M. *Systems Analysis Frameworks.* New York: John Wiley, 1970.

Leonard, V. A. *Police Patrol Organization.* Springfield, Ill.: Charles C. Thomas, 1970.

———. *The Police Communication System.* Springfield, Ill.: Charles C. Thomas, 1970.

———. *The Police Detective Function.* Springfield, Ill.: Charles C. Thomas, 1970.

Levine, Robert A. *Public Planning: Failure and Redirection.* New York: Basic Books, 1972.

Levy, F. K.; Thompson, G. L.; and Wiest, J. D. *Mathematical Basis of the Critical Path Method.* Pittsburgh: Carnegie Institute of Technology, 1962.

Lifton, W. M. *Working with Groups.* 2nd ed. New York: John Wiley, 1967.

Litterer, Joseph A. *Organizations: Structures and Behavior.* New York: John Wiley, 1963.

———. *The Analysis of Organizations.* New York: John Wiley, 1965.

Longenecker, Justin G. *Principles of Management and Organizational Behavior.* 2nd ed. Columbus, Ohio: Charles E. Merill, 1969.

Lopez, Felix M. *Evaluating Executive Decision Making: The In-Basket Technique.* New York: American Management Association, 1966.

Luft, Joseph. *Group Processes: Introduction to Group Dynamics.* Palo Alto, Calif.: National Press Books, 1970.

Lyden, Fremont J., and Miller, Ernest G. *Planning-Programming-Budgeting: Systems Approach to Management.* Chicago: Markham, 1972.

Lyden, F. J., et al., eds. *Policies, Decisions and Organization.* New York: Appleton-Century-Crofts, 1969.

McEwen, Thomas, project director. *Allocation of Patrol Manpower Resources in the St. Louis Police Department.* Washington, D.C.: International Association of Chiefs of Police, July 1966.

McGregor, Douglas. *Leadership and Motivation.* Boston: Massachusetts Institute of Technology Press, 1966.

———. *The Professional Manager.* New York: McGraw-Hill, 1967.

McLennan, Kenneth. *Managerial Skill and Knowledge.* Madison: University of Wisconsin, Industrial Relations Research Institute, 1967.

McMurry, Robert N. *Tested Techniques of Personnel Selection.* Chicago: Dartnell Corporation, 1966.

McPherson, Joseph H. *How Are They, Are We, Am I Doing? The Organization, Division, Group and Individual Performance Appraisal and Feedback System.* Midland, Tex.: Pendell, 1968.

Mack, Ruth P. *Planning on Uncertainty: Decision Making in Business and Government Administration.* New York: John Wiley, Interscience, 1972.

Madsen, K. B. *Theories of Motivation.* 4th ed. Kent, Ohio: Kent State University Press, 1968.

Mager, Robert F. *Preparing Instructional Objectives.* Palo Alto, Calif.: Fearon, 1962.

Maier, Norman R. F. *Frustration.* Ann Arbor: University of Michigan Press, 1961.

———. *Problem Solving Discussions and Conferences: Leadership Methods and Skills.* New York: McGraw-Hill, 1963.

Maier, Norman R. F., and Hayes, J. J. *Creative Management.* New York: John Wiley, 1962.

Mailick, Sidney, and Van Ness, Edward H., eds. *Concepts and Issues in Administrative Behavior.* Englewood Cliffs, N.J.: Prentice-Hall, 1962.

Malcolm, D. G. *Extensions and Applications of PERT as a System Management Tool.* Washington, D.C.: Armed Forces Management Association, 1961.

Manpower Administration, U.S. Department of Labor. *Handbook for Analyzing Jobs.* Washington, D.C.: U.S. Government Printing Office, 1972.

March, James, and Simon, Herbert A. *Organizations.* New York: John Wiley, 1965.

Marini, Frank, ed. *Toward a New Public Administration: The Minnowbrook Perspective.* Scranton, Pa.: Chandler, 1971.

Marrow, A. J.; Bowers, D. G.; and Seashore, S. E., eds. *Strategies of Organizational Change.* New York: Harper & Row, 1967.

Martin, Roscoe C., et al. *Decisions in Syracuse: A Metropolitan Action Study.* Bloomington: Indiana University Press, 1961.

Maslow, Abraham. *Eupsychian Management.* Homewood, Ill.: Richard D. Irwin, 1965.

Massie, Joseph L. *Essentials of Management.* Englewood Cliffs, N.J.: Prentice-Hall, 1964.

Megginson, Leon. *Personnel: Behavioral Approach to Administration.* Homewood, Ill.: Richard D. Irwin, 1967.

Merewitz, Leonard, and Sosnick, Stephen H. *The Budget's New Clothes: Critique of Planning-Programming-Budgeting and Benefit-Cost Analysis.* Chicago: Markham, 1972.

Mesarovic, Mihajlo D., ed. *Views on General Systems Theory.* New York: John Wiley, 1964.

Michigan State University, Institutes for Community Development. *Police Training in the Detroit Metropolitan Region: Recommendations for a Regional Approach.* Detroit: Metropolitan Fund, 1966.

Michigan State University, National Center on Police and Community Relations, School of Police Administration and Public Safety. *A National Survey of Police and Community Relations.* Washington, D.C.: U.S. Government Printing Office, 1967.

Miller, Delbert C. *Handbook of Research Design and Social Measurement.* 2nd ed. New York: David McKay, 1970.

Miller, D. W., and Starr, M. K. *Executive Decisions and Operations Research.* Englewood Cliffs, N.J.: Prentice-Hall, 1969.

Miller, Eric J., and Rice, Albert K. *Systems of Organization: The Control of Task and Sentient Boundaries.* London: Tavistock, 1967.

Miller, Harry L. *Teaching and Learning in Adult Education.* New York: Macmillan, 1964.

Miner, J. B. *The Management of Ineffective Performance.* New York: McGraw-Hill, 1963.

Mishan, E. J. *Cost-Benefit Analysis.* New York: Praeger, 1971.

Mockler, Robert. *Business Planning and Policy Formulation.* New York: Appleton-Century-Crofts, 1972.

Morris, Lud. *The Art of Motivating.* Boston: Industrial Education Institute, 1968.

Morse, Philip M., and Bacon, Laura W., eds. *Operations Research for Public Systems.* Cambridge: Massachusetts Institute of Technology Press, 1967.

Morse, Wilmer W. *Guidelines for Holding Disciplinary Hearings.* Chicago: Public Personnel Association, 1966.

Morton, Jack A. *Organizing for Innovation.* New York: McGraw-Hill, 1971.

Mott, Paul E. *Shift Work.* Ann Arbor: University of Michigan Press, 1965.

Munro, Jim L. *Administrative Behavior and Police Organization.* Cincinnati: W. H. Anderson, 1973.

Murphy, Thomas P. *Government Management Internships and Executive Development.* Lexington, Mass.: D. C. Heath, 1973.

Muth, Richard F. *Cities and Housing: The Spatial Pattern of Urban Residential Land Use.* Chicago: University of Chicago Press, 1969.

Myers, M. Scott. *Every Employee a Manager.* New York: McGraw-Hill, 1970.

National Institute of Law Enforcement and Criminal Justice. *Police Telecommunication Systems.* Washington, D.C.: U.S. Government Printing Office, 1971.

———. *Utilization of Helicopters for Police Air Mobility.* Washington, D.C.: U.S. Government Printing Office, 1971.

Neff, Walter S. *Work and Human Behavior.* New York: Atherton Press, 1968.

Neuschel, R. F. *Management by System.* 2nd ed. New York: McGraw-Hill, 1960.

Newman, A. D., and Rowbottom, R. W. *Organization Analysis: Guide to the Better Understanding of the Structural Problems of Organizations.* Carbondale: Southern Illinois University Press, 1968.

Newman, William H.; Sumner, Charles E.; and Warren, E. Kirby. *The Process of Management.* Englewood Cliffs, N.J.: Prentice-Hall, 1967.

Nierenberg, Gerard I. *Art of Negotiating.* New York: Hawthorn Books, 1968.

Nigro, Felix A. *Management-Employee Relations in the Public Service.* Chicago: Public Personnel Association, 1969.

Novick, David, ed. *Program Budgeting.* Cambridge: Harvard University Press, 1965.

O'Connor, George W. *Survey of Selection Methods.* Washington, D.C.: International Association of Chiefs of Police, 1962.

Odiorne, G. S. *How Managers Make Things Happen.* Englewood Cliffs, N.J.: Prentice-Hall, 1961.

———. *Management by Objectives.* New York: Pitman, 1965.

Office of Law Enforcement Assistance. *Crime Laboratories: Three Study Reports.* Washington, D.C.: U.S. Government Printing Office, 1966.

Olmstead, Joseph A. *Instructor's Guide to Performance Counseling.* Washington, D.C.: George Washington University, Human Resources Research Office, 1968.

Olson, Bruce T. *Police Expenditures.* U.S. Presidential Commission on Law Enforcement and Administration of Justice. Washington, D.C.: U.S. Government Printing Office, 1967.

Optner, Stanford L. *Systems Analysis for Business Management.* Englewood Cliffs, N.J.: Prentice-Hall, 1968.

Pappas, Nick, ed. *The Jail: Its Operations and Management.* Washington, D.C.: U.S. Bureau of Prisons, Department of Justice, 1970.

Parten, Mildred. *Surveys, Polls and Samples: Practical Procedures.* New York: Cooper Square, 1966.

Peabody, Robert L. *Organizational Authority.* New York: Atherton Press, 1964.

Perlman, Robert, and Jones, David. *Neighborhood Service Centers.* Washington, D.C.: Office of Juvenile Delinquency and Youth Development, Department of Health, Education and Welfare, 1967.

Perrow, Charles. *Organizational Analysis: A Sociological View.* Belmont, Calif.: Wadsworth, 1970.

Peter, Lawrence J., and Hull, Raymond J. *The Peter Principle.* New York: William Morrow, 1969.

Peters, Charles, and Branch, Taylor, eds. *Blowing the Whistle: Dissent in the Public Interest.* New York: Praeger, 1972.

Peters, Lynn H. *Management and Society.* Belmont, Calif.: Dickenson, 1968.

Pfiffner, John M. *The Function of the Police in a Democratic Society.* Los Angeles: University of Southern California, 1967.

Phelps, Edmund S., ed. *Private Wants and Public Needs.* New York: Norton, 1962.

Pierce, Lawrence C. *Politics of Fiscal Policy Formation.* Pacific Palisades, Calif.: Goodyear, 1971.

Pigors, Paul, and Myers, Charles A. *Personnel Administration: A Point of View and Method.* New York: McGraw-Hill, 1969.

Piven, Herman, and Alcabes, Abraham. *Education, Training and Manpower in Corrections and Law Enforcement.* Washington, D.C.: U.S. Government Printing Office, 1966.

Pomrenke, Norman E. *Law Enforcement Manual: Rules and Regulations.* Chapel Hill: Institute of Government, University of North Carolina, 1967.

Porter, Lyman W., and Lawler, Edward E. *Managerial Attitude and Performance.* Homewood, Ill.: Richard D. Irwin, 1968.

Press, Charles, and Arian, Alan. *Empathy and Ideology: Aspects of Administrative Innovation.* Chicago: Rand McNally, 1966.

Press, S. James. *Some Effects of an Increase in Police Manpower in the 20th Precinct of New York City.* Rand Study R-704-NYC. New York: New York City Rand Institute, 1971.

Public Personnel Association. *1966 Survey of Examination Appeal Procedures.* Chicago: Public Personnel Association, 1966.

———. *Survey of Probationary Period Practices.* Chicago: Public Personnel Association, 1968.

———. *Survey of Residence Requirements.* Chicago: Public Personnel Association, 1968.

———. *Survey of Selection Procedures.* Chicago: Public Personnel Association, 1966.

———. *Survey of Veteran Preference Policies.* Chicago: Public Personnel Association, 1968.

Puget Sound Governmental Conference, 1962. *Regional Joint County Jail District: Feasibility Study.* Seattle, Wash.: Puget Sound Governmental Conference, 1962.

Quade, E. S. *Systems Analysis Techniques for Planning-Programming-Budgeting.* Santa Monica, Calif.: Rand Corporation, 1966.

Quade, E. S., and Boucher, W. I., eds. *Systems Analysis and Policy Planning.* New York; American Elsevier, 1968.

Rabinovitz, Francine F. *City Politics and Planning.* New York: Atherton Press, 1969.

Raiffa, Howard, and Schlaifer, Robert. *Applied Statistical Decision Theory.*

Boston: Division of Research, Graduate School of Business Administration, Harvard University, 1961.

Randall, C. B. *The Folklore of Management.* New York: Mentor, 1962.

Ranney, David C. *Planning and Politics in the Metropolis.* Columbus, Ohio: Charles E. Merrill, 1969.

Rappaport, Alfred, ed. *Information for Decision Making.* Englewood Cliffs, N.J.: Prentice-Hall, 1970.

Raser, John R. *Simulation and Society: Exploration of Scientific Gaming.* Boston: Allyn & Bacon, 1969.

Reinke, Roger W. *Design and Operation of Police Communications Systems.* Washington, D.C.: International Association of Chiefs of Police, 1964.

Reuss, Henry S. *Revenue-Sharing: Crutch or Catalyst for State and Local Governments?* New York: Praeger, 1970.

Richards, Max D. and Greenlaw, Paul S. *Management Decision Making.* Homewood, Ill.: Rchard D. Irwin, 1966.

Richmond, S. B. *Operations Research for Management Decisions.* New York: Ronald Press, 1968.

Rieder, Robert J. *Law Enforcement Information Systems.* Springfield, Ill.: Charles C. Thomas, 1972.

Ripley, R. R., ed. *Public Policies and Their Politics.* New York: Norton, 1966.

Rivett, Patrick. *Introduction to Operations Research.* New York: Basic Books, 1968.

Roberts, Edward B. *The Dynamics of Research and Development.* New York: Harper & Row, 1964.

Roby, T. B. *Small Group Performance.* Chicago: Rand McNally, 1968.

Roman, Daniel D. *Research and Development Management: The Economics and Administration of Technology.* New York: Appleton-Century-Crofts, 1968.

Rome, B. K. and Rome, S. C. *Organizational Growth Through Decision Making: Computer Based Experiment in Educative Method.* New York: American Elsevier, 1971.

Sayles, Leonard R, and Strauss, George. *Human Behavior in Organizations.* Englewood Cliffs, N.J.: Prentice-Hall, 1966.

Schaller, Lyle E. *The Change Agent: The Strategy of Innovative Leadership.* New York: Abingdon Press, 1972.

Scheer, Wilbert E. *Personnel Director's Handbook.* Chicago: Dartnell Corporation, 1969.

Schein, Edgar H. *Organizational Psychology.* Englewood Cliffs, N.J.: Prentice-Hall, 1965.

Schein, Edgar H. and Bennis, Warren G. *Personal and Organizational Change Through Group Methods.* New York: John Wiley, 1965.

Schellenberger, R. E. *Managerial Analysis.* Homewood, Ill.: Irwin, 1969.

Schlesinger, James R. *Uses and Abuses of Analysis.* Washington, D.C.: U.S. Government Printing Office, 1968.

Schoderbek, Peter T. *Management Systems: Book of Readings.* New York: John Wiley, 1967.

Schwartz, Louis B., and Goldstein, Stephen R. *Police Guidance Manuals: Phila-*

delphia Model. Philadelphia: University of Pennsylvania Printing Office, 1968.

Scott, William G. *Human Relations in Management.* Homewood, Ill.: Richard D. Irwin, 1962.

————. *Management of Conflict: Appeal Systems in Organizations.* Homewood, Ill.: Dorsey Press, 1965.

Smalheiser, Irwin. *Analyzing the Application for Employment.* Davenport, Iowa: Personnel Associates, 1962.

Smelser, Neil J. *Theory of Collective Behavior.* New York: Free Press, 1962.

Smith, R. D. *Computer Applications in Police Manpower Distribution.* Washington, D.C.: International Association of Chiefs of Police, 1961.

Smithies, Arthur. *Government Decision-Making and the Theory of Choice.* Santa Monica, Calif.: Rand Corporation, 1964.

South Carolina ETV Network. *Potential Use of Educational Television to Accomplish the Objectives of the Omnibus Crime Bill.* Columbia: South Carolina ETV, Law Enforcement Division, January 1969.

Steiner, Gary A., ed. *The Creative Organization.* Chicago: University of Chicago Press, 1971.

Stenzel, Anne K., and Feeney, Helen M. *Volunteer Training and Development: Manual for Community Groups.* New York: Seabury Press, 1968.

Sterling, James W. *Changes in Role Concept of Police Officers.* Washington, D.C.: International Association of Chiefs of Police, 1968.

Stewart, Daniel K. *The Psychology of Communication.* New York: Funk & Wagnalls, 1968.

Strauss, George, and Sayles, Leonard R. *Personnel: The Human Problems of Management.* 2nd ed. Englewood Cliffs, N.J.: Prentice-Hall, 1967.

Strecher, Victor G. *Environment of Law Enforcement: A Community Relations Guide.* Englewood Cliffs, N.J.: Prentice-Hall, 1971.

Suojanen, Waino W. *The Dynamics of Management.* New York: Holt, Rinehart & Winston, 1966.

Swingle, Paul G., ed. *Structure of Conflict.* New York: Academic Press, 1970.

Systems Science Corporation. *A Regional Law Enforcement Systems Design.* Bloomington, Ind.: Systems Science Corporation, 1966.

Taguiri, Renato, and Litwin, George H., eds. *Organizational Climate: Explorations of a Concept.* Boston: Graduate School of Business Administration, Harvard University, 1968.

Tannenbaum, Robert; Wechsler, Irving R.; and Massarik, Fred, eds. *Leadership and Organization: Behavioral Science Approach.* New York: McGraw-Hill, 1961.

Terry, George R. *Principles of Management.* 5th ed. Homewood, Ill.: Richard D. Irwin, 1968.

Thompson, James D. *Organizations in Action.* New York: McGraw-Hill, 1967.

Thompson, James D., ed. *Approaches to Organizational Design.* Pittsburgh: University of Pittsburgh Press, 1966.

Traffic Institute. *Police Administration: A Bibliography.* Evanston, Ill.: Traffic Institute, Northwestern University, 1971.

United States Bureau of Employment Security. *Test Development Guide.* Rev. ed., 2 vols. Washington, D.C.: U.S. Government Printing Office, 1967.

United States Employment Service. *Suggestions for Control of Turnover and Absenteeism.* Washington, D.C.: U.S. Government Printing Office, 1962.

Urban Renewal Administration and Bureau of Public Roads. *Standard Long Use Coding Manual.* Washington, D.C.: U.S. Government Printing Office, 1965.

Uveges, Joseph A., Jr., ed. *The Dimensions of Public Administration: Introductory Readings.* Boston: Holbrook Press, 1971.

Vaid, K. N. *Papers on Absenteeism.* New York: Asia Publishing House, 1967.

Valentine, Raymond F. *The Goal-Setting Session.* New York: American Management Association, 1967.

Vogel, Joshua H. *Design of Subdivisions.* Seattle: University of Washington Press, 1965.

Vollmer, Howard M. *Organizational Design—An Exploratory Study.* Menlo Park, Calif.: Stanford Research Institute, 1967.

———*Organizational Design—Process and Concepts.* Menlo Park, Calif.: Stanford Research Institute, 1968.

Vollmer, H. M., and Mills, D. L., eds. *Professionalization.* Englewood Cliffs, N.J.: Prentice-Hall, 1966.

Vroom, V. H. *Some Personality Determinants of the Effects of Participation.* Englewood Cliffs, N.J.: Prentice-Hall, 1960.

Wallach, Irving A. *Police Function in a Negro Community.* Ford Foundation Grant 68-882. McLean, Va.: Research Analysis Corporation, 1970.

Walrod, Truman, ed. *Manual on Jail Administration.* Washington, D.C.: National Sheriff's Association, 1970.

Warner, K. O., and Hennessy, M. L. *Public Management at the Bargaining Table.* Chicago: Public Personnel Association, 1967.

Warr, Peter B., and Knapper, Christopher. *Perception of People and Events.* London: John Wiley, 1968.

Whisenand, Paul, and Cline, James. *Patrol Operations.* Englewood Cliffs, N.J.: Prentice-Hall, 1971.

Whisenand, Paul M., and Tamaru, Tug T. *Automated Police Information Systems.* New York: John Wiley, 1970.

Whisler, Thomas L. *Information Technology and Organizational Change.* Belmont, Calif.: Wadsworth, 1970.

Wickesberg, Albert K. *Management Organization.* New York: Appleton-Century-Crofts, 1966.

Wilcox, Robert F. *Criminal Justice Training by Television: California Model.* San Diego, Calif.: Institute of Public and Urban Affairs, S.D.S.C., February 1971.

Wileman, Fred A. *Guidelines for Discretion: Five Models for Local Law Enforcement Agencies.* Madison: University of Wisconsin, Institute of Governmental Affairs, 1970.

Wileman, Fred A., and Crisafi, Frank J., eds. *Guidelines for Discretion: Twelve*

Models for Local Law Enforcement Agencies. Madison: University of Winconsin, Institute of Governmental Affairs, 1971.

Wilensky, Harold L. *Organizational Intelligence: Knowledge and Policy in Government and Industry.* New York: Basic Books, 1967.

Williams, Earl. *Peer Group Evaluation.* Washington, D.C.: Civil Service Commission, U.S. Government Printing Office, 1968.

Williams, Oliver P. *Metropolitan Political Analysis: A Social Access Approach.* New York: Free Press, 1971.

Williams, Thomas H., and Griffin, Charles H. *Management Information: Quantitative Accent.* Homewood, Ill.: Richard D. Irwin, 1967.

Willmer, M. A. P. *Crime and Information Theory.* Chicago: Aldine, 1970.

Wilson, James Q., ed. *City Politics and Public Policy.* New York: John Wiley, 1968.

Wilson, Orlando W. *Police Administration.* 2nd ed. New York: McGraw-Hill, 1963.

Woll, Peter, ed. *Public Administration and Policy.* New York: Harper & Row, 1966.

Worthman, Max, and Luthans, Fred, eds. *Emerging Concepts in Management.* New York: Macmillan, 1969.

Wright, George O. *General Procedure for Systems Study.* Wright-Patterson Air Force Base, N.J.: Air Research and Development Command, 1960.

Wynne, G. Ray. *Police Transportation Management.* Oceanside, Calif.: Auto Book Press, 1965.

Yoder, Dale. *Personnel Management and Industrial Relations.* 6th ed. Englewood, Cliffs, N.J.: Prentice-Hall, 1970.

Young, Stanley. *Management: Systems Analysis.* Glenview, Ill.: Scott, Foresman, 1966.

Zaleznik, Abraham. *Human Dilemmas of Leadership.* New York: Harper & Row, 1966.

Zaleznik, Abraham; Dalton, Gene W.; and Bames, Louis B. *Orientation and Conflict in Career.* Boston: Graduate School of Business Administration, Harvard University, 1970.

Zimbardo, Philip, and Ebbesen, Ebbe. *Influencing Attitudes and Changing Behavior.* Reading, Mass.: Addison-Wesley, 1969.

Index

About the authors

Jack L. Kuykendall is assistant professor, Administration of Justice Department, San Jose State University. Previously he was assistant professor of police administration at the University of Alaska. He also served on the police force at Amarillo, Texas, for two years.

Professor Kuykendall is author of *Race, Crime, and Justice,* and also has written on his specialty for such magazines as *Police, Journal of California Law Enforcement, Criminology, Law and Order, Journal of Police Science and Administration,* and *Administration of Justice Journal.*

Peter C. Unsinger is also an assistant professor in the Administration of Justice Department at San Jose State University. He has had considerable experience working in county sheriffs' offices and has taught civil defense education (management) at the University of Idaho.

He has written a book for the Department of Justice entitled *Personnel Practices of Reserve/Auxiliary Law Enforcement Programs.* Among professional journals he has contributed to are *Journal of California Law Enforcement, Police Chief,* and *Law and Order.*